The Key to Theosophy

A Clear Exposition in the Form of Question and Answer of the Ethics, Science, and Philosophy for the Study of Which The Theosophical Society has been Founded.

H.P. Blavatsky

British Library Cataloguing in Publication Data

A catalogue record for this book is available from the British Library

ISBN-13: 978-1-908388-57-5

Printed and bound in Great Britain by Lightning Souce UK Ltd., 6 Precedent Drive, Rooksley, Milton Keynes MK13 8PR.

Dedicated by 'H.P.B.'
To all her Pupils,

That They may Learn
and Teach in their turn.

CONTENTS

Preface   7

Theosophy and The Theosophical Society - The Meaning of the Name   8

The Policy of the Theosophical Society   10

The Wisdom-Religion, Esoteric in All Ages   12

Theosophy is Not Buddhism   15

Exoteric and Esoteric Theosophy - What the Modern   16
Theosophical Society is Not

Theosophists and Members of the T.S   19

The Difference Between Theosophy and Occultism   21

The Difference Between Theosophy and Spiritualism   23

Why is Theosophy Accepted?   27

The Objects of the Society   29

The Common Origin of Man   30

Our Other Objects   34

On the Sacredness of the Pledge   35

The Relations of the T.S. to Theosophy - On Self-Improvement   36

The Abstract and the Concrete   38

The Fundamental Teachings of Theosophy - On God and Prayer   41

Is it Necessary to Pray?   43

Prayer Kills Self-Reliance   46

On the Source of the Human Soul   48

The Buddhist Teachings on the Above   49

Theosophical Teachings as to Nature and Man - The Unity of All in All   52

Evolution and Illusion   53

On The Septenary Constitution of Our Planet   57

The Septenary Nature of Man   56

The Distinction Between Soul and Spirit   58

The Greek Teachings   60

On the Various Postmortem States - The Physical and the Spiritual Man   62

On Eternal Reward and Punishment, and on Nirvana   67

On the Various Principles in Man   70

On Reincarnation or Rebirth - What is Memory According   73
to Theosophical Teaching?

Why Do We Not Remember Our Past Lives? 76

On Individuality and Personality 79

On the Reward and Punishment of the Ego 81

On the Kamaloka and Devachan - On the Fate of the Lower Principles 84

Why Theosophists Do Not Believe in the Return of Pure "Spirits" 86

A Few Words About the Skandhas 90

On Postmortem and Postnatal Consciousness 92

What is Really Meant by Annihilation 95

Definite Words for Definite Things 99

On the Nature of Our Thinking Principle - The Mystery of the Ego 102

The Complex Nature of Manas 105

The Doctrine is Taught in St. John's Gospel 107

On the Mysteries of Reincarnation - Periodical Rebirths 112

What is Karma? 115

Who Are Those Who Know? 123

The Difference Between Faith and Knowledge, Or 125
Blind and Reasoned Faith

Has God the Right to Forgive? 127

What is Practical Theosophy? Duty 129

The Relations of the T.S. to Political Reforms 132

On Self-Sacrifice 135

On Charity 137

Theosophy for the Masses 139

How Members Can Help the Society 141

What a Theosophist Ought Not to Do 141

On the Misconceptions About the T.S. - Theosophy and Asceticism 146

Theosophy and Marriage 148

Theosophy and Education 149

Why Then is There So Much Prejudice Against the T.S.? 153

Is the Theosophical Society A Money-Making Concern? 158

The Working Staff of the T.S. 160

The "Theosophical Mahatmas - Are They "Spirits of Light or 162
"Goblins Damned?

The Abuse of Sacred Names and Terms 168

Conclusion - The Future of the Theosophical Society 170

Annotated Glossary 173

Preface

The purpose of this book is exactly expressed in its title, *The Key to Theosophy,* and needs but few words of explanation. It is not a complete or exhaustive textbook of Theosophy, but only a key to unlock the door that leads to the deeper study. It traces the broad outlines of the Wisdom-Religion, and explains its fundamental principles; meeting, at the same time, the various objections raised by the average Western inquirer, and endeavouring to present unfamiliar concepts in a form as simple and in language as clear as possible. That it should succeed in making Theosophy intelligible without mental effort on the part of the reader, would be too much to expect; but it is hoped that the obscurity still left is of the thought and not of the language, is due to depth and not to confusion. To the mentally lazy or obtuse, Theosophy must remain a riddle; for in the world mental as in the world spiritual each man must progress by his own efforts. The writer cannot do the reader's thinking for him, nor would the latter be any the better off if such vicarious thought were possible. The need for such an exposition as the present has long been felt among those interested in the Theosophical Society and its work, and it is hoped that it will supply information, as free as possible from technicalities, to many whose attention has been awakened, but who, as yet, are merely puzzled and not convinced. Some care has been taken in disentangling some part of what is true from what is false in Spiritualistic teachings as to the postmortem life, and to showing the true nature of Spiritualistic phenomena. Previous explanations of a similar kind have drawn much wrath upon the writer's devoted head; the Spiritualists, like too many others, preferring to believe what is pleasant rather than what is true, and becoming very angry with anyone who destroys an agreeable delusion. For the past year Theosophy has been the target for every poisoned arrow of Spiritualism, as though the possessors of a half truth felt more antagonism to the possessors of the whole truth than those who had no share to boast of. Very hearty thanks are due from the author to many Theosophists who have sent suggestions and questions, or have otherwise contributed help during the writing of this book. The work will be the more useful for their aid, and that will be their best reward.

H.P. Blavatsky, 1889

Theosophy and The Theosophical Society
The Meaning of the Name

Q. Theosophy and its doctrines are often referred to as a newfangled religion. Is it a religion?

A. It is not. Theosophy is Divine Knowledge or Science.

Q. What is the real meaning of the term?

A. "Divine Wisdom", (Theosophia) or Wisdom of the gods, as (theogonia), genealogy of the gods. The word 'theos' means a god in Greek, one of the divine beings, certainly not "God" in the sense attached in our day to the term. Therefore, it is not "Wisdom of God", as translated by some, but Divine Wisdom such as that possessed by the gods. The term is many thousand years old.

Q. What is the origin of the name?

A. It comes to us from the Alexandrian philosophers, called lovers of truth, Philaletheians, from (phil) "loving", and (aletheia) "truth". The name Theosophy dates from the third century of our era, and began with Ammonius Saccas and his disciples, also called Analogeticists, who started the Eclectic Theosophical system. As explained by Professor Wilder, they were called so because of their practice of interpreting all sacred legends and narratives, myths and mysteries, by a rule or principle of analogy and correspondence: so that events which were related as having occurred in the external world were regarded as expressing operations and experiences of the human soul. They were also denominated Neo-Platonists. Though Theosophy, or the Eclectic Theosophical system, is generally attributed to the third century, yet, if Diogenes Laertius is to be credited, its origin is much earlier, as he attributed the system to an Egyptian priest, Pot-Amun, who lived in the early days of the Ptolemaic dynasty. The same author tells us that the name is Coptic, and signifies one consecrated to Amun, the God of Wisdom. Theosophy is the equivalent of Brahma-Vidya , divine knowledge.

Q. What was the object of this system?

A. First of all to inculcate certain great moral truths upon its disciples, and all those who were "lovers of the truth". Hence the motto adopted by the Theosophical Society: "There is no religion higher than truth". Eclectic Theosophy was divided under three heads:

1. Belief in one absolute, incomprehensible and supreme Deity, or infinite essence, which is the root of all nature, and of all that is, visible and invisible.

2. Belief in man's eternal immortal nature, because, being a radiation of the Universal Soul, it is of an identical essence with it.

3. Theurgy, or "divine work", or producing a work of gods; from theoi, "gods", and ergein, "to work".

The term is very old, but, as it belongs to the vocabulary of the mysteries, was not in popular use. It was a mystic belief - practically proven by initiated adepts and priests - that, by making oneself as pure as the incorporeal beings - i.e., by returning to one's pristine purity of nature-man could move the gods to impart to him Divine mysteries, and even cause them to become occasionally visible, either subjectively or objectively. It was the transcendental aspect of what is now called Spiritualism; but having been abused and misconceived by the populace, it had come to be regarded by some as necromancy, and was generally forbidden. A travestied practice of the theurgy of Iamblichus lingers still in the ceremonial magic of some modern Cabalists. Modern Theosophy avoids and rejects both these kinds of magic and "necromancy" as being very dangerous. Real divine theurgy requires an almost superhuman purity and holiness of life; otherwise it degenerates into mediumship or black magic. The immediate disciples of Ammonius Saccas, who was called *Theodidaktos,* "god-taught" - such as Plotinus and his follower Porphyry - rejected theurgy at first, but were finally reconciled to it through Iamblichus, who wrote a work to that effect entitled De Mysteriis, under the name of his own master, a famous Egyptian priest called Abammon. Ammonius Saccas was the son of Christian parents, and, having been repelled by dogmatic Spiritualistic Christianity from his childhood, became a Neo-Platonist, and like J. Boehme and other great seers and mystics, is said to have had divine wisdom revealed to him in dreams and visions. Hence his name of Theodidaktos. He resolved to reconcile every system of religion, and by demonstrating their identical origin to establish one universal creed based on ethics. His life was so blameless and pure, his learning so profound and vast, that several Church Fathers were his secret disciples. Clemens Alexandrinus speaks very highly of him. Plotinus, the "St. John" of Ammonius, was also a man universally respected and esteemed, and of the most profound learning and integrity. When thirty-nine years of age he accompanied the Roman Emperor Gordian and his army to the East, to be instructed by the sages of Bactria and India. He had a School of Philosophy in Rome. Porphyry, his disciple, whose real name was Malek (a Hellenized Jew), collected all the writings of his master. Porphyry was himself a great author, and gave an allegorical interpretation to some parts of Homer's writings. The system of meditation the Philaletheians resorted to was ecstasy, a system akin to Indian Yoga practice. What is known of the Eclectic School is due to Origen, Longinus, and Plotinus, the immediate disciples of Ammonius. The chief aim of the Founders of the Eclectic Theosophical School was one of the three objects of its modern successor, the Theosophical Society, namely, to reconcile all religions, sects, and nations under a common system of ethics, based on eternal verities.

Q. What have you to show that this is not an impossible dream; and that all the world's religions are based on the one and the same truth?

A. Their comparative study and analysis. The "Wisdom-Religion" was one in antiquity; and the sameness of primitive religious philosophy is proven to us by the identical doctrines taught to the Initiates during the mysteries, an institution once universally diffused. All the old worships indicate the existence of a single Theosophy anterior to them. The key that is to open one must open all; otherwise it cannot be the right key.

The Policy of the Theosophical Society

Q. In the days of Ammonius there were several ancient great religions, and numerous were the sects in Egypt and Palestine alone. How could he reconcile them?

A. By doing that which we again try to do now. The Neo-Platonists were a large body, and belonged to various religious philosophies; so do our Theosophists.

It was under Philadelphus that Judaism established itself in Alexandria, and forthwith the Hellenic teachers became the dangerous rivals of the College of Rabbis of Babylon. As the author of The Eclectic Philosophy very pertinently remarks:

The Buddhist, Vedantic, and Magian systems were expounded along with the philosophies of Greece at that period. It was not wonderful that thoughtful men supposed that the strife of words ought to cease, and considered it possible to extract one harmonious system from these various teachings ... Panaetius, Athenagoras, and Clement were thoroughly instructed in Platonic philosophy, and comprehended its essential unity with the Oriental systems.

In those days, the Jew Aristobulus affirmed that the ethics of Aristotle represented the esoteric teachings of the Law of Moses; Philo Judaeus endeavored to reconcile the pentateuch with the Pythagorean and Platonic philosophy; and Josephus proved that the Essenes of Carmel were simply the copyists and followers of the Egyptian Therapeutae (the healers). So it is in our day. We can show the line of descent of every Christian religion, as of every, even the smallest, sect. The latter are the minor twigs or shoots grown on the larger branches; but shoots and branches spring from the same trunk - the wisdomreligion. To prove this was the aim of Ammonius, who endeavored to induce Gentiles and Christians, Jews and Idolaters, to lay aside their contention and strife, remembering only that they were all in possession of the same truth under various vestments, and were all the children of a common mother. This is the aim of Theosophy likewise. Says Mosheim of Ammonius:

Conceiving that not only the philosophers of Greece, but also all those of the different barbarian nations, were perfectly in unison with each other with regard to every essential point, he made it his business so to expound the thousand tenets of all these various sects as to show they had all originated from one and the same source, and tended all to one and the same end.

If the writer on Ammonius in the *Edinburgh Encyclopedia* knows what he is talking about, then he describes the modern Theosophists, their beliefs, and their work, for he says, speaking of the Theodidaktos:

He adopted the doctrines which were received in Egypt (the esoteric were those of India) concerning the Universe and the Deity, considered as constituting one great whole; concerning the eternity of the world ... and established a system

10

of moral discipline which allowed the people in general to live according to the laws of their country and the dictates of nature, but required the wise to exalt their mind by contemplation.

Q. What is your authority for saying this of the ancient Theosophists of Alexandria?

A. An almost countless number of well-known writers. Mosheim, one of them, says that: Ammonius taught that the religion of the multitude went hand-in-hand with philosophy, and with her had shared the fate of being by degrees corrupted and obscured with mere human conceits, superstitions, and lies; that it ought, therefore, to be brought back to its original purity by purging it of this dross and expounding it upon philosophical principles; and the whole Christ had in view was to reinstate and restore to its primitive integrity the wisdom of the ancients; to reduce within bounds the universally prevailing dominion of superstition; and in part to correct, and in part to exterminate the various errors that had found their way into the different popular religions. This, again, is precisely what the modern Theosophists say. Only while the great Philaletheian was supported and helped in the policy he pursued by two Church Fathers, Clement and Athenagoras, by all the learned Rabbis of the Synagogue, the Academy and the Groves, and while he taught a common doctrine for all, we, his followers on the same line, receive no recognition, but, on the contrary, are abused and persecuted. People 1,500 years ago are thus shown to have been more tolerant than they are in this enlightened century.

Q. Was he encouraged and supported by the Church because, notwithstanding his heresies, Ammonius taught Christianity and was a Christian?

A. Not at all. He was born a Christian, but never accepted Church Christianity. As said of him by the same writer: He had but to propound his instructions according to the ancient pillars of Hermes, which Plato and Pythagoras knew before, and from them constituted their philosophy. Finding the same in the prologue of the Gospel according to St. John, he very properly supposed that the purpose of Jesus was to restore the great doctrine of wisdom in its primitive integrity. The narratives of the Bible and the stories of the gods he considered to be allegories illustrative of the truth, or else fables to be rejected. As says the *Edinburgh Encyclopedia*: Moreover, he acknowledged that Jesus Christ was an excellent man and the "friend of God", but alleged that it was not his design entirely to abolish the worship of demons (gods), and that his only intention was to purify the ancient religion.

The Wisdom-Religion, Esoteric in All Ages

Q. Since Ammonius never committed anything to writing, how can one feel sure that such were his teachings?

A. Neither did Buddha, Pythagoras, Confucius, Orpheus, Socrates, or even Jesus, leave behind them any writings. Yet most of these are historical personages, and their teachings have all survived. The disciples of Ammonius (among whom Origen and Herennius) wrote treatises and explained his ethics. Certainly the latter are as historical, if not more so, than the Apostolic writings. Moreover, his pupils - Origen, Plotinus, and Longinus (counselor of the famous Queen Zenobia) - have all left voluminous records of the Philaletheian System - so far, at all events, as their public profession of faith was known, for the school was divided into exoteric and esoteric teachings.

Q. How have the latter tenets reached our day, since you hold that what is properly called the wisdomreligion was esoteric?

A. The wisdom-religion was ever one, and being the last word of possible human knowledge, was, therefore, carefully preserved. It preceded by long ages the Alexandrian Theosophists, reached the modern, and will survive every other religion and philosophy.

Q. Where and by whom was it so preserved?

A. Among Initiates of every country; among profound seekers after truth - their disciples; and in those parts of the world where such topics have always been most valued and pursued: in India, Central Asia, and Persia.

Q. Can you give me some proofs of its esotericism?

A. The best proof you can have of the fact is that every ancient religious, or rather philosophical, cult consisted of an esoteric or secret teaching, and an exoteric (outward public) worship. Furthermore, it is a well-known fact that the mysteries of the ancients comprised with every nation the "greater" (secret) and "Lesser" (public) mysteries - e.g., in the celebrated solemnities called the Eleusinia, in Greece. From the Hierophants of Samothrace, Egypt, and the initiated Brahmins of the India of old, down to the later Hebrew Rabbis, all preserved, for fear of profanation, their real bona fide beliefs secret. The Jewish Rabbis called their secular religious series the Merkabah (the exterior body), "the vehicle", or, the covering which contains the hidden soul - i.e., their highest secret knowledge. Not one of the ancient nations ever imparted through its priests its real philosophical secrets to the masses, but allotted to the latter only the husks. Northern Buddhism has its "greater" and its "lesser" vehicle, known as the Mahayana, the esoteric, and the Hinayana, the exoteric, Schools. Nor can you blame them for such secrecy; for surely you would not think of feeding your flock of sheep on learned dissertations on botany instead of on grass? Pythagoras called his Gnosis "the knowledge of things that are", or [translit. Greek] "he gnosis ton onton" and preserved that knowledge for his pledged disciples only: for those who could digest such mental food and feel satisfied; and he pledged them to silence and secrecy. Occult alphabets and secret ciphers are the development of the old Egyptian hieratic writings, the secret of which was, in the days of old, in the possession only of the Hierogrammatists, or initiated Egyptian priests. Ammonius Saccas, as his biographers tell us, bound his pupils by oath not to divulge his higher doctrines except to those who had already been instructed in preliminary knowledge, and who were also bound by a pledge. Finally, do we not find the same even in early Christianity, among the Gnostics, and even in the teachings of Christ? Did he not speak to the multitudes in parables which had a two-fold meaning, and explain his reasons only to his disciples? He says: To you it is given to know the mysteries of the kingdom of heaven; but unto them that are without, all these things are done in parables The Essenes of Judea and Carmel made similar distinctions, dividing their adherents into neophytes, brethren, and the perfect, or those initiated. Examples might be brought from every country to this effect.

Q. Can you attain the "Secret Wisdom" simply by study? Encyclopedias define Theosophy pretty much as Webster's Dictionary does, i.e.,as ... *supposed intercourse with God and superior spirits, and consequent attainment of superhuman knowledge by physical means and chemical processes.* Is this so?

A. I think not. Nor is there any lexicographer capable of explaining, whether to himself or others, how superhuman knowledge can be attained by physical or chemical processes. Had Webster said "by metaphysical and alchemical processes", the definition would be approximately correct: as it is, it is absurd. Ancient Theosophists claimed, and so do the modern, that the infinite cannot be known by the finite -i.e., sensed by the finite Self - but that the divine essence could be communicated to the higher Spiritual Self in a state of ecstasy. This condition can hardly be attained, like hypnotism, by "physical and chemical means".

Q. What is your explanation of it?

A. Real ecstasy was defined by Plotinus as "the liberation of the mind from its finite consciousness, becoming one and identified with the infinite". This is the highest condition, says Professor Wilder, but not one of permanent duration, and it is reached only by the very, very few. It is, indeed, identical with that state which is known in India as *Samadhi*. The latter is practiced by the Yogis, who facilitate it physically by the greatest abstinence in food and drink, and mentally by an incessant endeavor to purify and elevate the mind. Meditation is silent and unuttered prayer, or, as Plato expressed it,

... the ardent turning of the soul toward the divine; not to ask any particular good (as in the common meaning of prayer), but for good itself - for the universal Supreme Good ...- of which we are a part on earth, and out of the essence of which we have all emerged. Therefore, adds Plato, *Remain silent in the presence*

of the divine ones, till they remove the clouds from thy eyes and enable thee to see by the light which issues from themselves, not what appears as good to thee, but what is intrinsically good.

This is what the scholarly author of The Eclectic Philosophy, Professor Alexander Wilder, F.T.S., describes as "spiritual photography": 'The soul is the camera in which facts and events, future, past, and present, are alike fixed; and the mind becomes conscious of them. Beyond our everyday world of limits all is one day or state - the past and future comprised in the present. ... Death is the last ecstasies on earth. Then the soul is freed from the constraint of the body, and its nobler part is united to higher nature and becomes partaker in the wisdom and foreknowledge of the higher beings'.

Real Theosophy is, for the mystics, that state which Apollonius of Tyana was made to describe thus: I *can see the present and the future as in a clear mirror. The sage need not wait for the vapours of the earth and the corruption of the air to foresee events ... The theoi, or gods, see the future; common men the present, sages that which is about to take place.* "The Theosophy of the Sages" he speaks of is well expressed in the assertion, "The Kingdom of God is within us".

Q. Theosophy, then, is not, as held by some, a newly devised scheme?

A. Only ignorant people can thus refer to it. It is as old as the world, in its teachings and ethics, if not in name, as it is also the broadest and most catholic system among all.

Q. How comes it, then, that Theosophy has remained so unknown to the nations of the Western Hemisphere? Why should it have been a sealed book to races confessedly the most cultured and advanced?

A. We believe there were nations as cultured in days of old and certainly more spiritually "advanced" than we are. But there are several reasons for this willing ignorance. One of them was given by St. Paul to the cultured Athenians - a loss, for long centuries, of real spiritual insight, and even interest, owing to their too great devotion to things of sense and their long slavery to the dead letter of dogma and ritualism. But the strongest reason for it lies in the fact that real Theosophy has ever been kept secret.

Q. You have brought forward proofs that such secrecy has existed; but what was the real cause for it?

A. The causes for it were: 1. The perversity of average human nature and its selfishness, always tending to the gratification of personal desires to the detriment of neighbors arid next of kin. Such people could never be entrusted with divine secrets. 2. Their unreliability to keep the sacred and divine knowledge from desecration. It is the latter that led to the perversion of the most sublime truths and symbols, and to the gradual transformation of things spiritual into anthropomorphic, concrete, and gross imagery - in other words, to the dwarfing of the godidea and to idolatry.

Theosophy is Not Buddhism

Q. You are often spoken of as "Esoteric Buddhists". Are you then all followers of Gautama Buddha?

A. No more than musicians are all followers of Wagner. Some of us are Buddhists by religion; yet there are far more Hindus and Brahmins than Buddhists among us, and more Christian-born Europeans and Americans than converted Buddhists. The mistake has arisen from a misunderstanding of the real meaning of the title of Mr. Sinnett's excellent work, *Esoteric Buddhism*, which last word ought to have been spelt with one, instead of two, d's, as then Budhism would have meant what it was intended for, merely "Wisdom - ism" (Bodha, bodhi, "intelligence", "wisdom") instead of Buddhism, Gautama's religious philosophy. Theosophy, as already said, is the wisdom-religion.

Q. What is the difference between Buddhism, the religion founded by the Prince of Kapilavastu, and Budhism, the "Wisdomism" which you say is synonymous with Theosophy?

A. Just the same difference as there is between the secret teachings of Christ, which are called "the mysteries of the Kingdom of Heaven", and the later ritualism and dogmatic theology of the Churches and Sects. Buddha means the "Enlightened" by Bodha, or understanding, Wisdom. This has passed root and branch into the esoteric teachings that Gautama imparted to his chosen Arhats only.

Q. But some Orientalists deny that Buddha ever taught any esoteric doctrine at all?

A. They may as well deny that Nature has any hidden secrets for the men of science. Further on I will prove it by Buddha's conversation with his disciple Ananda. His esoteric teachings were simply the Gupta-Vidya(secret knowledge) of the ancient Brahmins, the key to which their modern successors have, with few exceptions, completely lost. And this Vidya has passed into what is now known as the inner teachings of the Mahayana school of Northern Buddhism. Those who deny it are simply ignorant pretenders to Orientalism. I advise you to read the Rev. Mr. Edkin's *Chinese Buddhism* - especially the chapters on the Exoteric and Esoteric schools and teachings - and then compare the testimony of the whole ancient world upon the subject.

Q. But are not the ethics of Theosophy identical with those taught by Buddha?

A. Certainly, because these ethics are the soul of the Wisdom-Religion, and were once the common property of the initiates of all nations. But Buddha was the first to embody these lofty ethics in his public teachings, and to make them the foundation and the very essence of his public system. It is herein that lies the immense difference between exoteric Buddhism and every other religion. For while in other religions ritualism and dogma hold the first and most important place, in Buddhism it is the ethics which have always been the most insisted upon. This accounts for the resemblance, amounting almost to identity, between the ethics of Theosophy and those of the religion of Buddha.

Q. Are there any great points of difference?

A. One great distinction between Theosophy and exoteric Buddhism is that the latter, represented by the Southern Church, entirely denies (a) the existence of any Deity, and (b) any conscious postmortem life, or even any self-conscious surviving individuality in man. Such at least is the teaching of the Siamese sect, now considered as the purest form of exoteric Buddhism. And it is so, if we refer only to Buddha's public teachings; the reason for such reticence on his part I will give further on. But the schools of the Northern Buddhist Church, established in those countries to which his initiated Arhats retired after the Master's death, teach all that is now called Theosophical doctrines, because they form part of the knowledge of the initiates - thus proving how the truth has been sacrificed to the dead-letter by the toozealous orthodoxy of Southern Buddhism. But how much grander and more noble, more philosophical and scientific, even in its dead-letter, is this teaching than that of any other Church or religion. Yet Theosophy is not Buddhism.

Exoteric and Esoteric Theosophy
What the Modern Theosophical Society is Not

Q. Your doctrines, then, are not a revival of Buddhism, nor are they entirely copied from the Neo-Platonic Theosophy?

A. They are not. But to these questions I cannot give you a better answer than by quoting from a paper read on "Theosophy" by Dr. J.D. Buck, F.T.S., No living Theosophist has better expressed and understood the real essence of Theosophy than our honored friend Dr. Buck: The Theosophical Society was organized for the purpose of promulgating the Theosophical doctrines, and for the promotion of the Theosophic life. The present Theosophical Society is not the first of its kind. I have a volume entitled: *Theosophical Transactions of the Philadelphian Society,* published in London in 1697; and another with the following title: Introduction to Theosophy, or the Science of the Mystery of Christ; that is, of Deity, Nature, and Creature, embracing the philosophy of all the working powers of life, magical and spiritual, ant forming a practical guide to the most sublime purity, sanctity, and evangelical perfection; also to the attainment of divine vision, and the holy angelic arts, potencies, and other prerogatives of the regeneration.

- published in London in 1855. The following is the dedication of this volume: To the students of Universities, Colleges, and schools of Christendom: To Professors of Metaphysical, Mechanical, and Natural Science in all its forms: To men and women of Education generally, of fundamental orthodox faith: To Deists, Arians, Unitarians, Swedenborgians, and other defective and ungrounded creeds, rationalists, and skeptics of every kind: To just-minded and enlightened Mohammedans, Jews, and oriental Patriarch-religionists: but especially to the gospel minister and missionary, whether to the barbaric or intellectual peoples, this introduction to Theosophy, or the science of the ground and mystery of all things, is most humbly and affectionately dedicated. In the following year (1856) another volume was issued, royal octavo, of 600 pages, diamond type, of Theosophical Miscellanies. Of the last-named work 500 copies only were issued, for gratuitous distribution to Libraries and Universities. These earlier movements, of which there were many, originated within the Church, with persons of great piety and earnestness, and of unblemished character; and all of these writings were in orthodox form, using the Christian expressions, and, like the writings of the eminent Churchman William Law, would only be distinguished by the ordinary reader for their great earnestness and piety. These were one and all but attempts to derive and explain the deeper meanings and original import of the Christian Scriptures, and to illustrate and unfold the Theosophic life. These works were soon forgotten, and are now generally unknown. They sought to reform the clergy and revive genuine piety, and were never welcomed. That one word, Heresy, was sufficient to bury them in the limbo of all such Utopias. At the time of the Reformation John Reuchlin made a similar attempt with the same result, though he was the intimate and trusted friend of Luther. Orthodoxy never desired to be informed and enlightened. These reformers were informed, as was Paul by Festus, that too much learning had made them mad, and that it would be dangerous to go farther. Passing by the verbiage, which was partly a matter of habit and education with these writers, and partly due to religious restraint through secular power, and coming to the core of the matter, these writings were Theosophical in the strictest sense, and pertain solely to man's knowledge of his own nature and the higher life of the soul. The present Theosophical Movement has sometimes been declared to be an attempt to convert Christendom to Buddhism, which means simply that the word Heresy has lost its terrors and relinquished its power. Individuals in every age have more or less clearly apprehended the Theosophical doctrines and wrought them into the fabric of their lives. These doctrines belong exclusively to no religion, and are confined to no society or time. They are the birthright of every human soul. Such a thing as orthodoxy must be wrought out by each individual according to his nature and his needs, and according to his varying experience. This may explain why those who have imagined Theosophy to be a new religion have hunted in vain for its creed and its ritual. Its creed is Loyalty to Truth, and its ritual "To honor every truth by use".

How little this principle of Universal Brotherhood is understood by the masses of mankind, how seldom its transcendent importance is recognized, may be seen in the diversity of opinion and fictitious interpretations regarding the Theosophical Society. This Society was organized on this one principle, the essential Brotherhood of Man, as herein briefly outlined and imperfectly set forth. It has been assailed as Buddhist and anti-Christian, as though it could be both these together, when both Buddhism and Christianity, as set forth by their inspired founders, make brotherhood the one essential of doctrine and of life. Theosophy has been also regarded as something new under the sun, or, at best as old mysticism masquerading under a new name. While it is true that many Societies founded upon, and united to support, the principles of altruism, or essential brotherhood, have borne various names, it is also true that many have also been called Theosophic, and with principles and aims as the present society bearing that name. With these societies, one and all, the essential doctrine has been the same, and all else has been incidental, though this does not obviate the fact that many persons are attracted to the incidentals who overlook or ignore the essentials.

No better or more explicit answer - by a man who is one of our most esteemed and earnest Theosophists - could be given to your questions.

Q. Which system do you prefer or follow, in that case, besides Buddhist ethics?

A. None, and all. We hold to no religion, as to no philosophy in particular: we cull the good we find in each. But here, again, it must be stated that, like all other ancient systems, Theosophy is divided into Exoteric and Esoteric Sections.

Q. What is the difference?

A. The members of the Theosophical Society at large are free to profess whatever religion or philosophy they like, or none if they so prefer, provided they are in sympathy with, and ready to carry out one or more of the three objects of the Association. The Society is a philanthropic and scientific body for the propagation of the idea of brotherhood on practical instead of theoretical lines. The Fellows may be Christians or Muslims, Jews or Parsees, Buddhists or Brahmins, Spiritualists or Materialists, it does not matter; but every member must be either a philanthropist, or a scholar, a searcher into ryan and other old literature, or a psychic student. In short, he has to help, if he can, in the carrying out of at least one of the objects of the program. Otherwise he has no reason for becoming a "Fellow". Such are the majority of the exoteric Society, composed of "attached" and "unattached" members. These may, or may not, become Theosophists de facto. Members they are, by virtue of their having joined the Society; but the latter cannot make a Theosophist of one who has no sense for the divine fitness of things, or of him who understands Theosophy in his own - if the expression may be used - sectarian and egotistic way. "Handsome is, as handsome does" could be paraphrased in this case and be made to run: "Theosophist is, who Theosophy does".

Theosophists and Members of the T.S.

Q. This applies to lay members, as I understand. And what of those who pursue the esoteric study of Theosophy; are they the real Theosophists?

A. Not necessarily, until they have proven themselves to be such. They have entered the inner group and pledged themselves to carry out, as strictly as they can, the rules of the occult body. This is a difficult undertaking, as the foremost rule of all is the entire renunciation of one's personality - i.e., a pledged member has to become a thorough altruist, never to think of himself, and to forget his own vanity and pride in the thought of the good of his fellow-creatures, besides that of his fellow-brothers in the esoteric circle. He has to live, if the esoteric instructions shall profit him, a life of abstinence in everything, of selfdenial and strict morality, doing his duty by all men. The few real Theosophists in the T.S. are among these members.

A. This does not imply that outside of the T.S. and the inner circle, there are no Theosophists; for there are, and more than people know of; certainly far more than are found among the lay members of the T.S.

Q. Then what is the good of joining the so-called Theosophical Society in that case? Where is the incentive?

A. None, except the advantage of getting esoteric instructions, the genuine doctrines of the "Wisdom-Religion", and if the real program is carried out, deriving much help from mutual aid and sympathy. Union is strength and harmony, and well-regulated simultaneous efforts produce wonders. This has been the secret of all associations and communities since mankind existed.

Q. But why could not a man of well-balanced mind and singleness of purpose, one, say, of indomitable energy and perseverance, become an Occultist and even an Adept if he works alone?

A. He may; but there are ten thousand chances against one that he will fail. For one reason out of many others, no books on Occultism or Theurgy exist in our day which give out the secrets of alchemy or medieval Theosophy in plain language. All are symbolical or in parables; and as the key to these has been lost for ages in the West, how can a man learn the correct meaning of what he is reading and studying? Therein lies the greatest danger, one that leads to unconscious black magic or the most helpless mediumship. He who has not an Initiate for a master had better leave the dangerous study alone. Look around you and observe. While two-thirds of civilized society ridicule the mere notion that there is anything in Theosophy, Occultism, Spiritualism, or in the Cabala, the other third is composed of the most heterogeneous and opposite elements. Some believe in the mystical, and even in the supernatural (!), but each believes in his own way. Others will rush single-handed into the study of the Cabala, Psychism, Mesmerism, Spiritualism, or some form or another of Mysticism.

Result: no two men think alike, no two are agreed upon any fundamental occult principles, though many are those who claim for themselves the ultima thule of knowledge, and would make outsiders believe that they are full-blown adepts. Not only is there no scientific and accurate knowledge of Occultism accessible in the West - not even of true astrology, the only branch of Occultism which, in its exoteric teachings, has definite laws and a definite system - but no one has any idea of what real Occultism means. Some limit ancient wisdom to the cabala and the Jewish Zohar, which each interprets in his own way according to the dead-letter of the Rabbinical methods. Others regard Swedenborg or Boehme as the ultimate expressions of the highest wisdom; while others again see in mesmerism the great secret of ancient magic. One and all of those who put their theory into practice are rapidly drifting, through ignorance, into black magic. Happy are those who escape from it, as they have neither test nor criterion by which they can distinguish between the true and the false.

Q. Are we to understand that the inner group of the T.S. claims to learn what it does from real initiates or masters of esoteric wisdom?

A. Not directly. The personal presence of such masters is not required. Suffice it if they give instructions to some of those who have studied under their guidance for years, and devoted their whole lives to their service. Then, in turn, these can give out the knowledge so imparted to others, who had no such opportunity. A portion of the true sciences is better than a mass of undigested and misunderstood learning. An ounce of gold is worth a ton of dust.

Q. But how is one to know whether the ounce is real gold or only a counterfeit?

A. A tree is known by its fruit, a system by its results. When our opponents are able to prove to us that any solitary student of Occultism throughout the ages has become a saintly adept like Ammonius Saccas, or even a Plotinus, or a Theurgist like Iamblichus, or achieved feats such as are claimed to have been done by St. Germain, without any master to guide him, and all this without being a medium, a selfdeluded psychic, or a charlatan - then shall we confess ourselves mistaken. But till then, Theosophists prefer to follow the proven natural law of the tradition of the Sacred Science. There are mystics who have made great discoveries in chemistry and physical sciences, almost bordering on alchemy and Occultism; others who, by the sole aid of their genius, have rediscovered portions, if not the whole, of the lost alphabets of the "Mystery language", and are, therefore, able to read correctly Hebrew scrolls; others still, who, being seers, have caught wonderful glimpses of the hidden secrets of Nature. But all these are specialists. One is a theoretical inventor, another a Hebrew, i.e.,a Sectarian Cabalist, a third a Swedenborg of modern times, denying all and everything outside of his own particular science or religion. Not one of them can boast of having produced a universal or even a national benefit thereby, not even to himself. With the exception of a few healers - of that class which the Royal College of Physicians or Surgeons would call quacks - none have helped with their science Humanity, nor even a number of men of the same community. Where are the Chaldeans of old, those who wrought marvelous cures, "not by charms but by simples"? Where is an Apollonius of Tyana, who healed the sick and raised the dead under any climate and circumstances? We know some specialists of the former class in Europe, but none of the latter - except in Asia, where the secret of the Yogi, "to live in death", is still preserved.

Q. Is the production of such healing adepts the aim of Theosophy?

A. Its aims are several; but the most important of all are those which are likely to lead to the relief of human suffering under any or every form, moral as well as physical. And we believe the former to be far more important than the latter. Theosophy has to inculcate ethics; it has to purify the soul, if it would relieve the physical body, whose ailments, save cases of accidents, are all hereditary. It is not by studying Occultism for selfish ends, for the gratification of one's personal ambition, pride, or vanity, that one can ever reach the true goal: that of helping suffering mankind. Nor is it by studying one single branch of the esoteric philosophy that a man becomes an Occultist, but by studying, if not mastering, them all.

Q. Is help, then, to reach this most important aim, given only to those who study the esoteric sciences?

A. Not at all. Every lay member is entitled to general instruction if he only wants it; but few are willing to become what is called "working members", and most prefer to remain the drones of Theosophy. Let it be understood that private research is encouraged in the T.S., provided it does not infringe the limit which separates the exoteric from the esoteric, the *blind* from the conscious magic.

The Difference Between Theosophy and Occultism

Q. You speak of Theosophy and Occultism; are they identical?

A. By no means. A man may be a very good Theosophist indeed, whether in or outside of the Society, without being in any way an Occultist. But no one can be a true Occultist without being a real Theosophist; otherwise he is simply a black magician, whether conscious or unconscious.

Q. What do you mean?

A. I have said already that a true Theosophist must put in practice the loftiest moral ideal, must strive to realize his unity with the whole of humanity, and work ceaselessly for others. Now, if an Occultist does not do all this, he must act selfishly for his own personal benefit; and if he has acquired more practical power than other ordinary men, he becomes forthwith a far more dangerous enemy to the world and those around him than the average mortal. This is clear.

Q. Then is an Occultist simply a man who possesses more power than other people?

A. Far more - if he is a practical and really learned Occultist, and not one only in name. Occult sciences are not, as described in Encyclopedias,

... those imaginary sciences of the Middle Ages which related to the supposed action or influence of Occult qualities or supernatural powers, as alchemy, magic, necromancy, and astrology ...- for they are real, actual, and very dangerous sciences. They teach the secret potency of things in Nature, developing and cultivating the hidden powers "latent in man", thus giving him tremendous advantages over more ignorant mortals. Hypnotism, now become so common and a subject of serious scientific inquiry, is a good instance in point. Hypnotic power has been discovered almost by accident, the way to it having been prepared by mesmerism; and now an able hypnotist can do almost anything with it, from forcing a man, unconsciously to himself, to play the fool, to making him commit a crime - often by proxy for the hypnotist, and for the benefit of the latter. Is not this a terrible power if left in the hands of unscrupulous persons? And please to remember that this is only one of the minor branches of Occultism.

Q. But are not all these Occult sciences, magic, and sorcery, considered by the most cultured and learned people as relics of ancient ignorance and superstition?

A. Let me remind you that this remark of yours cuts both ways. The "most cultured and learned" among you regard also Christianity and every other religion as a relic of ignorance and superstition. People begin to believe now, at any rate, in hypnotism, and some - even of the most cultured - in Theosophy and phenomena. But who among them, except preachers and blind fanatics, will confess to a belief in Biblical miracles? And this is where the point of difference comes in. There are very good and pure Theosophists who may believe in the supernatural, divine miracles included, but no Occultist will do so. For an Occultist practices *scientific Theosophy,* based on accurate knowledge of Nature's secret workings; but a Theosophist, practicing the powers called abnormal, minus the light of Occultism, will simply tend toward a dangerous form of mediumship, because, although holding to Theosophy and its highest conceivable code of ethics, he practices it in the dark, on sincere but blind faith. Anyone, Theosophist or Spiritualist, who attempts to cultivate one of the branches of Occult science - e.g.,Hypnotism, Mesmerism, or even the secrets of producing physical phenomena, etc. - without the knowledge of the philosophic rationale of those powers, is like a rudderless boat launched on a stormy ocean.

The Difference Between Theosophy and Spiritualism

Q. But do you not believe in Spiritualism?

A. If by "Spiritualism" you mean the explanation which Spiritualists give of some abnormal phenomena, then decidedly *we do not*. They maintain that these manifestations are all produced by the "spirits" of departed mortals, generally their relatives, who return to earth, they say, to communicate with those they have loved or to whom they are attached. We deny this point blank. We assert that the spirits of the dead cannot return to earth - save in rare and exceptional cases, of which I may speak later; nor do they communicate with men except by *entirely subjective* means. That which does appear objectively, is only the phantom of the ex-physical man. But in psychic, and so to say, "Spiritual" Spiritualism, we do believe, most decidedly.

Q. Do you reject the phenomena also?

A. Assuredly not - save cases of conscious fraud.

Q. How do you account for them, then?

A. In many ways. The causes of such manifestations are by no means so simple as the Spiritualists would like to believe. Foremost of all, the deus ex machina of the so-called "materializations" is usually the astral body or "double" of the medium or of someone present. This astral body is also the producer or operating force in the manifestations of slate-writing, "Davenport"-like manifestations, and so on.

Q. You say usually - then what is it that produces the rest?

A. That depends on the nature of the manifestations. Sometimes the astral remains, the Kamalokic "shells" of the vanished personalities that were; at other times, Elementals. Spirit is a word of manifold and wide significance. I really do not know what Spiritualists mean by the term; but what we understand them to claim is that the physical phenomena are produced by the reincarnating Ego, the Spiritual and immortal "individuality". And this hypothesis we entirely reject. The Conscious Individuality of the disembodied cannot materialize, nor can it return from its own mental Devachanic sphere to the plane of terrestrial objectivity.

Q. But many of the communications received from the "spirits" show not only intelligence, but a knowledge of facts not known to the medium, and sometimes even not consciously present to the mind of the investigator, or any of those who compose the audience.

A. This does not necessarily prove that the intelligence and knowledge you speak of belong to spirits, or emanate from disembodied souls. Somnambulists have been known to compose music and poetry and to solve mathematical problems while in their trance state, without having ever learnt music or mathematics. Others, answered intelligently to questions put to them, and even, in several cases, spoke languages, such as Hebrew and Latin, of which they were entirely ignorant when awake - all this in a state of profound sleep. Will you, then, maintain that this was caused by "spirits"?

Q. But how would you explain it?

A. We assert that the divine spark in man being one and identical in its essence with the Universal Spirit, our "spiritual Self" is practically omniscient, but that it cannot manifest its knowledge owing to the impediments of matter. Now the more these impediments are removed, in other words, the more the physical body is paralyzed, as to its own independent activity and consciousness, as in deep sleep or deep trance, or, again, in illness, the more fully can the inner Self manifest on this plane. This is our explanation of those truly wonderful phenomena of a higher order, in which undeniable intelligence and knowledge are exhibited. As to the lower order of manifestations, such as physical phenomena and the platitudes and common talk of the general "spirit", to explain even the most important of the teachings we hold upon the subject would take up more space and time than can be allotted to it at present. We have no desire to interfere with the belief of the Spiritualists any more than with any other belief. The responsibility must fall on the believers in "spirits". And at the present moment, while still convinced that the higher sort of manifestations occur through the disembodied souls, their leaders and the most learned and intelligent among the Spiritualists are the first to confess that not all the phenomena are produced by spirits. Gradually they will come to recognize the whole truth; but meanwhile we have no right nor desire to proselytise them to our views. The less so, as in the cases of purely psychic and spiritual manifestations we believe in the intercommunication of the spirit of the living man with that of disembodied personalities.

We say that in such cases it is not the spirits of the dead who descend on earth, but the spirits of the living that ascend to the pure spiritual Souls. In truth there is neither ascending nor descending, but a change of state or condition for the medium. The body of the latter becoming paralyzed, or "entranced", the spiritual Ego is free from its trammels, and finds itself on the same plane of consciousness with the disembodied spirits. Hence, if there is any spiritual attraction between the two they can communicate, as often occurs in dreams. The difference between a mediumistic and a non-sensitive nature is this: the liberated spirit of a medium has the opportunity and facility of influencing the passive organs of its entranced physical body, to make them act, speak, and write at its will. The Ego can make it repeat, echo-like, and in the human language, the thoughts and ideas of the disembodied entity, as well as its own. But the non-receptive or non-sensitive organism of one who is very positive cannot be so influenced. Hence, although there is hardly a human being whose Ego does not hold free intercourse, during the sleep of his body, with those whom it loved and lost, yet, on account of the positiveness and non-receptivity of its physical envelope and brain, no recollection, or a very dim, dream-like remembrance, lingers in the memory of the person once awake.

Q. This means that you reject the philosophy of Spiritualism in toto?

A. If by "philosophy" you mean their crude theories, we do. But they have no philosophy, in truth. Their best, their most intellectual and earnest defenders say so. Their fundamental and only unimpeachable truth, namely, that phenomena occur through mediums controlled by invisible forces and intelligences - no one, except a blind materialist of the "Huxley big toe" school, will or can deny. With regard to their philosophy, however, let me read to you what the able editor of Light, than whom the Spiritualists will find no wiser nor more devoted champion, says of them and their philosophy.

This is what "M.A. Oxon", one of the very few philosophical Spiritualists, writes, with respect to their lack of organization and blind bigotry: It is worthwhile to look steadily at this point, for it is of vital moment. We have an experience and a knowledge beside which all other knowledge is comparatively insignificant. The ordinary Spiritualist waxes wroth if anyone ventures to impugn his assured knowledge of the future and his absolute certainty of the life to come. Where other men have stretched forth feeble hands groping into the dark future, he walks boldly as one who has a chart and knows his way. Where other men have stopped short at a pious aspiration or have been content with a hereditary faith, it is his boast that he knows what they only believe, and that out of his rich stores he can supplement the fading faiths built only upon hope. He is magnificent in his dealings with man's most cherished expectations. He seems to say:

You hope for that which I can demonstrate. You have accepted a traditional belief in what I can experimentally prove according to the strictest scientific method. The old beliefs are fading; come out from them and be separate. They contain as much falsehood as truth. Only by building on a sure foundation of demonstrated fact can your superstructure be stable. All round you old faiths are toppling. Avoid the crash and get you out.

When one comes to deal with this magnificent person in a practical way, what is the result? Very curious and very disappointing. He is so sure of his ground that he takes no trouble to ascertain the interpretation which others put upon his facts. The wisdom of the ages has concerned itself with the explanation of what he rightly regards as proven; but he does not turn a passing glance on its researches. He does not even agree altogether with his brother Spiritualist. It is the story over again of the old Scotch body who, together with her husband, formed a "kirk". They had exclusive keys to Heaven, or, rather, she had, for she was "na certain aboot Jamie". So the infinitely divided and subdivided and re-subdivided sects of Spiritualists shake their heads, and are "na certain aboot" one another. Again, the collective experience of mankind is solid and unvarying on this point that union is strength, and disunion a source of weakness and failure. Shoulder to shoulder, drilled and disciplined, a rabble becomes an army, each man a match for a hundred of the untrained men that may be brought against it. Organization in every department of man's work means success, saving of time and labor, profit and development. Want of method, want of plan, haphazard work, fitful energy, undisciplined effort - these mean bungling failure. The voice of humanity attests the truth. Does the Spiritualist accept the verdict and act on the conclusion? Verily, no. He refuses to organize. He is a law unto himself, and a thorn in the side of his neighbors.

Q. I was told that the Theosophical Society was originally founded to crush Spiritualism and belief in the survival of the individuality in man?

A. You are misinformed. Our beliefs are all founded on that immortal individuality. But then, like so many others, you confuse personality with individuality. Your Western psychologists do not seem to have established any clear distinction between the two. Yet it is precisely that difference which gives the keynote to the understanding of Eastern philosophy, and which lies at the root of the divergence between the Theosophical and Spiritualistic teachings. And though it may draw upon us still more the hostility of some Spiritualists, yet I must state here that it is Theosophy which is the true and unalloyed Spiritualism, while the modern scheme of that name is, as now practiced by the masses, simply transcendental materialism.

Q. Please explain your idea more clearly.

A. What I mean is that though our teachings insist upon the identity of spirit and matter, and though we say that spirit is potential matter, and matter simply crystallized spirit (e.g., as ice is solidified steam), yet since the original and eternal condition of all is not spirit but meta-spirit, so to speak, we maintain that the term spirit can only be applied to the true individuality.

Q. But what is the distinction between this "true individuality" and the "I" or "Ego" of which we are all conscious?

A. Before I can answer you, we must argue upon what you mean by "I" or "Ego". We distinguish between the simple fact of self-consciousness, the simple feeling that "I am I", and the complex thought that "I am Mr. Smith" or "Mrs. Brown". Believing as we do in a series of births for the same Ego, or reincarnation, this distinction is the fundamental pivot of the whole idea. You see "Mr. Smith" really means a long series of daily experiences strung together by the thread of memory, and forming what Mr. Smith calls "himself". But none of these "experiences" are really the "I" or the Ego, nor do they give "Mr. Smith" the feeling that he is himself, for he forgets the greater part of his daily experiences, and they produce the feeling of Egoity in him only while they last. We Theosophists, therefore, distinguish between this bundle of "experiences". which we call the false (because so finite and evanescent)personality, and that element in man to which the feeling of "I am I" is due. It is this "I am I" which we call the true individuality; and we say that this "Ego" or individuality plays, like an actor, many parts on the stage of life. Let us call every new life on earth of the same Ego at night on the stage of a theater. One night the actor, or "Ego", appears as "Macbeth", the next as "Shylock", the third as "Romeo", the fourth as "Hamlet" or "King Lear", and so on, until he has run through the whole cycle of incarnations. The Ego begins his life-pilgrimage as a sprite, an "Ariel", or a

"Puck"; he plays the part of a super, is a soldier, a servant, one of the chorus; rises then to "speaking parts", plays leading roles, interspersed with insignificant parts, till he finally retires from the stage as "Prospero", the magician.

Q. I understand. You say, then, that this true Ego cannot return to earth after death. But surely the actor is at liberty, if he has preserved the sense of his individuality, to return if he likes to the scene of his former actions?

A. We say not, simply because such a return to earth would be incompatible with any state of unalloyed bliss after death, as I am prepared to prove. We say that man suffers so much unmerited misery during his life, through the fault of others with whom he is associated, or because of his environment, that he is surely entitled to perfect rest and quiet, if not bliss, before taking up again the burden of life. However, we can discuss this in detail later.

Why is Theosophy Accepted?

Q. I understand to a certain extent; but I see that your teachings are far more complicated and metaphysical than either Spiritualism or current religious thought. Can you tell me, then, what has caused this system of Theosophy which you support to arouse so much interest and so much animosity at the same time?

A. There are several reasons for it, I believe; among other causes that may be mentioned is:

1. The great reaction from the crassly materialistic theories now prevalent among scientific teachers.

2. General dissatisfaction with the artificial theology of the various Christian Churches, and the number of daily increasing and conflicting sects.

3. An ever-growing perception of the fact that the creeds which are so obviously self - and mutually contradictory *cannot be true*, and that claims which are unverified cannot be real. This natural distrust of conventional religions is only strengthened by their complete failure to preserve morals and to purify society and the masses.

4. A conviction on the part of many, and knowledge by a few, that there must be somewhere a philosophical and religious system which shall be scientific and not merely speculative.

5. A belief, perhaps, that such a system must be sought for in teachings far antedating any modern faith.

Q. But how did this system come to be put forward just now?

A. Just because the time was found to be ripe, which fact is shown by the determined effort of so many earnest students to reach the truth, at whatever cost and wherever it may be concealed. Seeing this, its custodians permitted that some portions at least of that truth should be proclaimed. Had the formation of the Theosophical Society been postponed a few years longer, one half of the civilized nations would have become by this time rank materialists, and the other half anthropomorphists and phenomenalists.

Q. Are we to regard Theosophy in any way as a revelation?

A. In no way whatever - not even in the sense of a new and direct disclosure from some higher, supernatural, or, at least, superhuman beings; but only in the sense of an "unveiling" of old, very old, truths to minds hitherto ignorant of them, ignorant even of the existence and preservation of any such archaic knowledge.

It has become "fashionable", especially of late, to deride the notion that there ever was, in the mysteries of great and civilized peoples, such as the Egyptians, Greeks, or Romans, anything but priestly imposture. Even the Rosicrucians were no better than half lunatics, half knaves. Numerous books have been written on them; and tyros, who had hardly heard the name a few years before, sallied out as profound critics and Gnostics on the subject of alchemy, the fire-philosophers, and mysticism in general. Yet a long series of the Hierophants of Egypt, India, Chaldea, and Arabia are known, along with the greatest philosophers and sages of Greece and the West, to have included under the designation of wisdom and divine science all knowledge, for they considered the base and origin of every art and science as essentially divine. Plato regarded the mysteries as most sacred, and Clemens Alexandrinus, who had been himself initiated into the Eleusinian mysteries, has declared "that the doctrines taught therein contained in them the end of all human knowledge". Were Plato and Clemens two knaves or two fools, we wonder, or - both?

Q. You spoke of "Persecution". If truth is as represented by Theosophy, why has it met with such opposition, and with no general acceptance?

A. For many and various reasons again, one of which is the hatred felt by men for "innovations", as they call them. Selfishness is essentially conservative, and hates being disturbed. It prefers an easy-going, unexacting lie to the greatest truth, if the latter requires the sacrifice of one's smallest comfort. The power of mental inertia is great in anything that does not promise immediate benefit and reward. Our age is preeminently unspiritual and matter of fact. Moreover, there is the unfamiliar character of Theosophic teachings; the highly abstruse nature of the doctrines, some of which contradict flatly many of the human vagaries cherished by sectarians, which have eaten into the very core of popular beliefs. If we add to this the personal efforts and great purity of life exacted of those who would become the disciples of the inner circle, and the very limited class to which an entirely unselfish code appeals, it will be easy to perceive the reason why Theosophy is doomed to such slow, uphill work. It is essentially the philosophy of those who suffer, and have lost all hope of being helped out of the mire of life by any other means. Moreover, the history of any system of belief or morals, newly introduced into a foreign soil, shows that its beginnings were impeded by every obstacle that obscurantism and selfishness could suggest. "The crown of the innovator is a crown of thorns" indeed! No pulling down of old, worm-eaten buildings can be accomplished without some danger.

Q. All this refers rather to the ethics and philosophy of the T.S. Can you give me a general idea of the Society itself, its objects and statutes?

A. This was never made secret. Ask, and you shall receive accurate answers.

Q. But I heard that you were bound by pledges?

A. Only in the Arcane or "Esoteric" Section.

Q. And also, that some members after leaving did not regard themselves bound by them. Are they right?

A. This shows that their idea of honor is an imperfect one. How can they be right? As well said in *The Path*, our theosophical organ at New York, treating of such a case:

Suppose that a soldier is tried for infringement of oath and discipline, and is dismissed from the service. In his rage at the justice he has called down, and of whose penalties he was distinctly forewarned, the soldier turns to the enemy with false information - a spy and traitor - as a revenge upon his former Chief, and claims that his punishment has released him from his oath of loyalty to a cause.

Is he justified, think you? Don't you think he deserves being called a dishonourable man, a coward?

Q. I believe so; but some think otherwise.

A. So much the worse for them. But we will talk on this subject later, if you please.

The Objects of the Society

Q. What are the objects of the "Theosophical Society"?

A. They are three, and have been so from the beginning.

1. To form the nucleus of a Universal Brotherhood of Humanity without distinction of race, color, or creed.

2. To promote the study of Aryan[2] and other Scriptures, of the World's religions and sciences, and to vindicate the importance of old Asiatic literature, namely, of the Brahmanical, Buddhist, and Zoroastrian philosophies.

3. To investigate the hidden mysteries of Nature under every aspect possible, and the psychic and spiritual powers latent in man especially. These are, broadly stated, the three chief objects of the Theosophical Society.

2. H.P.B. means the original Indo-Germanic race from Northern India (see the glossary at the end of this file)

Q. Can you give me some more detailed information upon these?

A. We may divide each of the three objects into as many explanatory clauses as may be found necessary.

Q. Then let us begin with the first. What means would you resort to, in order to promote such a feeling of brotherhood among races that are known to be of the most diversified religions, customs, beliefs, and modes of thought?

A. Allow me to add that which you seem unwilling to express. Of course we know that with the exception of two remnants of races - the Parsees and the Jews - every nation is divided, not merely against all other nations, but even against itself. This is found most prominently among the so-called civilized Christian nations. Hence your wonder, and the reason why our first object appears to you a Utopia. Is it not so?

Q. Well, yes; but what have you to say against it?

A. Nothing against the fact; but much about the necessity of removing the causes which make Universal Brotherhood a Utopia at present.

Q. What are, in your view, these causes?

A. First and foremost, the natural selfishness of human nature. This selfishness, instead of being eradicated, is daily strengthened and stimulated into a ferocious and irresistible feeling by the present religious education, which tends not only to encourage, but positively to justify it. People's ideas about right and wrong have been entirely perverted by the literal acceptance of the Jewish Bible. All the unselfishness of the altruistic teachings of Jesus has become merely a theoretical subject for pulpit oratory; while the precepts of practical selfishness taught in the Mosaic Bible, against which Christ so vainly preached, have become ingrained into the innermost life of the Western nations. "An eye for an eye and a tooth for a tooth" has come to be the first maxim of your law. Now, I state openly and fearlessly, that the perversity of this doctrine and of so many others Theosophy alone can eradicate.

The Common Origin of Man

Q. How?

A. Simply by demonstrating on logical, philosophical, metaphysical, and even scientific grounds that: (a) All men have spiritually and physically the same origin, which is the fundamental teaching of Theosophy. (b) As mankind is essentially of one and the same essence, and that essence is one - infinite, uncreate, and eternal, whether we call it God or Nature - nothing, therefore, can affect one nation or one man without affecting all other nations and all other men.

This is as certain and as obvious as that a stone thrown into a pond will, sooner or later, set in motion every single drop of water therein.

Q. But this is not the teaching of Christ, but rather a pantheistic notion.

A. That is where your mistake lies. It is purely Christian, although not Judaic, and therefore, perhaps, your Biblical nations prefer to ignore it.

Q. This is a wholesale and unjust accusation. Where are your proofs for such a statement?

A. They are ready at hand. Christ is alleged to have said: "Love each other" and "Love your enemies"; for... *if ye love them (only) which love you, what reward (or merit) have ye? Do not even the publicans the same? And if you salute your brethren only, what do ye more than others? Do not even publicans so?*

These are Christ's words. But Genesis says "Cursed be Canaan, a servant of servants shall he be unto his brethren". And, therefore, Christian but Biblical people prefer the law of Moses to Christ's law of love. They base upon the Old Testament, which panders to all their passions, their laws of conquest, annexation, and tyranny over races which they call inferior. What crimes have been committed on the strength of this infernal (if taken in its dead letter) passage in Genesis, history alone gives us an idea, however inadequate.

At the close of the Middle Ages slavery, under the power of moral forces, had mainly disappeared from Europe; but two momentous events occurred which overbore the moral power working in European society and let loose a swarm of curses upon the earth such as mankind had scarcely ever known. One of these events was the first voyaging to a populated and barbarous coast where human beings were a familiar article of traffic; and the other the discovery of a new world, where mines of glittering wealth were open, provided labor could be imported to work them. For four hundred years men and women and children were torn from all whom they knew and loved, and were sold on the coast of Africa to foreign traders; they were chained below decks - the dead often with the living-during the horrible "middle passage", and, according to Bancroft, an impartial historian, two hundred and fifty thousand out of three and a quarter millions were thrown into the sea on that fatal passage, while the remainder were consigned to nameless misery in the mines, or under the lash in the cane and rice fields. The guilt of this great crime rests on the Christian Church. "In the name of the most Holy Trinity" the Spanish Government (Roman Catholic) concluded more than ten treaties authorizing the sale of five hundred thousand human beings; in 1562 Sir John Hawkins sailed on his diabolical errand of buying slaves in Africa and selling them in the West Indies in a ship which bore the sacred name of Jesus; while Elizabeth, the Protestant Queen, rewarded him for his success in this first adventure of Englishmen in that inhuman traffic by allowing him to wear as his crest "a demi-Moor in his proper color, bound with a cord, or, in other words, a manacled Negro slave".

Q. I have heard you say that the identity of our physical origin is proved by science, that of our spiritual origin by the Wisdom-Religion. Yet we do not find

Darwinists exhibiting great fraternal affection.

A. Just so. This is what shows the deficiency of the materialistic systems, and proves that we Theosophists are in the right. The identity of our physical origin makes no appeal to our higher and deeper feelings. Matter, deprived of its soul and spirit, or its divine essence, cannot speak to the human heart. But the identity of the soul and spirit, of real, immortal man, as Theosophy teaches us, once proven and deep-rooted in our hearts, would lead us far on the road of real charity and brotherly goodwill.

Q. But how does Theosophy explain the common origin of man?

A-1- By teaching that the root of all nature, objective and subjective, and everything else in the universe, visible and invisible, is, was, and ever will be one absolute essence, from which all starts, and into which everything returns. This is Aryan (See remark on the use of the word Aryan a while back) philosophy, fully represented only by the Vedantins, and the Buddhist system. With this object in view, it is the duty of all Theosophists to promote in every practical way, and in all countries, the spread of non-sectarian education.

Q. What do the written statutes of your Society advise its members to do besides this? On the physical plane, I mean?

A. In order to awaken brotherly feeling among nations we have to assist in the international exchange of useful arts and products, by advice, information, and cooperation with all worthy individuals and associations (provided, however, add the statutes, "that no benefit or percentage shall be taken by the Society or the 'Fellows' for its or their corporate services"). For instance, to take a practical illustration. The organization of Society, depicted by Edward Bellamy, in his magnificent work Looking Backwards, admirably represents the Theosophical idea of what should be the first great step towards the full realization of universal brotherhood. The state of things he depicts falls short of perfection, because selfishness still exists and operates in the hearts of men. But in the main, selfishness and individualism have been overcome by the feeling of solidarity and mutual brotherhood; and the scheme of life there described reduces the causes tending to create and foster selfishness to a minimum.

Q. Then as a Theosophist you will take part in an effort to realize such an ideal?

A. Certainly; and we have proved it by action. Have not you heard of the Nationalist clubs and party which have sprung up in America since the publication of Bellamy's book? They are now coming prominently to the front, and will do so more and more as time goes on. Well, these clubs and this party were started in the first instance by Theosophists. One of the first, the Nationalist Club of Boston, Massachusetts, has Theosophists for President and Secretary, and the majority of its executive belong to the T.S. In the constitution of all their clubs, and of the party they are forming, the influence of Theosophy and of the Society is plain, for they all take as their basis, their first and fundamental principle, the Brotherhood of Humanity as taught by Theosophy. In their declaration of Principles they state:

The principle of the Brotherhood of Humanity is one of the eternal truths that govern the world's progress on lines which distinguish human nature from brute nature.

What can be more Theosophical than this? But it is not enough. What is also needed is to impress men with the idea that, if the root of mankind is one, then there must also be one truth which finds expression in all the various religions-except in the Jewish, as you do not find it expressed even in the Cabala.

Q. This refers to the common origin of religions, and you may be right there. But how does it apply to practical brotherhood on the physical plane?

A. First, because that which is true on the metaphysical plane must be also true on the physical. Secondly, because there is no more fertile source of hatred and strife than religious differences. When one party or another thinks himself the sole possessor of absolute truth, it becomes only natural that he should think his neighbor absolutely in the clutches of Error or the Devil. But once get a man to see that none of them has the whole truth, but that they are mutually complementary, that the complete truth can be found only in the combined views of all, after that which is false in each of them has been sifted out - then true brotherhood in religion will be established. The same applies in the physical world.

Q. Please explain further.

A. Take an instance. A plant consists of a root, a stem, and many shoots and leaves. As humanity, as a whole, is the stem which grows from the spiritual root, so is the stem the unity of the plant. Hurt the stem and it is obvious that every shoot and leaf will suffer. So it is with mankind.

Q. Yes, but if you injure a leaf or a shoot, you do not injure the whole plant.

A. And therefore you think that by injuring one man you do not injure humanity? But how do you know? Are you aware that even materialistic science teaches that any injury, however, slight, to a plant will affect the whole course of its future growth and development? Therefore, you are mistaken, and the analogy is perfect. If, however, you overlook the fact that a cut in the finger may often make the whole body suffer, and react on the whole nervous system, I must all the more remind you that there may well be other spiritual laws, operating on plants and animals as well as on mankind, although, as you do not recognize their action on plants and animals, you may deny their existence.

Q. What laws do you mean?

A. We call them Karmic laws; but you will not understand the full meaning of the term unless you study Occultism. However, my argument did not rest on the assumption of these laws, but really on the analogy of the plant. Expand the idea, carry it out to a universal application, and you will soon find that in true philosophy every physical action has its moral and everlasting effect. Hurt a man by doing him bodily harm; you may think that his pain and suffering cannot spread by any means to his neighbors, least of all to men of other nations. We affirm t*hat it will, in good time.* Therefore, we say, that unless every man is brought to understand and accept *as an axiomatic truth* that by having wronged one man we wrong not only ourselves but the whole of humanity in the long run, no brotherly feelings such as preached by all the great Reformers, preeminently by Buddha and Jesus, are possible on earth.

Our Other Objects

Q. Will you now explain the methods by which you propose to carry out the second object?

A. To collect for the library at our headquarters of Adyar, Madras - and by the Fellows of their Branches for their local libraries - all the good works upon the world's religions that we can. To put into written form correct information upon the various ancient philosophies, traditions, and legends, and disseminate the same in such practicable ways as the translation and publication of original works of value, and extracts from and commentaries upon the same, or the oral instructions of persons learned in their respective departments.

Q. And what about the third object, to develop in man his latent spiritual or psychic powers?

A. This has to be achieved also by means of publications, in those places where no lectures and personal teachings are possible. Our duty is to keep alive in man his spiritual intuitions. To oppose and counteract - after due investigation and proof of its irrational nature - bigotry in every form, religious, scientific, or social, and cant above all, whether as religious sectarianism or as belief in miracles or anything supernatural. What we have to do is to seek to obtain *knowledge* of all the laws of nature, and to diffuse it. To encourage the study of those laws least understood by modern people, the so-called Occult Sciences, *based on the true knowledge of nature*, instead of, as at present, on *superstitious beliefs based on blind faith and authority.* Popular folklore and traditions, however fanciful at times, when sifted may lead to the discovery of long-lost, but important, secrets of nature. The Society, therefore, aims at pursuing this line of inquiry, in the hope of widening the field of scientific and philosophical observation.

On the Sacredness of the Pledge

Q. Have you any ethical system that you carry out in the Society?

A. The ethics are there, ready and clear enough for whomsoever would follow them. They are the essence and cream of the world's ethics, gathered from the teachings of all the world's great reformers. Therefore, you will find represented therein Confucius and Zoroaster, Lao-tzu and the Bhagavad-Gita , the precepts of Gautama Buddha and Jesus of Nazareth, of Hillel and his school, as of Pythagoras, Socrates, Plato, and their schools.

Q. Do the members of your Society carry out these precepts? I have heard of great dissensions and quarrels among them.

A. Very naturally, since although the reform (in its present shape) may be called new, the men and women to be reformed are the same human, sinning natures as of old. As already said, the earnest working members are few; but many are the sincere and well-disposed persons, who try their best to live up to the Society's and their own ideals. Our duty is to encourage and assist individual fellows in selfimprovement, intellectual, moral, and spiritual; not to blame or condemn those who fail. We have, strictly speaking, no right to refuse admission to anyone - especially in the Esoteric Section of the Society, wherein "he who enters is as one newly born". But if any member, his sacred pledges on his word of honor and immortal Self notwithstanding, chooses to continue, after that "new birth", with the new man, the vices or defects of his old life, and to indulge in them still in the Society, then, of course, he is more than likely to be asked to resign and withdraw; or, in case of his refusal, to be expelled. We have the strictest rules for such emergencies.

Q. Can some of them be mentioned?

A. They can. To begin with, no Fellow in the Society, whether exoteric or esoteric, has a right to force his personal opinions upon another Fellow. It is not lawful for any officer of the Parent Society to express in public, by word or act, any hostility to, or preference for, any one section, religious or philosophical, more than another. All have an equal right to have the essential features of their religious belief laid before the tribunal of an impartial world. And no officer of the Society, in his capacity as an officer, has the right to preach his own sectarian views and beliefs to members assembled, except when the meeting consists of his co-religionists. After due warning, violation of this rule shall be punished by suspension or expulsion. This is one of the offenses in the Society at large. As regards the inner section, now called the Esoteric, the following rules have been laid down and adopted, so far back as 1880. No Fellow shall put to his selfish use any knowledge communicated to him by any member of the first section (now a higher "degree"); violation of the rule being punished by expulsion. Now, however, before any such knowledge can be imparted, the applicant has to bind himself by a solemn oath not to use it for selfish purposes, nor to reveal anything said except by permission.

Q. But is a man expelled, or resigning, from the section free to reveal anything he may have learned, or to break any clause of the pledge he has taken?

A. Certainly not. His expulsion or resignation only relieves him from the obligation of obedience to the teacher, and from that of taking an active part in the work of the Society, but surely not from the sacred pledge of secrecy.

Q. But is this reasonable and just?

A. Most assuredly. To any man or woman with the slightest honourable feeling a pledge of secrecy taken even on one's word of honor, much more to one's Higher Self - the God within - is binding till death. And though he may leave the Section and the Society, no man or woman of honor will think of attacking or injuring a body to which he or she has been so pledged.

Q. But is not this going rather far?

A. Perhaps so, according to the low standard of the present time and morality. But if it does not bind as far as this, what use is a pledge at all? How can anyone expect to be taught secret knowledge, if he is to be at liberty to free himself from all the obligations he had taken, whenever he pleases? What security, confidence, or trust would ever exist among men, if pledges such as this were to have no really binding force at all? Believe me, the law of retribution (Karma) would very soon overtake one who so broke his pledge, and perhaps as soon as the contempt of every honourable man would, even on this physical plane. As well expressed in the New York Path just cited on this subject,

A pledge once taken, is *forever binding in both the moral and the occult worlds*. If we break it once and are punished, that does not justify us in breaking it again, and so long as we do, so long will the mighty lever of the Law (of Karma) react upon us.

The Relations of the T.S. to Theosophy
On Self-Improvement

Q. Is moral elevation, then, the principal thing insisted upon in your Society?

A. Undoubtedly! He who would be a true Theosophist must bring himself to live as one.

Q. If so, then, as I remarked before, the behavior of some members strangely belies this fundamental rule.

A. Indeed it does. But this cannot be helped among us, any more than amongst those who call themselves Christians and act like fiends. This is no fault of our statutes and rules, but that of human nature. Even in some exoteric public branches, the members pledge themselves on their "Higher Self" to live the life prescribed by Theosophy. They have to bring their Divine Self to guide their every thought and action, every day and at every moment of their lives. A true Theosophist ought "to deal justly and walk humbly".

Q. What do you mean by this?

A. Simply this: the one self has to forget itself for the many selves. Let me answer you in the words of a true Philaletheian, an F.T.S., who has beautifully expressed it in 'The Theosophist': *What every man needs first is to find himself, and then take an honest inventory of his subjective possessions, and, bad or bankrupt as it may be, it is not beyond redemption if we set about it in earnest.*

But how many do? All are willing to work for their own development and progress; very few for those of others. To quote the same writer again: *Men have been deceived and deluded long enough; they must break their idols, put away their shams, and go to work for themselves - nay, there is one little word too much or too many, for he who works for himself had better not work at all; rather let him work himself for others, for all. For every flower of love and charity he plants in his neighbor's garden, a loathsome weed will disappear from his own, and so this garden of the gods - Humanity - shall blossom as a rose. In all Bibles, all religions, this is plainly set forth - but designing men have at first misinterpreted and finally emasculated, materialized, besotted them. It does not require a new revelation. Let every man be a revelation unto himself. Let once man's immortal spirit take possession of the temple of his body, drive out the money-changers and every unclean thing, and his own divine humanity will redeem him, for when he is thus at one with himself he will know the "builder of the Temple".*

Q. This is pure Altruism, I confess.

A. It is. And if only one Fellow of the T.S. out of ten would practice it ours would be a body of elect indeed. But there are those among the outsiders who will always refuse to see the essential difference between Theosophy and the Theosophical Society, the idea and its imperfect embodiment. Such would visit every sin and shortcoming of the vehicle, the human body, on the pure spirit which sheds thereon its divine light. Is this just to either? They throw stones at an association that tries to work up to, and for the propagation of, its ideal with most tremendous odds against it. Some vilify the Theosophical Society only because it presumes to attempt to do that in which other systems - Church and State Christianity preeminently - have failed most egregiously; others because they would fain preserve the existing state of things: Pharisees and Sadducees in the seat of Moses, and publicans and sinners reveling in high places, as under the Roman Empire during its decadence. Fair-minded people, at any rate, ought to remember that the man who does all he can, does as much as he who has achieved the most, in this world of relative possibilities. This is a simple truism, an axiom supported for believers in the Gospels by the parable of the talents given by their Master: the servant who doubled his two talents was rewarded as much as that other fellow-servant who had received five. To every man it is given "according to his several ability".

Q. Yet it is rather difficult to draw the line of demarcation between the abstract and the concrete in this case, as we have only the latter to form our judgment by.

A. Then why make an exception for the T.S.? Justice, like charity, ought to begin at home. Will you revile and scoff at the "Sermon on the Mount" because your social, political and even religious laws have, so far, not only failed to carry out its precepts in their spirit, but even in their dead letter? Abolish the oath in Courts, Parliament, Army and everywhere, and do as the Quakers do, if you will call yourselves Christians. Abolish the Courts themselves, for if you would follow the Commandments of Christ, you have to give away your coat to him who deprives you of your cloak, and turn your left cheek to the bully who smites you on the right. "Resist not evil, love your enemies, bless them that curse you, do good to them that hate you", for "whosoever shall break one of the least of these Commandments and shall teach men so, he shall be called the least in the Kingdom of Heaven", and "whosoever shall say 'Thou fool' shall be in danger of hell fire". And why should you judge, if you would not be judged in your turn? Insist that between Theosophy and the Theosophical Society there is no difference, and forthwith you lay the system of Christianity and its very essence open to the same charges, only in a more serious form.

Q. Why *more* serious?

A. Because, while the leaders of the Theosophical Movement, recognizing fully their shortcomings, try all they can do to amend their ways and uproot the evil existing in the Society; and while their rules and bylaws are framed in the spirit of Theosophy, the Legislators and the Churches of nations and countries which call themselves Christian do the reverse. Our members, even the worst among them, are no worse than the average Christian. Moreover, if the Western Theosophists experience so much difficulty in leading the true Theosophical life, it is because they are all the children of their generation. Every one of them was a Christian, bred and brought up in the sophistry of his Church, his social customs, and even his paradoxical laws. He was this before he became a Theosophist, or rather, a member of the Society of that name, as it cannot be too often repeated that between the abstract ideal and its vehicle there is a most important difference.

The Abstract and the Concrete

Q. Please elucidate this difference a little more.

A. The Society is a great body of men and women, composed of the most heterogeneous elements. Theosophy, in its abstract meaning, is Divine Wisdom, or the aggregate of the knowledge and wisdom that underlie the Universe - the homogeneity of eternal good; and in its concrete sense it is the sum total of the same as allotted to man by nature, on this earth, and no more. Some members earnestly endeavor to realize and, so to speak, to objectivize Theosophy in their lives; while others desire only to know of, not to practice it; and others still may have joined the Society merely out of curiosity, or a passing interest, or perhaps, again, because some of their friends belong to it. How, then, can the system be judged by the standard of those who would assume the name without any right to it? Is poetry or its muse to be measured only by those would-be poets who afflict our ears? The Society can be regarded as the embodiment of Theosophy only in its abstract motives; it can never presume to call itself its concrete vehicle so long as human imperfections and weaknesses are all represented in its body; otherwise the Society would be only repeating the great error and the outflowing sacrilege of the so-called Churches of Christ. If Eastern comparisons may be permitted, Theosophy is the shoreless ocean of universal truth, love, and wisdom, reflecting its radiance on the earth, while the Theosophical Society is only a visible bubble on that reflection. Theosophy is divine nature, visible and invisible, and its Society human nature trying to ascend to its divine parent. Theosophy, finally, is the fixed eternal sun, and its Society the evanescent comet trying to settle in an orbit to become a planet, ever revolving within the attraction of the sun of truth. It was formed to assist in showing to men that such a thing as Theosophy exists, and to help them to ascend towards it by studying and assimilating its eternal verities.

Q. I thought you said you had no tenets or doctrines of your own?

A. No more we have. The Society has no wisdom of its own to support or teach. It is simply the storehouse of all the truths uttered by the great seers, initiates, and prophets of historic and even prehistoric ages; at least, as many as it can get. Therefore, it is merely the channel through which more or less of truth, found in the accumulated utterances of humanity's great teachers, is poured out into the world.

Q. But is such truth unreachable outside of the society? Does not every Church claim the same?

A. Not at all. The undeniable existence of great initiates - true "Sons of God" - shows that such wisdom was often reached by isolated individuals, never, however, without the guidance of a master at first. But most of the followers of such, when they became masters in their turn, have dwarfed the Catholicism of these teachings into the narrow groove of their own sectarian dogmas. The commandments of a chosen master alone were then adopted and followed, to the exclusion of all others - if followed at all, note well, as in the case of the Sermon on the Mount. Each religion is thus a bit of the divine truth, made to focus a vast panorama of human fancy which claimed to represent and replace that truth.

Q. But Theosophy, you say, is not a religion?

A. Most assuredly it is not, since it is the essence of all religion and of absolute truth, a drop of which only underlies every creed. To resort once more to metaphor. Theosophy, on earth, is like the white ray of the spectrum, and every religion only one of the seven prismatic colors. Ignoring all the others, and cursing them as false, every special colored ray claims not only priority, but to be that white ray itself, and anathematizes even its own tints from light to dark, as heresies. Yet, as the sun of truth rises higher and higher on the horizon of man's perception, and each colored ray gradually fades out until it is finally reabsorbed in its turn, humanity will at last be cursed no longer with artificial polarizations, but will find itself bathing in the pure colorless sunlight of eternal truth. And this will be Theosophia.

Q. Your claim is, then, that all the great religions are derived from Theosophy, and that it is by assimilating it that the world will be finally saved from the curse of its great illusions and errors?

A. Precisely so. And we add that our Theosophical Society is the humble seed which, if watered and left to live, will finally produce the Tree of Knowledge of Good and Evil which is grafted on the Tree of Life Eternal. For it is only by studying the various great religions and philosophies of humanity, by comparing them dispassionately and with an unbiased mind, that men can hope to arrive at the truth. It is especially by finding out and noting their various points of agreement that we may achieve this result. For no sooner do we arrive - either by study, or by being taught by someone who knows - at their inner meaning, than we find, almost in every case, that it expresses some great truth in Nature.

Q. We have heard of a Golden Age that was, and what you describe would be a Golden Age to be realized at some future day. When shall it be?

A. Not before humanity, as a whole, feels the need of it. A maxim in the Persian Javidan Khirad says: Truth is of two kinds - one manifest and self-evident; the other demanding incessantly new demonstrations and proofs. It is only when this latter kind of truth becomes as universally obvious as it is now dim, and therefore liable to be distorted by sophistry and casuistry; it is only when the two kinds will have become once more one, that all people will be brought to see alike.

Q. But surely those few who have felt the need of such truths must have made up their minds to believe in something definite? You tell me that, the Society having no doctrines of its own, every member may believe as he chooses and accept what he pleases. This looks as if the Theosophical Society was bent upon reviving the confusion of languages and beliefs of the Tower of Babel of old. Have you no beliefs in common?

A. What is meant by the Society having no tenets or doctrines of its own is, that no special doctrines or beliefs are obligatory on its members; but, of course, this applies only to the body as a whole. The Society, as you were told, is divided into an outer and an inner body. Those who belong to the latter have, of course, a philosophy, or - if you so prefer it - a religious system of their own.

Q. May we be told what it is?

A. We make no secret of it. It was outlined a few years ago in *The Theosophist* and *Esoteric Buddhism*, and may be found still more elaborated in *The Secret Doctrine.* It is based on the oldest philosophy of the world, called the Wisdom-Religion or the Archaic Doctrine. If you like, you may ask questions and have them explained.

The Fundamental Teachings of Theosophy
On God and Prayer

Q. Do you believe in God?

A. That depends what you mean by the term.

Q. I mean the God of the Christians, the Father of Jesus, and the Creator: the Biblical God of Moses, in short.

A. In such a God we do not believe. We reject the idea of a personal, or an extra-cosmic and anthropomorphic God, who is but the gigantic shadow of *man,* and not of man at his best, either. The God of theology, we say - and prove it - is a bundle of contradictions and a logical impossibility. Therefore, we will have nothing to do with him.

Q. State your reasons, if you please.

A. They are many, and cannot all receive attention. But here are a few. This God is called by his devotees infinite and absolute, is he not?

Q. I believe he is.

A. Then, if infinite - i.e.,limitless - and especially if absolute, how can he have a form, and be a creator of anything? Form implies limitation, and a beginning as well as an end; and, in order to create, a Being must think and plan. How can the absolute be supposed to think - i.e.,to have any relation whatever to that which is limited, finite, and conditioned? This is a philosophical, and a logical absurdity. Even the Hebrew Cabala rejects such an idea, and therefore, makes of the one and the Absolute Deific Principle an infinite Unity called Ain-Soph (Ain-Soph (Greek: toh pan, epeiros), the boundless or limitless, in and of nature, the non-existing that IS, but that is not *a* Being)

In order to create, the Creator has to become active; and as this is impossible for absoluteness, the infinite principle had to be shown becoming the cause of evolution (not creation) in an indirect way - i.e., through the emanation from itself (another absurdity, due this time to the translators of the Cabala) of the Sephiroth.

How can the non-active eternal principle emanate or emit? The Parabrahman of the Vedantins does nothing of the kind; nor does the Ain-Soph of the Chaldean Cabala. It is an eternal and periodical law which causes an active and creative force (the logos) to emanate from the ever-concealed and incomprehensible one principle at the beginning of every Maha -Manvantara, or new cycle of life.

Q. How about those Cabalists, who, while being such, still believe in Jehovah, or the Tetragrammaton?

A. They are at liberty to believe in what they please, as their belief or disbelief can hardly affect a selfevident fact. The Jesuits tell us that two and two are not always four to a certainty, since it depends on the will of God to make $2 + 2 = 5$. Shall we accept their sophistry for all that?

Q. Then you are Atheists?

A. Not that we know of, and not unless the epithet of "Atheist" is to be applied to those who disbelieve in an anthropomorphic God. We believe in a Universal Divine Principle, the root of all, from which all proceeds, and within which all shall be absorbed at the end of the great cycle of Being.

Q. This is the old, old claim of Pantheism. If you are Pantheists, you cannot be Deists; and if you are not Deists, then you have to answer to the name of Atheists.

A. Not necessarily so. The term Pantheism is again one of the many abused terms, whose real and primitive meaning has been distorted by blind prejudice and a one-sided view of it. If you accept the Christian etymology of this compound word, and form it of *pan*, "all", and *theos*, "god", and then imagine and teach that this means that every stone and every tree in Nature is a God or the one God, then, of course, you will be right, and make of Pantheists fetish-worshippers, in addition to their legitimate name. But you will hardly be as successful if you etymologize the word *Pantheism* esoterically, and as we do.

Q. What is, then, your definition of it?

A. Let me ask you a question in my turn. What do you understand by Pan, or Nature?

Q. Nature is, I suppose, the sum total of things existing around us; the aggregate of causes and effects in the world of matter, the creation or universe.

A. Hence the personified sum and order of known causes and effects; the total of all finite agencies and forces, as utterly disconnected from an intelligent Creator or Creators, and perhaps "conceived of as a single and separate force" - as in your encyclopedias?

Q. Yes, I believe so.

A. Well, we neither take into consideration this objective and material nature, which we call an evanescent illusion, nor do we mean by Nature, in the sense of its accepted derivation from the Latin Natura (becoming, from nasci, to be born). When we speak of the Deity and make it identical, hence coeval, with Nature, the eternal and uncreate nature is meant, and not your aggregate of flitting shadows and finite unrealities. We leave it to the hymn-makers to call the visible sky or heaven, God's Throne, and our earth of mud His footstool. Our deity is neither in a paradise, nor in a particular tree, building, or mountain: it is everywhere, in every atom of the visible as of the invisible Cosmos, in, over, and around every invisible atom and divisible molecule; for it is the mysterious power of evolution and involution, the omnipresent, omnipotent, and even omniscient creative potentiality.

Q. Stop! Omniscience is the prerogative of something that thinks, and you deny to your Absoluteness the power of thought.

A. We deny it to the absolute, since thought is something limited and conditioned. But you evidently forget that in philosophy absolute unconsciousness is also absolute consciousness, as otherwise it would not be *absolute*.

Q. Then your Absolute thinks?

A. No, it does not; for the simple reason that it is *Absolute Thought* itself. Nor does it exist, for the same reason, as it is absolute existence, and *Be-ness*, not a Being. Read the superb Cabalistic poem by Solomon Ben Jehudah Gabirol, in the Kether-Malchut, and you will understand:

> *Thou art one, the root of all numbers, but not as an element of numeration; for unity admits not of multiplication, change, or form.*
> *Thou art one, and in the secret of Thy unity the wisest of men are lost, because they know it not.*
> *Thou art one, and Thy unity is never diminished, never extended, and cannot be changed.*
> *Thou art one, and no thought of mine can fix for Thee a limit, or define Thee.*
> *Thou art, but not as one existent, for the understanding and vision of mortals cannot attain to Thy existence, nor determine for Thee the where, the how and the why ...*

In short, our Deity is the eternal, incessantly evolving, not creating, builder of the universe; that *universe itself unfolding* out of its own essence, not being made. It is a sphere, without circumference, in its symbolism, which has but one ever-acting attribute embracing all other existing or thinkable attributes - itself. It is the one law, giving the impulse to manifested, eternal, and immutable laws, within that nevermanifesting, because absolute law, which in its manifesting periods is The ever-Becoming.

Q. I once heard one of your members remarking that Universal Deity, being everywhere, was in vessels of dishonour, as in those of honor, and, therefore, was present in every atom of my cigar ash! Is this not rank blasphemy?

A. I do not think so, as simple logic can hardly be regarded as blasphemy. Were we to exclude the Omnipresent Principle from one single mathematical point of the universe, or from a particle of matter occupying any conceivable space, could we still regard it as infinite?

Is it Necessary to Pray?

Q. Do you believe in prayer, and do you ever pray?

A. We do not. We act, instead of talking.

Q. You do not offer prayers even to the Absolute Principle?

A. Why should we? Being well-occupied people, we can hardly afford to lose time in addressing verbal prayers to a pure abstraction. The Unknowable is capable of relations only in its parts to each other, but is non-existent as regards any finite relations. The visible universe depends for its existence and phenomena on its mutually acting forms and their laws, not on prayer or prayers.

Q. Do you not believe at all in the efficacy of prayer?

A. Not in prayer taught in so many words and repeated externally, if by prayer you mean the outward petition to an unknown God as the addressee, which was inaugurated by the Jews and popularized by the Pharisees.

Q. Is there any other kind of prayer?

A. Most decidedly; we call it will-prayer, and it is rather an internal command than a petition.

Q. To whom, then, do you pray when you do so?

A. To "our Father in heaven" - in its esoteric meaning.

Q. Is that different from the one given to it in theology?

A. Entirely so. An Occultist or a Theosophist addresses his prayer to *his Father which is in secret*, not to an extra-cosmic and therefore finite God; and that "Father" is in man himself.

Q. Then you make of man a God?

A. Please say "God" and not a God. In our sense, the inner man is the only God we can have cognizance of. And how can this be otherwise? Grant us our postulate that God is a universally diffused, infinite principle, and how can man alone escape from being soaked through by, and in, the Deity? We call our "Father in heaven" that deific essence of which we are cognizant within us, in our heart and spiritual consciousness, and which has nothing to do with the anthropomorphic conception we may form of it in our physical brain or its fancy: "Know ye not that ye are the temple of God, and that the spirit of (the absolute) God dwelleth in you?"

One often finds in Theosophical writings conflicting statements about the Christos principle in man. Some call it the sixth principle (Buddhi), others the seventh (Atma). If Christian Theosophists wish to make use of such expressions, let them be made philosophically correct by following the analogy of the old Wisdom-Religion symbols. We say that Christos is not only one of the three higher principles, but all the three regarded as a Trinity. This Trinity represents the Holy Ghost, the Father, and the Son, as it answers to abstract spirit, differentiated spirit, and embodied spirit. Krishna and Christ are philosophically the same principle under its triple aspect of manifestation. In the Bhagavad-Gita we find Krishna calling himself indifferently Atma, the abstract Spirit, Kshetrajna, the Higher or reincarnating Ego, and the Universal Self, all names which, when transferred from the Universe to man, answer to *Atma, Buddhi,* and *Manas.* The Anugita is full of the same doctrine.

Yet, let no man anthropomorphize that essence in us. Let no Theosophist, if he would hold to divine, not human truth, say that this "God in secret" listens to, or is distinct from, either finite man or the infinite essence - for all are one. Nor, as just remarked, that a prayer is a petition. It is a mystery rather; an occult process by which finite and conditioned thoughts and desires, unable to be assimilated by the absolute spirit which is unconditioned, are translated into spiritual wills and the will; such process being called "spiritual transmutation". The intensity of our ardent aspirations changes prayer into the "philosopher's stone", or that which transmutes lead into pure gold. The only homogeneous essence, our "will-prayer" becomes the active or creative force, producing effects according to our desire.

Q. Do you mean to say that prayer is an occult process bringing about physical results?

A. I do. *Will*-Power becomes a living power. But woe unto those Occultists and Theosophists, who, instead of crushing out the desires of the lower personal ego or physical man, and saying, addressing their *Higher* Spiritual Ego immersed in Atma-Buddhic light, "Thy will be done, not mine", etc., send up waves of will-power for selfish or unholy purposes! For this is black magic, abomination, and spiritual sorcery. Unfortunately, all this is the favorite occupation of our Christian statesmen and generals, especially when the latter are sending two armies to murder each other. Both indulge before action in a bit of such sorcery, by offering respectively prayers to the same God of Hosts, each entreating his help to cut its enemies' throats.

Q. David prayed to the Lord of Hosts to help him smite the Philistines and slay the Syrians and the Moabites, and "the Lord preserved David whithersoever he went". In that we only follow what we find in the Bible.

A. Of course you do. But since you delight in calling yourselves Christians, not Israelites or Jews, as far as we know, why do you not rather follow that which Christ says? And he distinctly commands you not to follow "them of old times", or the Mosaic law, but bids you do as he tells you, and warns those who would kill by the sword, that they, too, will perish by the sword. Christ has given you one prayer of which you have made a lip prayer and a boast, and which none but the *true* Occultist understands. In it you say, in your dead-sense meaning: "Forgive us our debts, as we forgive our debtors", which you never do. Again, he told you *to love your enemies and do good to them that hate you.* It is surely not the "meek prophet of Nazareth" who taught you to pray to your "Father" to slay, and give you victory over your enemies! This is why we reject what you call "prayers".

Q. But how do you explain the universal fact that all nations and peoples have prayed to, and worshiped a God or Gods? Some have adored and propitiated devils and harmful spirits, but this only proves the universality of the belief in the efficacy of prayer.

A. It is explained by that other fact that prayer has several other meanings besides that given it by the Christians. It means not only a pleading or petition, but meant, in days of old, far more an invocation and incantation. The mantra, or the rhythmically chanted prayer of the Hindus, has precisely such a meaning, as the Brahmins hold themselves higher than the common devas or "Gods". A prayer may be an appeal or an incantation for malediction, and a curse (as in the case of two armies praying simultaneously for mutual destruction) as much as for blessing. And as the great majority of people are intensely selfish, and pray only for themselves, asking to be given their "daily bread" instead of working for it, and begging God not to lead them "into temptation" but to deliver them (the memorialists only) from evil, the result is, that prayer, as now understood, is doubly pernicious: (a) It kills in man self-reliance; (b) It develops in him a still more ferocious selfishness and egotism than he is already endowed with by nature. I repeat, that we believe in "communion" and simultaneous action in unison with our "Father in secret"; and in rare moments of ecstatic bliss, in the mingling of our higher soul with the universal essence, attracted as it is towards its origin and center, a state, called during life Samadhi, and after death, Nirvana. We refuse to pray to created finite beings - i.e., gods, saints, angels, etc., because we regard it as idolatry. We cannot pray to the absolute for reasons explained before; therefore, we try to replace fruitless and useless prayer by meritorious and good-producing actions.

Q. Christians would call it pride and blasphemy. Are they wrong?

A. Entirely so. It is they, on the contrary, who show Satanic pride in their belief that the Absolute or the Infinite, even if there was such a thing as the possibility of any relation between the unconditioned and the conditioned-will stoop to listen to every foolish or egotistical prayer. And it is they again, who virtually blaspheme, in teaching that an Omniscient and Omnipotent God needs uttered prayers to know what he has to do! This - understood esoterically - is corroborated by both Buddha and Jesus. The one says: *Seek nought from the helpless Gods-pray not! but rather act; for darkness will not brighten. Ask nought from silence, for it can neither speak nor hear.*

And the other - Jesus - recommends: "Whatsoever ye shall ask in my name (that of Christos) that will I do". Of course, this quotation, if taken in its literal sense, goes against our argument. But if we accept it esoterically, with the full knowledge of the meaning of the term Christos which to us represents Atma-Buddhi-Manas, the "self", it comes to this: the only God we must recognize and pray to, or rather act in unison with, is that spirit of God of which our body is the temple, and in which it dwelleth.

Prayer Kills Self-Reliance

Q. But did not Christ himself pray and recommend prayer?

A. It is so recorded, but those "prayers" are precisely of that kind of communion just mentioned with one's "Father in secret". Otherwise, and if we identify Jesus with the universal deity, there would be something too absurdly illogical in the inevitable conclusion that he, the "very God himself" prayed to himself, and separated the will of that God from his own!

Q. One argument more; an argument, moreover, much used by some Christians. They say, I feel that I am not able to conquer any passions and weaknesses in my own strength. But when I pray to Jesus Christ I feel that he gives me strength and that in His power I am able to conquer.

A. No wonder. If "Christ Jesus" is God, and one independent and separate from him who prays, of course everything is, and *must* be possible to "a mighty God". But, then, where's the merit, or justice either, of such a conquest? Why should the pseudo-conqueror be rewarded for something done which has cost him only prayers? Would you, even a simple mortal man, pay your labourer a full day's wage if you did most of his work for him, he sitting under an apple tree, and praying to you to do so, all the while? This idea of passing one's whole life in moral idleness, and having one's hardest work and duty done by another - whether God or man - is most revolting to us, as it is most degrading to human dignity.

Q. Perhaps so, yet it is the idea of trusting in a personal Savior to help and strengthen in the battle of life, which is the fundamental idea of modern Christianity. And there is no doubt that, subjectively, such belief is efficacious; i.e., that those who believe do feel themselves helped and strengthened.

A. Nor is there any more doubt, that some patients of "Christian" and "Mental Scientists" - the great "*Deniers*"- are also sometimes cured; nor that hypnotism, and suggestion, psychology, and even mediumship, will produce such results, as often, if not oftener. You take into consideration, and string on the thread of your argument, successes alone. And how about ten times the number of failures? Surely you will not presume to say that failure is unknown even with a sufficiency of blind faith, among fanatical Christians?

Q. But how can you explain those cases which are followed by full success? Where does a Theosophist look to for power to subdue his passions and selfishness?

A. To his Higher Self, the divine spirit, or the God in him, and to his *Karma*. How long shall we have to repeat over and over again that the tree is known by its fruit, the nature of the cause by its effects? You speak of subduing passions, and becoming good through and with the help of God or Christ. We ask, where do you find more virtuous, guiltless people, abstaining from sin and crime, in Christendom or Buddhism - in Christian countries or in heathen lands? Statistics are there to give the answer and corroborate our claims. According to the last census in Ceylon and India, in the comparative table of crimes committed by Christians, Muslims, Hindus, Eurasians, Buddhists, etc., etc., on two millions of population taken at random from each, and covering the misdemeanours of several years, the proportion of crimes committed by the Christian stands as 15 to 4 as against those committed by the Buddhist population. No Orientalist, no historian of any note, or traveler in Buddhist lands, from Bishop Bigandet and Abbé Huc, to Sir William Hunter and every fair-minded official, will fail to give the palm of virtue to Buddhists before Christians. Yet the former (not the true Buddhist Siamese sect, at all events) do not believe in either God or a future reward, outside of this earth. They do not pray, neither priests nor laymen. "Pray!" they would exclaim in wonder, "to whom, or what?"

Q. Then they are truly Atheists.

A. Most undeniably, but they are also the most virtue-loving and virtuekeeping men in the whole world. Buddhism says: Respect the religions of other men and remain true to your own; but Church Christianity, denouncing all the gods of other nations as devils, would doom every *non*-Christian to eternal perdition.

Q. Does not the Buddhist priesthood do the same?

A. Never. They hold too much to the wise precept found in the Dhammapada to do so, for they know that, If any man, whether he be learned or not, consider himself so great as to despise other men, he is like a blind man holding a candle-blind himself, he illumines others.

On the Source of the Human Soul

Q. How, then, do you account for man being endowed with a Spirit and Soul? Whence these?

A. From the Universal Soul. Certainly not bestowed by a personal God. Whence the moist element in the jelly-fish? From the Ocean which surrounds it, in which it lives and breathes and has its being, and whither it returns when dissolved.

Q. So you reject the teaching that Soul is given, or breathed into man, by God?

A. We are obliged to. The "Soul" spoken of in Genesis is, as therein stated, the "living Soul" or Nephesh (the vital, animal soul) with which God (we say "nature" and *immutable* law) endows man like every animal. Is not at all the thinking soul or mind; least of all is it the *immortal Spirit*.

Q. Well, let us put it otherwise: is it God who endows man with a human *rational* Soul and immortal Spirit?

A. Again, in the way you put the question, we must object to it. Since we believe in no personal God, how can we believe that he endows man with anything? But granting, for the sake of argument, a God who takes upon himself the risk of creating a new Soul for every new-born baby, all that can be said is that such a God can hardly be regarded as himself endowed with any wisdom or prevision. Certain other difficulties and the impossibility of reconciling this with the claims made for the mercy, justice, equity and omniscience of that God, are so many deadly reefs on which this theological dogma is daily and hourly broken.

Q. What do you mean? What difficulties?

A. I am thinking of an unanswerable argument offered once in my presence by a Singhalese Buddhist priest, a famous preacher, to a Christian missionary - one in no way ignorant or unprepared for the public discussion during which it was advanced. It was near Colombo, and the Missionary had challenged the priest Megattivati to give his reasons why the Christian God should not be accepted by the "heathen". Well, the Missionary came out of that forever memorable discussion second best, as usual.

Q. I should be glad to learn in what way.

A. Simply this: the Buddhist priest premised by asking the padre whether his God had given commandments to Moses only for men to keep, but to be broken by God himself. The missionary denied the supposition indignantly. Well, said his opponent,

... you tell us that God makes no exceptions to this rule, and that no Soul can be born without his will. Now God forbids adultery, among other things, and yet you say in the same breath that it is he who creates every baby born, and he who endows it with a Soul. Are we then to understand that the millions of children born in crime and adultery are your God's work? That your God forbids and punishes the breaking of his laws; and that, nevertheless, he creates daily and hourly souls for just such children? According to the simplest logic, your God is an accomplice in the crime; since, but for his help and interference, no such children of lust could be born. Where is the justice of punishing not only the guilty parents but even the innocent babe for that which is done by that very God, whom yet you exonerate from any guilt himself?

The missionary looked at his watch and suddenly found it was getting too late for further discussion.

Q. You forget that all such inexplicable cases are mysteries, and that we are forbidden by our religion to pry into the mysteries of God.

A. No, we do not forget, but simply reject such impossibilities. Nor do we want you to believe as we do. We only answer the questions you ask. We have, however, another name for your "mysteries".

The Buddhist Teachings on the Above

Q. What does Buddhism teach with regard to the Soul?

A. It depends whether you mean exoteric, popular Buddhism, or its esoteric teachings. The former explains itself in The Buddhist Catechism in this wise: Soul it considers a word used by the ignorant to express a false idea. If everything is subject to change, then man is included, and every material part of him must change. That which is subject to change is not permanent, so there can be no immortal survival of a changeful thing.

This seems plain and definite. But when we come to the question that the new personality in each succeeding rebirth is the aggregate of "Skandhas", or the attributes, of the old personality, and ask whether this new aggregation of Skandhas is a new being likewise, in which nothing has remained of the last, we read that:

In one sense it is a new being, in another it is not. During this life the Skandhas are continually changing, while the man A.B. of forty is identical as regards personality with the youth A.B. of eighteen, yet by the continual waste and reparation of his body and change of mind and character, he is a different being. Nevertheless, the man in his old age justly reaps the reward or suffering consequent upon his thoughts and actions at every previous stage of his life. So the new being of the rebirth, being the same individuality as before (but not the same personality), with but a changed form, or new aggregation of Skandhas, justly reaps the consequences of his actions and thoughts in the previous existence. This is abstruse metaphysics, and plainly does not express disbelief in Soul by any means.

Q. Is not something like this spoken of in *Esoteric Buddhism*?

A. It is, for this teaching belongs both to Esoteric Budhism or Secret Wisdom, and to the exoteric Buddhism, or the religious philosophy of Gautama Buddha.

Q. But we are distinctly told that most of the Buddhists do not believe in the Soul's immortality?

A. No more do we, if you mean by Soul the personal Ego, or life - Soul - Nephesh.But every learned Buddhist believes in the individual or divine Ego. Those who do not, err in their judgment. They are as mistaken on this point, as those Christians who mistake the theological interpolations of the later editors of the Gospels about damnation and hellfire, for verbatim utterances of Jesus. Neither Buddha nor "Christ" ever wrote anything themselves, but both spoke in allegories and used "dark sayings", as all true Initiates did, and will do for a long time yet to come. Both Scriptures treat of all such metaphysical questions very cautiously, and both, Buddhist and Christian records, sin by that excess of exotericism; the dead letter meaning far overshooting the mark in both cases.

Q. Do you mean to suggest that neither the teachings of Buddha nor those of Christ have been heretofore rightly understood?

A. What I mean is just as you say. Both Gospels, the Buddhist and the Christian, were preached with the same object in view. Both reformers were ardent philanthropists and practical altruists - preaching most unmistakably Socialism of the noblest and highest type, self-sacrifice to the bitter end. "Let the sins of the whole world fall upon me that I may relieve man's misery and suffering!" cries Buddha. "I would not let one cry whom I could save!" exclaims the Prince-beggar, clad in the refuse rags of the burial-grounds. "Come unto me all ye that labor and are heavy laden and I will give you rest", is the appeal to the poor and the disinherited made by the "Man of Sorrows", who hath not where to lay his head. The teachings of both are boundless love for humanity, charity, forgiveness of injury, forgetfulness of self, and pity for the deluded masses; both show the same contempt for riches, and make no difference between meum and tuum. Their desire was, without revealing to all the sacred mysteries of initiation, to give the ignorant and the misled, whose burden in life was too heavy for them, hope enough and an inkling into the truth sufficient to support them in their heaviest hours. But the object of both Reformers was frustrated, owing to excess of zeal of their later followers. The words of the Masters having been misunderstood and misinterpreted, behold the consequences!

Q. But surely Buddha must have repudiated the soul's immortality, if all the Orientalists and his own Priests say so!

A. The Arhats began by following the policy of their Master and the majority of the subsequent priests were not initiated, just as in Christianity; and so, little by little, the great esoteric truths became almost lost. A proof in point is, that, out of the two existing sects in Ceylon, the Siamese believes death to be the absolute annihilation of individuality and personality, and the other explains Nirvana, as we Theosophists do.

Q. But why, in that case, do Buddhism and Christianity represent the two opposite poles of such belief?

A. Because the conditions under which they were preached were not the same. In India the Brahmins, jealous of their superior knowledge, and excluding from it every caste save their own, had driven millions of men into idolatry and almost fetishism. Buddha had to give the death-blow to an exuberance of unhealthy fancy and fanatical superstition resulting from ignorance, such as has rarely been known before or after. Better a philosophical atheism than such ignorant worship for those: Who cry upon their gods and are not heard - Or are not heeded … - and who live and die in mental despair. He had to arrest first of all this muddy torrent of superstition, to uproot errors before he gave out the truth. And as he could not give out all, for the same good reason as Jesus, who reminds his disciples that the Mysteries of Heaven are not for the unintelligent masses, but for the elect alone, and therefore "spake he to them in parables" - so his caution led Buddha to conceal too much. He even refused to say to the monk Vacchagotta whether there was, or was not an Ego in man. When pressed to answer, "the Exalted one maintained silence".

Buddha gives to Ananda, his *initiated* disciple, who inquires for the reason of this silence, a plain and unequivocal answer in the dialogue translated by Oldenburg from the Samyutta-Nikaya: If I, Ananda, when the wandering monk Vacchagotta asked me: "Is there the Ego?" had answered "The Ego is", then that, Ananda, would have confirmed the doctrine of the Samanas and Brahmans, who believed in permanence. *If I, Ananda, when the wandering monk Vacchagotta asked me, "Is there not the Ego?" had answered, "The Ego is not", then that, Ananda, would have confirmed the doctrine of those who believed in annihilation. If I, Ananda, when the wandering monk Vacchagotta asked me, "Is there the Ego?" had answered, "The Ego is", would that have served my end, Ananda, by producing in him the knowledge: all existences (dhamma) are non-ego? But if I, Ananda, had answered, "The Ego is not", then that, Ananda, would only have caused the wandering monk Vacchagotta to be thrown from one bewilderment to another: "My Ego, did it not exist before? But now it exists no longer!"* This shows, better than anything, that

Gautama Buddha withheld such difficult metaphysical doctrines from the masses in order not to perplex them more. What he meant was the difference between the personal temporary Ego and the Higher Self, which sheds its light on the imperishable Ego, the spiritual "I" of man.

Q. This refers to Gautama, but in what way does it touch the Gospels?

A. Read history and think over it. At the time the events narrated in the Gospels are alleged to have happened, there was a similar intellectual fermentation taking place in the whole civilized world, only with opposite results in the East and the West. The old gods were dying out. While the civilized classes drifted in the train of the unbelieving Sadducees into materialistic negations and mere dead-letter Mosaic form in Palestine, and into moral dissolution in Rome, the lowest and poorer classes ran after sorcery and strange gods, or became hypocrites and Pharisees. Once more the time for a spiritual reform had arrived. The cruel, anthropomorphic and jealous God of the Jews, with his sanguinary laws of "an eye for eye and tooth for tooth", of the shedding of blood and animal sacrifice, had to be relegated to a secondary place and replaced by the merciful "Father in Secret". The latter had to be shown, not as an extra-Cosmic God, but as a divine Savior of the man of flesh, enshrined in his own heart and soul, in the poor as in the rich. No more here than in India, could the secrets of initiation be divulged, lest by giving that which is holy to the dogs, and casting pearls before swine, both the *Revealer* and the things revealed should be trodden under foot. Thus, the reticence of both Buddha and Jesus - whether the latter lived out the historic period allotted to him or not, and who equally abstained from revealing plainly the Mysteries of Life and Death-led in the one case to the blank negations of Southern Buddhism, and in the other, to the three clashing forms of the Christian Church and the 300 sects in Protestant England alone.

Theosophical Teachings as to Nature and Man
The Unity of All in All

Q. Having told me what God, the Soul and Man are not, in your views, can you inform me what they are, according to your teachings?

A. In their origin and in eternity the three, like the universe and all therein, are one with the absolute Unity, the unknowable deific essence I spoke about some time back. We believe in no creation, but in the periodical and consecutive appearances of the universe from the subjective onto the objective plane of being, at regular intervals of time, covering periods of immense duration.

Q. Can you elaborate the subject?

A. Take as a first comparison and a help towards a more correct conception, the solar year, and as a second, the two halves of that year, producing each a day and a night of six months' duration at the North Pole. Now imagine, if you can, instead of a Solar year of 365 days, eternity. Let the sun represent the universe, and the polar days and nights of six months each - *days and nights lasting each 182 trillions and quadrillions of years*, instead of 182 days each. As the sun arises every morning on our *objective* horizon out of its (to us) *subjective* and antipodal space, so does the Universe emerge periodically on the plane of objectivity, issuing from that of subjectivity - the antipodes of the former. This is the "Cycle of Life". And as the sun disappears from our horizon, so does the Universe disappear at regular periods, when the "Universal night" sets in. The Hindus call such alternations the "Days and Nights of Brahm", or the time of *Manvantara* and that of *Pralaya* (dissolution). The Westerns may call them Universal Days and Nights if they prefer. During the latter (the nights) *All is in All*; every atom is resolved into one Homogeneity.

Evolution and Illusion

Q. But who is it that creates each time the Universe?

A. No one creates it. Science would call the process evolution; the pre-Christian philosophers and the Orientalists called it emanation: we, Occultists and Theosophists, see in it the only universal and eternal reality casting a periodical reflection of itself on the infinite Spatial depths. This reflection, which you regard as the objective *material universe*, we consider as a temporary *illusion* and nothing else. That alone which is eternal is real.

Q. At that rate, you and I are also illusions.

A. As flitting personalities, today one person, tomorrow another - we are. Would you call the sudden flashes of the aurora borealis, the Northern lights, a "reality", though it is as real as can be while you look at it? Certainly not; it is the cause that produces it, if permanent and eternal, which is the only reality, while the other is but a passing illusion.

Q. All this does not explain to me how this illusion called the universe originates; how the conscious to be, proceeds to manifest itself from the unconsciousness that is.

A. It is unconsciousness *only* to our finite consciousness. Verily may we paraphrase St. John and say:

... *and (*Absolute) *light* (which is darkness) *shineth in darkness* (which is illusionary material light); *and the darkness comprehendeth it not.*

This absolute light is also absolute and immutable law. Whether by radiation or emanation - we need not quarrel over terms - the universe passes out of its homogeneous subjectivity onto the first plane of manifestation, of which planes there are seven, we are taught. With each plane it becomes more dense and material until it reaches this, our plane, on which the only world approximately known and understood in its physical composition by Science, is the planetary or Solar system - one *sui generis*, we are told.

Q. What do you mean by *sui generis*?

A. I mean that, though the fundamental law and the universal working of laws of Nature are uniform, still our Solar system (like every other such system in the millions of others in Cosmos) and even our Earth, has its own program of manifestations differing from the respective programs of all others. We speak of the inhabitants of other planets and imagine that if they are men, i.e., thinking entities, they must be as we are. The fancy of poets and painters and sculptors never fails to represent even the angels as a beautiful copy of man - *plus* wings. We say that all this is an error and a delusion; because, if on this little earth alone one finds such a diversity in its flora, fauna, and mankind - from the seaweed to the cedar of Lebanon, from the jellyfish to the elephant, from the Bushman and negro to the Apollo Belvedere - alter the conditions cosmic and planetary, and there must be as a result quite a different flora, fauna, and mankind. The same laws will fashion quite a different set of things and beings even on this our plane, including in it all our planets. How much more different then must be external nature in other Solar systems, and how foolish is it to judge of other stars and worlds and human beings by our own, as physical science does!

Q. But what are your data for this assertion?

A. What science in general will never accept as proof - the cumulative testimony of an endless series of Seers who have testified to this fact. Their spiritual visions, real explorations by, and through, physical and spiritual senses untrammelled by blind flesh, were systematically checked and compared one with the other, and their nature sifted. All that was not corroborated by unanimous and collective experience was rejected, while that only was recorded as established truth which, in various ages, under different climes, and throughout an untold series of incessant observations, was found to agree and receive constantly further corroboration. The methods used by our scholars and students of the psycho-spiritual sciences do not differ from those of students of the natural and physical sciences, as you may see. Only our fields of research are on two different planes, and our instruments are made by no human hands, for which reason perchance they are only the more reliable. The retorts, accumulators, and microscopes of the chemist and naturalist may get out of order; the telescope and the astronomer's horological instruments may get spoiled; our recording instruments are beyond the influence of weather or the elements.

Q. And therefore you have implicit faith in them?

A. Faith is a word not to be found in theosophical dictionaries: we say knowledge based, on observation and experience. There is this difference, however, that while the observation and experience of physical science lead the Scientists to about as many "working" hypotheses as there are minds to evolve them, our *knowledge* consents to add to its lore only those facts which have become undeniable, and which are fully and absolutely demonstrated. We have no two beliefs or hypotheses on the same subject.

Q. Is it on such data that you came to accept the strange theories we find in *Esoteric Buddhism*?

A. Just so. These theories may be slightly incorrect in their minor details, and even faulty in their exposition by lay students; they are facts in nature, nevertheless, and come nearer the truth than any scientific hypothesis.

On The Septenary Constitution of Our Planet

Q. I understand that you describe our earth as forming part of a chain of earths?

A. We do. But the other six "earths" or globes, are not on the same plane of objectivity as our earth is; therefore we cannot see them.

Q. Is that on account of the great distance?

A. Not at all, for we see with our naked eye planets and even stars at immeasurably greater distances; but it is owing to those six globes being outside our physical means of perception, or plane of being. It is not only that their material density, weight, or fabric are entirely different from those of our earth and the other known planets; but they are (to us) on an entirely different layer of space, so to speak; a layer not to be perceived or felt by our physical senses. And when I say "layer", please do not allow your fancy to suggest to you layers like strata or beds laid one over the other, for this would only lead to another absurd misconception. What I mean by "layer" is that plane of infinite space which by its nature cannot fall under our ordinary waking perceptions, whether mental or physical; but which exists in nature outside of our normal mentality or consciousness, outside of our three-dimensional space, and outside of our division of time. Each of the seven fundamental planes (or layers) in space - of course as a whole, as the pure space of Locke's definition, not as our finite space - has its own objectivity and subjectivity, its own space and time, its own consciousness and set of senses. But all this will be hardly comprehensible to one trained in the modern ways of thought.

Q. What do you mean by a different set of senses? Is there anything on our human plane that you could bring as an illustration of what you say, just to give a clearer idea of what you may mean by this variety of senses, spaces, and respective perceptions?

A. None; except, perhaps, that which for Science would be rather a handy peg on which to hang a counter argument. We have a different set of senses in dreamlife, have we not? We feel, talk, hear, see, taste and function in general on a different plane; the change of state of our consciousness being evidenced by the fact that a series of acts and events embracing years, as we think, pass ideally through our mind in one instant. Well, that extreme rapidity of our mental operations in dreams, and the perfect naturalness, for the time being, of all the other functions, show us that we are on quite another plane. Our philosophy teaches us that, as there are seven fundamental forces in nature, and seven planes of being, so there are seven states of consciousness in which man can live, think, remember and have his being. To enumerate these here is impossible, and for this one has to turn to the study of Eastern metaphysics. But in these two states - the waking and the dreaming - every ordinary mortal, from a learned philosopher down to a poor untutored savage, has a good proof that such states differ.

Q. You do not accept, then, the well-known explanations of biology and physiology to account for the dream state?

A. We do not. We reject even the hypotheses of your psychologists, preferring the teachings of Eastern Wisdom. Believing in seven planes of Kosmic being and states of Consciousness, with regard to the Universe or the Macrocosm, we stop at the fourth plane, finding it impossible to go with any degree of certainty beyond. But with respect to the Microcosm, or man, we speculate freely on his seven states and principles.

Q. How do you explain these?

A. We find, first of all, two distinct beings in man; the spiritual and the physical, the man who thinks, and the man who records as much of these thoughts as he is able to assimilate. Therefore we divide him into two distinct natures; the upper or the spiritual being, composed of three principles or *aspects*; and the lower or the physical quaternary, composed of *four* - in all *seven*.

The Septenary Nature of Man

Q. Is it what we call Spirit and Soul, and the man of flesh?

A. It is not. That is the old Platonic division. Plato was an Initiate, and therefore could not go into forbidden details; but he who is acquainted with the archaic doctrine finds the seven in Plato's various combinations of Soul and Spirit. He regarded man as constituted of two parts - one eternal, formed of the same essence as the Absoluteness, the other mortal and corruptible, deriving its constituent parts from the minor "created" Gods. Man is composed, he shows, of (1) A mortal body, (2) An immortal principle, and (3) A "separate mortal kind of Soul". It is that which we respectively call the physical man, the Spiritual Soul or Spirit, and the animal Soul (the Nous and psuche). This is the division adopted by Paul, another Initiate, who maintains that there is a psychical body which is sown in the corruptible (astral soul or body), and a spiritual body that is raised in incorruptible substance. Even James corroborates the same by saying that the "wisdom" (of our lower soul) descendeth not from the above, but is terrestrial ("psychical", "demoniacal", see the Greek text) while the other is heavenly wisdom. Now so plain is it that Plato and even Pythagoras, while speaking but of three principles, give them seven separate functions, in their various combinations, that if we contrast our teachings this will become quite plain. Let us take a cursory view of these seven aspects by drawing two tables.

LOWER QUATERNARY

SANSCRIT TERMS	EXOTERIC MEANING	EXPLANATORY
a. Rupa, or Suthula-Sarira	a. Physical Body	a. Is the vehicle of all the other 'principles' during life
b. Prana	b. Life, or Vital Principle	b. Necessary only to a, c, d and functions of the lower *Manas*, which embrace all those limited to the physical brain
c. Linga Sharira	c. Astral Body	c The *Double*, the Phantom Body
d. Kama Rupa	d. The seat of animal desires and passions	d This is the centre of the animal man, where lies the line of demarcation which the mortal man from the immortal enitity

THE UPPER IMPERISHABLE TRIAD

SANSCRIT TERMS	EXOTERIC MEANING	EXPLANATORY
e. Manas - a dual principle in its functions	e. Mind, Intelligence; which is the higher human mind, whose light/radiation links the *Monad,* for the lifetime, the the mortal man.	e. The future state & Karmic destiny of man depends on whether manas moves down to Kama rupa (animal passions)or up to *Buddhi*, the Spiritual *Ego*. In the latter. the higher consciousness of individ-ual Spiritual aspirations of *mind* (Manas), assimilating Buddhi. are absorbed by it & form the *Ego* which goes into Devachanic bliss.
f. Buddhi	f. The Spiritual Soul	f. The vehicle of pure universal spirit
g. Atma	g. Spirit	g. One with the Absolute, as its radiation

NB In Mr. Sinnett's *Esoteric Buddhism* d, e, and f, are respectively called the Animal, the Human, and the Spiritual Souls, which answers as well. Though the principles in *Esoteric Buddhism* are numbered, this is, strictly speaking, useless. The dual Monad alone (Atma-Buddhi) is susceptible of being thought of as the two highest numbers (the sixth and seventh). As to all others, since that principle only which is predominant in man has to be considered as the first and foremost, no numeration is possible as a general rule. In some men it is the higher Intelligence (Manas or the fifth) which dominates the rest; in others the Animal Soul (Kamarupa) that reigns supreme, exhibiting the most bestial instincts, etc.

Now what does Plato teach? He speaks of the interior man as constituted of two parts - one immutable and always the same, formed of the same substance as Deity, and the other mortal and corruptible. These "two parts" are found in our upper Triad, and the lower Quaternary (see table above,). He explains that when the Soul, psuche, "allies herself to the Nous (divine spirit or substance), she does everything aright and felicitously", but the case is otherwise when she attaches herself to Anoia, (folly, or the irrational animal Soul). Here, then, we have Manas (or the Soul in general) in its two aspects: when attaching itself to Anoia (our Kamarupa, or the "Animal Soul" in Esoteric Buddhism) it runs towards entire annihilation, as far as the personal Ego is concerned; when allying itself to the Nous (Atma-Buddhi) it merges into the immortal, imperishable Ego, and then its spiritual consciousness of the personal that was, becomes immortal.

The Distinction Between Soul and Spirit

Q. Do you really teach, as you are accused of doing by some Spiritualists and French Spiritists, the annihilation of every personality?

A. We do not. But as this question of the duality - the individuality of the Divine Ego, and the personality of the human animal - involves that of the possibility of the real immortal Ego appearing in Séance rooms as a "materialized spirit", which we deny as already explained, our opponents have started the nonsensical charge.

Q. You have just spoken of psuche running towards its entire annihilation if it attaches itself to Anoia. What did Plato, and do you mean by this?

A. The entire annihilation of the personal consciousness, as an exceptional and rare case, I think. The general and almost invariable rule is the merging of the personal into the individual or immortal consciousness of the Ego, a transformation or a divine transfiguration, and the entire annihilation only of the lower quaternary. Would you expect the man of flesh, or the temporary personality,his shadow, the "astral", his animal instincts and even physical life, to survive with the "spiritual Ego" and become everlasting, eternal? Naturally all this ceases to exist, either at, or soon after corporeal death. It becomes in time entirely disintegrated and disappears from view, being annihilated as a whole.

Q. Then you also reject resurrection in the flesh?

A. Most decidedly we do! Why should we, who believe in the archaic esoteric philosophy of the Ancients, accept the unphilosophical speculations of the later Christian theology, borrowed from the Egyptian and Greek exoteric Systems of the Gnostics?

Q. The Egyptians revered Nature-Spirits, and deified even onions: your Hindus are idolaters,to this day; the Zoroastrians worshiped, and do still worship, the Sun; and the best Greek philosophers were either dreamers or materialists - witness Plato and Democritus. How can you compare!

A. It may be so in your modern Christian and even Scientific catechism; it is not so for unbiased minds. The Egyptians revered the "One-Only-One", as Nout; and it is from this word that Anaxagoras got his denomination Nous, or as he calls it, nous autokrates, "the Mind or Spirit Self-potent", the archetes kinedeos , the leading motor, or primum-mobile of all. With him the Nous was God, and the logos was man, his emanation. The Nous is the spirit (whether in Kosmos or in man), and the logos, whether Universe or astral body, the emanation of the former, the physical body being merely the animal. Our external powers perceive phenomena; our Nous alone is able to recognize their noumena. It is the logos alone, or the noumenon, that survives, because it is immortal in its very nature and essence, and the logos in man is the Eternal Ego, that which reincarnates and lasts forever. But how can the evanescent or external shadow, the temporary clothing of that divine Emanation which returns to the source whence it proceeded, be that which is raised in incorruptibility?

Q. Still you can hardly escape the charge of having invented a new division of man's spiritual and psychic constituents; for no philosopher speaks of them, though you believe that Plato does.

A. And I support the view. Besides Plato, there is Pythagoras, who also followed the same idea. Says Plutarch: *Plato and Pythagoras distribute the soul into two parts, the rational (noetic) and irrational (agnoia); that part of the soul of man which is rational is eternal; for though it be not God, yet it is the product of an eternal deity, but that part of the soul which is divested of reason (agnoia) dies.*

The modern term Agnostic comes from Agnosis,a cognate word. We wonder why Mr. Huxley, the author of the word, should have connected his great intellect with "the soul divested of reason" which dies? Is it the exaggerated humility of the modern materialist? Pythagoras described the Soul as a self-moving Unit (monad) composed of three elements, the Nous(Spirit), the phren (mind), and the thumos (life, breath or the Nephesh of the Cabalists) which three correspond to our "Atma-buddhi", (higher Spirit-Soul), to Manas (the Ego), and to Kamarupa in conjunction with the lower reflection of Manas. That which the Ancient Greek philosophers termed Soul, in general, we call Spirit, or Spiritual Soul, Buddhi, as the vehicle of

59

Atma (the Agathon,or Plato's Supreme Deity). The fact that Pythagoras and others state that phren and thumos are shared by us with the brutes, proves that in this case the lower Manasic reflection (instinct) and Kamarupa (animal living passions) are meant. And as Socrates and Plato accepted the clue and followed it, if to these five, namely, Agathon (Deity or Atma),Psuche (Soul in its collective sense), Nous (Spirit or Mind), Phren (physical mind), and Thumos (Kamarupa or passions) we add the eidolon of the Mysteries, the shadowy form or the human double, and the physical body,it will be easy to demonstrate that the ideas of both Pythagoras and Plato were identical with ours. Even the Egyptians held to the Septenary division. In its exit, they taught, the Soul (Ego) had to pass through its seven chambers, or principles, those it left behind, and those it took along with itself. The only difference is that, ever bearing in mind the penalty of revealing Mystery-doctrines, which was death, they gave out the teaching in a broad outline, while we elaborate it and explain it in its details. But though we do give out to the world as much as is lawful, even in our doctrine more than one important detail is withheld, which those who study the esoteric philosophy and are pledged to silence,are alone entitled to know.

The Greek Teachings

Q. We have magnificent Greek and Latin, Sanskrit and Hebrew scholars. How is it that we find nothing in their translations that would afford us a clue to what you say?

A. Because your translators, their great learning notwithstanding, have made of the philosophers, the Greeks especially, misty instead of mystic writers. Take as an instance Plutarch, and read what he says of "the principles" of man. That which he describes was accepted literally and attributed to metaphysical superstition and ignorance. Let me give you an illustration in point. Says Plutarch: *Man is compound; and they are mistaken who think him to be compounded of two parts only. For they imagine that the understanding (brain intellect) is a part of the soul (the upper Triad), but they err in this no less than those who make the soul to be a part of the body, i.e., those who make of the Triad part of the corruptible mortal quaternary.For the understanding (nous) as far exceeds the soul, as the soul is better and diviner than the body. Now this composition of the soul (psuche) with the understanding (nous) makes reason; and with the body (or thumos, the animal soul) passion; of which the one is the beginning or principle of pleasure and pain, and the other of virtue and vice. Of these three parts conjoined and compacted together, the earth has given the body, the moon the soul, and the sun the understanding to the generation of man.*

This last sentence is purely allegorical, and will be comprehended only by those who are versed in the esoteric science of correspondences and know which planet is related to every principle. Plutarch divides the latter into three groups, and makes of the body a compound of physical frame, astral shadow, and breath, or the triple lower part, which "from earth was taken and to earth returns"; of the middle principle and the instinctual soul, the second part, derived from and through and ever influenced by the moon; and only of the higher part or the Spiritual Soul, with the Atmic and Manasic elements in it does he make a direct emanation of the Sun, who stands here for Agathon the Supreme Deity. This is proven by what he says further as follows: *Now of the deaths we die, the one makes man two of three and the other one of (out of) two. The former is in the region and jurisdiction of Demeter, whence the name given to the Mysteries, telein , resembled that given to death, teleutan. The Athenians also heretofore called the deceased sacred to Demeter. As for the other death, it is in the moon or region of Persephone.*

Here you have our doctrine, which shows man a septenary during life; a quintile just after death, in Kamaloka; and a threefold Ego, Spirit-Soul, and consciousness in Devachan. This separation, first in "the Meadows of Hades", as Plutarch calls the Kamaloka, then in Devachan, was part and parcel of the performances during the sacred Mysteries, when the candidates for initiation enacted the whole drama of death, and the resurrection as a glorified spirit, by which name we mean Consciousness. This is what Plutarch means when he says: And as with the one, the terrestrial, so with the other celestial Hermes doth dwell. This suddenly and with violence plucks the soul from the body; but Prospina mildly and in a long time disjoins the understanding from the soul. (Proserpina, or Persephone, stands here for postmortem Karma, which is said to regulate the separation of the lower from the higher principles: the Soul, as Nephesh, the breath of animal life, which remains for a time in Kamaloka, from the higher compound Ego, which goes into the state of Devachan, or bliss.) For this reason she is called Monogenes, only begotten, or rather begetting one alone; for the better part of man becomes alone when it is separated by her.Now both the one and the other happens thus according to nature. It is ordained by Fate (Fatum or Karma) that every soul, whether with or without understanding (mind), when gone out of the body, should wander for a time, though not all for the same, in the region lying between the earth and moon (Kamaloka). For those that have been unjust and dissolute suffer then the punishment due to their offenses; but the good and virtuous are there detained till they are purified, and have, by expiation, purged out of them all the infections they might have contracted from the contagion of the body, as if from foul health, living in the mildest part of the air, called the Meadows of Hades, where they must remain for a certain prefixed and appointed time. And then, as if they were returning from a wandering pilgrimage or long exile into their country, they have a taste of joy, such as they principally receive who are initiated into Sacred Mysteries, mixed with trouble, admiration, and each one's proper and peculiar hope.

This is Nirvanic bliss, and no Theosophist could describe in plainer though esoteric language the mental joys of Devachan, where every man has his paradise around him, erected by his consciousness. But you must beware of the general error into which too many even of our Theosophists fall. Do not imagine that because man is called septenary, then quintuple and a triad, he is a compound of seven, five, or three entities;or, as well expressed by a Theosophical writer, of skins to be peeled off like the skins of an onion. The principles, as already said, save the body, the life, and the astral eidolon,all of which disperse at death, are simply aspects and states of consciousness. There is but one real man, enduring through the cycle of life and immortal in essence, if not in form, and this is Manas, the Mind-man or embodied Consciousness. The objection made by the materialists, who deny the possibility of mind and consciousness acting without matter is worthless in our case. We do not deny the soundness of their argument; but we simply ask our opponents,

Are you acquainted with all the states of matter,you who knew hitherto but of three? And how do you know whether that which we refer to as absolute consciousness or Deity forever invisible and unknowable, be not that which, though it eludes forever our human finite conception, is still universal Spirit-matter or matter-Spirit *in its absolute infinitude*? It is then one of the lowest, and in its manvantaric manifestations fractioned-aspects of this Spirit-matter, which is the conscious Ego that creates its own paradise, a fool's paradise, it may be, still a state of bliss.

Q. But what is Devachan?

A. The "land of gods" literally; a condition, a state of mental bliss. Philosophically a mental condition analogous to, but far more vivid and real than, the most vivid dream. It is the state after death of most mortals.

On the Various Postmortem States
The Physical and the Spiritual Man

Q. I am glad to hear you believe in the immortality of the Soul.

A. Not of "the Soul", but of the divine Spirit; or rather in the immortality of the reincarnating Ego.

Q. What is the difference?

A. A very great one in our philosophy, but this is too abstruse and difficult a question to touch lightly upon. We shall have to analyze them separately, and then in conjunction. We may begin with Spirit.

We say that the Spirit (the "Father in secret" of Jesus), or Atma, is no individual property of any man, but is the Divine essence which has no body, no form, which is imponderable, invisible and indivisible, that which does not exist and yet is, as the Buddhists say of Nirvana. It only overshadows the mortal; that which enters into him and pervades the whole body being only its omnipresent rays, or light, radiated through Buddhi, its vehicle and direct emanation. This is the secret meaning of the assertions of almost all the ancient philosophers, when they said that "the rational part of man's soul" never entered wholly into the man, but only overshadowed him more or less through the irrational spiritual Soul or Buddhi. Buddhi is irrational in the sense that as a pure emanation of the Universal mind it can have no individual reason of its own on this plane of matter, but like the Moon, who borrows her light from the Sun and her life from the Earth, so Buddhi, receiving its light of Wisdom from Atma, gets its rational qualities from Manas. Per se, as something homogeneous, it is devoid of attributes.

Q. I laboured under the impression that the "Animal Soul" alone was irrational, not the Divine.

A. You have to learn the difference between that which is negatively, or passively "irrational", because undifferentiated, and that which is irrational because too active and positive. Man is a correlation of spiritual powers, as well as a correlation of chemical and physical forces, brought into function by what we call principles.

Q. I have read a good deal upon the subject, and it seems to me that the notions of the older philosophers differed a great deal from those of the medieval Cabalists, though they do agree in some particulars.

A. The most substantial difference between them and us is this. While we believe with the Neo-Platonists and the Eastern teachings that the spirit (Atma) never descends hypostatically into the living man, but only showers more or less its radiance on the inner man (the psychic and spiritual compound of the astral principles), the Cabalists maintain that the human Spirit, detaching itself from the ocean of light and Universal Spirit, enters man's Soul, where it remains throughout life imprisoned in the astral capsule. All Christian Cabalists still maintain the same, as they are unable to break quite loose from their anthropomorphic and Biblical doctrines.

Q. And what do you say?

A. We say that we only allow the presence of the radiation of Spirit (or Atma) in the astral capsule, and so far only as that spiritual radiancy is concerned. We say that man and Soul have to conquer their immortality by ascending towards the unity with which, if successful, they will be finally linked and into which they are finally, so to speak, absorbed. The individualization of man after death depends on the spirit, not on his soul and body. Although the word personality, in the sense in which it is usually understood, is an absurdity if applied literally to our immortal essence, still the latter is, as our individual Ego, a distinct entity, immortal and eternal, per se. It is only in the case of black magicians or of criminals beyond redemption, criminals who have been such during a long series of lives - that the shining thread, which links the spirit to the personal soul from the moment of the birth of the child, is violently snapped, and the disembodied entity becomes divorced from the personal soul, the latter being annihilated without leaving the smallest impression of itself on the former. If that union between the lower, or personal Manas, and the individual reincarnating Ego, has not been effected during life, then the former is left to share the fate of the lower animals, to gradually dissolve into ether, and have its personality annihilated. But even then the Ego remains a distinct being. It (the spiritual Ego) only loses one Devachanic state - after that special, and in that case indeed useless, life - as that idealized Personality,and is reincarnated, after enjoying for a short time its freedom as a planetary spirit almost immediately.

Q. It is stated in *Isis Unveiled* that such planetary Spirits or Angels, "the gods of the Pagans or the Archangels of the Christians", will never be men on our planet.

A. Quite right. Not "such", but some classes of higher Planetary Spirits. They will never be men on this planet, because they are liberated Spirits from a previous, earlier world, and as such they cannot rebecome men on this one. Yet all these will live again in the next and far higher Maha-Manvantara, after this "great Age", and "Brahma pralaya", (a little period of 16 figures or so) is over. For you must have heard, of course, that Eastern philosophy teaches us that mankind consists of such "Spirits" imprisoned in human bodies? The difference between animals and men is this: the former are ensouled by the principles potentially,the latter actually. Do you understand now the difference?

Q. Yes; but this specialization has been in all ages the stumbling-block of metaphysicians.

A. It was. The whole esotericism of the Buddhist philosophy is based on this mysterious teaching, understood by so few persons, and so totally misrepresented by many of the most learned modern scholars. Even metaphysicians are too inclined to confound the effect with the cause. An Ego who has won his immortal life as spirit will remain the same inner self throughout all his rebirths on earth; but this does not imply necessarily that he must either remain the Mr. Smith or Mr. Brown he was on earth, or lose his individuality. Therefore, the astral soul and the terrestrial body of man may, in the dark hereafter, be absorbed into the cosmical ocean of sublimated elements, and cease to feel his last personal Ego (if it did not deserve to soar higher), and the divine Ego still remain the same unchanged entity, though this terrestrial experience of his emanation may be totally obliterated at the instant of separation from the unworthy vehicle.

Q. If the "Spirit", or the divine portion of the soul, is preexistent as a distinct being from all eternity, as Origen, Synesius, and other semi-Christians and semi-Platonic philosophers taught, and if it is the same, and nothing more than the metaphysically-objective soul, how can it be otherwise than eternal? And what matters it in such a case, whether man leads a pure life or an animal, if, do what he may, he can never lose his individuality?

A. This doctrine, as you have stated it, is just as pernicious in its consequences as that of vicarious atonement. Had the latter dogma, in company with the false idea that we are all immortal, been demonstrated to the world in its true light, humanity would have been bettered by its propagation.

Let me repeat to you again. Pythagoras, Plato, Timaeus of Locris, and the old Alexandrian School, derived the Soul of man (or his higher principles and attributes) from the Universal World Soul, the latter being, according to their teachings, Aether(Pater-Zeus). Therefore, neither of these principles can be unalloyed essence of the Pythagorean Monas, or our Atma-Buddhi,because the Anima Mundi is but the effect, the subjective emanation or rather radiation of the former. Both the human Spirit (or the individuality), the reincarnating Spiritual Ego, and Buddhi, the Spiritual soul, are preexistent. But, while the former exists as a distinct entity, an individualization, the soul exists as preexisting breath, an unscient [lacking in knowledge] portion of an intelligent whole. Both were originally formed from the Eternal Ocean of light; but as the Fire-Philosophers, the medieval Theosophists, expressed it, there is a visible as well as invisible spirit in fire. They made a difference between the anima bruta and the anima divina. Empedocles firmly believed all men and animals to possess two souls; and in Aristotle we find that he calls one the reasoning soul,nous , and the other, the animal soul, psuche . According to these philosophers, the reasoning soul comes from within the universal soul, and the other from without.

Q. Would you call the Soul, i.e., the human thinking Soul, or what you call the Ego-matter?

A. Not matter, but substance assuredly; nor would the word matter, if prefixed with the adjective, primordial, be a word to avoid. That matter, we say, is coeternal with Spirit, and is not our visible, tangible, and divisible matter, but its extreme sublimation. Pure Spirit is but one remove from the no- Spirit, or the absolute all .Unless you admit that man was evolved out of this primordial Spirit-matter, and represents a regular progressive scale of principles from meta-Spirit down to the grossest matter, how can we ever come to regard the inner man as immortal, and at the same time as a spiritual Entity and a mortal man?

Q. Then why should you not believe in God as such an Entity?

A. Because that which is infinite and unconditioned can have no form, and cannot be a being, not in any Eastern philosophy worthy of the name, at any rate. An "entity" is immortal, but is so only in its ultimate essence, not in its individual form. When at the last point of its cycle, it is absorbed into its primordial nature; and it becomes spirit, when it loses its name of Entity. Its immortality as a form is limited only to its life cycle or the Maha-Manvantara; after which it is one and identical with the Universal Spirit, and no longer a separate Entity. As to the personal Soul - by which we mean the spark of consciousness that preserves in the Spiritual Ego the idea of the personal "I" of the last incarnation - this lasts, as a separate distinct recollection, only throughout the Devachanic period; after which time it is added to the series of other innumerable incarnations of the Ego, like the remembrance in our memory of one of a series of days, at the end of a year. Will you bind the infinitude you claim for your God to finite conditions? That alone which is indissolubly cemented by Atma (i.e., Buddhi-Manas) is immortal. The Soul of man (i.e., of the personality)per se is neither immortal, eternal nor divine. Says The Zohar: *The soul, when sent to this earth, puts on an earthly garment, to preserve herself here, so she receives above a shining garment, in order to be able to look without injury into the mirror, whose light proceeds from the Lord of Light.*

Moreover, The Zohar teaches that the soul cannot reach the abode of bliss, unless she has received the "holy kiss", or the reunion of the soul with the substance from which she emanated - spirit. All souls are dual, and, while the latter is a feminine principle, the spirit is masculine. While imprisoned in body, man is a trinity, unless his pollution is such as to have caused his divorce from the spirit. "Woe to the soul which prefers to her divine husband (spirit) the earthly wedlock with her terrestrial body", records a text of The Book of the Keys, a Hermetic work. Woe indeed, for nothing will remain of that personality to be recorded on the imperishable tablets of the Ego's memory.

Q. How can that which, if not breathed by God into man, yet is on your own confession of an identical substance with the divine, fail to be immortal?

A. Every atom and speck of matter, not of substance only, is imperishable in its essence, but not in its individual consciousness. Immortality is but one's unbroken consciousness; and the personal consciousness can hardly last longer than the personality itself, can it? And such consciousness, as I already told you, survives only throughout Devachan, after which it is reabsorbed, first, in the individual,and then in the universal consciousness. Better enquire of your theologians how it is that they have so sorely jumbled up the Jewish Scriptures. Read the Bible, if you would have a good proof that the writers of the Pentateuch, and Genesis especially, never regarded nephesh, that which God breathes into Adam, as the immortal soul. Here are some instances: "And God created ... every nephesh (life) that moveth", meaning animals; and it is said: "And man became a nephesh" (living soul), which shows that the word nephesh was indifferently applied to immortal man and to mortal beast. "And surely your blood of your nepheshim (lives) will I require; at the hand of every beast will I require it, and at the hand of man", "Escape for nephesh" (escape for thy life, it is translated). "Let us not kill him", reads the English version. "Let us not kill his nephesh", is the Hebrew text. "Nephesh for nephesh", says Leviticus. "He that killeth any man shall surely be put to death", literally "He that smiteth the nephesh of a man"; and from verse 18 and following it reads: "And he that killeth a beast (nephesh) shall make it good ... Beast for beast", whereas the original text has it "nephesh for nephesh". How could man kill that which is immortal? And this explains also why the Sadducees denied the immortality of the soul, as it also affords another proof that very probably the Mosaic Jews - the uninitiated at any rate - never believed in the soul's survival at all.

On Eternal Reward and Punishment, and on Nirvana

Q. It is hardly necessary, I suppose, to ask you whether you believe in the Christian dogmas of Paradise and Hell, or in future rewards and punishments as taught by the Orthodox churches?

A. As described in your catechisms, we reject them absolutely; least of all would we accept their eternity. But we believe firmly in what we call the Law of Retribution, and in the absolute justice and wisdom guiding this Law, or Karma. Hence we positively refuse to accept the cruel and unphilosophical belief in eternal reward or eternal punishment. We say with Horace:

> *Let rules be fixed that may our rage contain,*
> *And punish faults with a proportioned pain;*
> *But do not flay him who deserves alone*
> *A whipping for the fault that he has done.*

This is a rule for all men, and a just one. Have we to believe that God, of whom you make the embodiment of wisdom, love and mercy, is less entitled to these attributes than mortal man?

Q. Have you any other reasons for rejecting this dogma?

A. Our chief reason for it lies in the fact of reincarnation. As already stated, we reject the idea of a new soul created for every newly-born babe. We believe that every human being is the bearer, or Vehicle, of an Ego coeval with every other Ego; because all Egos are of the same essence and belong to the primeval emanation from one universal infinite Ego. Plato calls the latter the logos (or the second manifested God); and we, the manifested divine principle, which is one with the universal mind or soul, not the anthropomorphic, extra-cosmic and personal God in which so many Theists believe. Pray do not confuse.

Q. But where is the difficulty, once you accept a manifested principle, in believing that the soul of every new mortal is created by that Principle, as all the Souls before it have been so created?

A. Because that which is impersonal can hardly create, plan and think, at its own sweet will and pleasure. Being a universal Law, immutable in its periodical manifestations, those of radiating and manifesting its own essence at the beginning of every new cycle of life, it is not supposed to create men, only to repent a few years later of having created them. If we have to believe in a divine principle at all, it must be in one which is as absolute harmony, logic, and justice, as it is absolute love, wisdom, and impartiality; and a God who would create every soul for the space of one brief span of life, regardless of the fact whether it has to animate the body of a wealthy, happy man, or that of a poor suffering wretch, hapless from birth to death though he has done nothing to deserve his cruel fate - would be rather a senseless fiend than a God. Why, even the Jewish philosophers, believers in the Mosaic Bible (esoterically, of course), have never entertained such an idea; and, moreover, they believed in reincarnation, as we do.

Q. Can you give me some instances as a proof of this?

A. Most decidedly I can. Philo Judaeus says: *The air is full of them (of souls); those which are nearest the earth, descending to be tied to mortal bodies, palindromousi authis , return to other bodies, being desirous to live in them.*

In The Zohar, the soul is made to plead her freedom before God: *Lord of the Universe! I am happy in this world, and do not wish to go into another world, where I shall be a handmaid, and be exposed to all kinds of pollution.* The doctrine of fatal necessity, the everlasting immutable law, is asserted in the answer of the Deity: *"Against thy will thou becomest an embryo, and against thy will thou art born".* Light would be incomprehensible without darkness to make it manifest by contrast; good would be no longer good without evil to show the priceless nature of the boon; and so personal virtue could claim no merit, unless it had passed through the furnace of temptation. Nothing is eternal and unchangeable, save the concealed Deity. Nothing that is finite - whether because it had a beginning, or must have an end - can remain stationary. It must either progress or recede; and a soul which thirsts after a reunion with its spirit, which alone confers upon it immortality, must purify itself through cyclic transmigrations onward toward the only land of bliss and eternal rest, called in The Zohar,"The Palace of Love" ; in the Hindu religion, "Moksha"; among the Gnostics, "The Pleroma of Eternal Light"; and by the Buddhists, "Nirvana". And all these states are temporary, not eternal.

Q. Yet there is no reincarnation spoken of in all this.

A. A soul which pleads to be allowed to remain where she is, must be preexistent,and not have been created for the occasion. In The Zohar,however, there is a still better proof. Speaking of the reincarnating Egos (the rational souls), those whose last personality has to fade out entirely, it is said: *All souls which have alienated themselves in heaven from the Holy One - blessed be His Name - have thrown themselves into an abyss at their very existence, and have anticipated the time when they are to descend once more on earth.*

"The Holy One" means here, esoterically, the Atma, or Atma-Buddhi.

Q. Moreover, it is very strange to find Nirvana spoken of as something synonymous with the Kingdom of Heaven, or the Paradise, since according to every Orientalist of note Nirvana is a synonym of annihilation!

A. Taken literally, with regard to the personality and differentiated matter, not otherwise. These ideas on reincarnation and the trinity of man were held by many of the early Christian Fathers. It is the jumble made by the translators of the New Testament and ancient philosophical treatises between soul and spirit, that has occasioned the many misunderstandings. It is also one of the many reasons why Buddha, Plotinus, and so many other Initiates are now accused of having longed for the total extinction of their souls - "absorption unto the Deity", or "reunion with the universal soul", meaning, according to modern ideas, annihilation. The personal soul must, of course, be disintegrated into its particles, before it is able to link its purer essence forever with the immortal spirit. But the translators of both the Acts and the Epistles,who laid the foundation of the Kingdom of Heaven, and the modern commentators on the Buddhist Sutra of the Foundation of the Kingdom of Righteousness, have muddled the sense of the great apostle of Christianity as of the great reformer of India. The former have smothered the word psuchikos , so that no reader imagines it to have any relation with soul; and with this confusion of soul and spirit together, Bible readers get only a perverted sense of anything on the subject. On the other hand, the interpreters of Buddha have failed to understand the meaning and object of the Buddhist four degrees of Dhyana. Ask the Pythagoreans, "Can that spirit, which gives life and motion and partakes of the nature of light, be reduced to nonentity?". "Can even that sensitive spirit in brutes which exercises memory, one of the rational faculties, die and become nothing?" observe the Occultists. In Buddhist philosophy annihilation means only a dispersion of matter, in whatever form or semblance of form it may be, for everything that has form is temporary, and is, therefore, really an illusion. For in eternity the longest periods of time are as a wink of the eye. So with form. Before we have time to realize that we have seen it, it is gone like an instantaneous flash of lightning, and passed forever. When the Spiritual entity breaks loose forever from every particle of matter, substance, or form, and rebecomes a Spiritual breath: then only does it enter upon the eternal and unchangeable Nirvana, lasting as long as the cycle of life has lasted - an eternity, truly. And then that Breath, existing in Spirit, is nothing because it is all;as a form, a semblance, a shape, it is completely annihilated; as absolute Spirit it still is, for it has become Be-ness itself. The very word used, "absorbed in the universal essence", when spoken of the "Soul" as Spirit, means "union with". It can never mean annihilation, as that would mean eternal separation.

Q. Do you not lay yourself open to the accusation of preaching annihilation by the language you yourself use? You have just spoken of the Soul of man returning to its primordial elements.

A. But you forget that I have given you the differences between the various meanings of the word Soul, and shown the loose way in which the term Spirit has been hitherto translated. We speak of an animal, a human, and a spiritual, Soul, and distinguish between them. Plato, for instance, calls "rational Soul" that which we call Buddhi, adding to it the adjective of "spiritual", however; but that which we call the reincarnating Ego, Manas, he calls Spirit, Nous,etc., whereas we apply the term Spirit, when standing alone and without any qualification, to Atma alone. Pythagoras repeats our archaic doctrine when stating that the Ego (Nous) is eternal with Deity; that the soul only passed through various stages to arrive at divine excellence; while thumos returned to the earth, and even the phren, the lower Manas,was eliminated. Again, Plato defines Soul (Buddhi) as "the motion that is able to move itself". "Soul", he adds (Laws X.), "*is the most ancient of all things, and the commencement of motion*", thus calling Atma-

Buddhi "Soul", and Manas "Spirit", which we do not.

Soul was generated prior to body, and body is posterior and secondary, as being according to nature, ruled over by the ruling soul. The soul which administers all things that are moved in every way, administers likewise the heavens. Soul then leads everything in heaven, and on earth, and in the sea, by its movements - the names of which are, to will, to consider to take care of, to consult. to form opinions true and false, to be in a state of joy, sorrow, confidence, fear, hate, love, together with all such primary movements as are allied to these ... Being a goddess herself, she ever takes as an ally Nous, a god, and disciplines all things correctly and happily; but when with Annoia - not nous - it works out everything the contrary.

In this language, as in the Buddhist texts, the negative is treated as essential existence. Annihilation comes under a similar exegesis. The positive state is essential being, but no manifestation as such. When the spirit, in Buddhist parlance, enters Nirvana, it loses objective existence, but retains subjective being. To objective minds this is becoming absolute "nothing"; to subjective, No-thing, nothing to be displayed to sense. Thus, their Nirvana means the certitude of individual immortality in Spirit, not in Soul, which, though "the most ancient of all things", is still - along with all the other Gods - a finite emanation, in forms and individuality, if not in substance.

Q. I do not quite seize the idea yet, and would be thankful to have you explain this to me by some illustrations.

A. No doubt it is very difficult to understand, especially to one brought up in the regular orthodox ideas of the Christian Church. Moreover, I must tell you one. thing; and this is that unless you have studied thoroughly well the separate functions assigned to all the human principles and the state of all these after death, you will hardly realize our Eastern philosophy.

On the Various Principles in Man

Q. I have heard a good deal about this constitution of the "inner man" as you call it, but could never make "head or tail on't" as Gabalis expresses it.

A. Of course, it is most difficult, and, as you say, "puzzling" to understand correctly and distinguish between the various aspects,called by us the principles of the real Ego. It is the more so as there exists a notable difference in the numbering of those principles by various Eastern schools, though at the bottom there is the same identical substratum of teaching.

Q. Do you mean the Vedantins, as an instance? Don't they divide your seven principles into five only?

A.They do; but though I would not presume to dispute the point with a learned Vedantin, I may yet state as my private opinion that they have an obvious reason for it. With them it is only that compound spiritual aggregate which consists of various mental aspects that is called Man at all, the physical body being in their view something beneath contempt, and merely an illusion. Nor is the Vedanta the only philosophy to reckon in this manner. Lao-tzu, in his Tao Te Ching, mentions only five principles, because he, like the Vedantins, omits to include two principles, namely, the spirit (Atma) and the physical body, the latter of which, moreover, he calls "the cadaver". Then there is the Taraka Raja-Yoga School. Its teaching recognizes only three principles in fact; but then, in reality, their Sthulopadhi, or the physical body, in its waking conscious state, their Sukshmopadhi, the same body in Svapna,or the dreaming state, and their Karanopadhi or "causal body", or that which passes from one incarnation to another, are all dual in their aspects, and thus make six. Add to this Atma, the impersonal divine principle or the immortal element in Man, undistinguished from the Universal Spirit, and you have the same seven again. They are welcome to hold to their division; we hold to ours. [See 'Secret Doctrine', part 1, p. 182 for a clearer exposition]

Q. Then it seems almost the same as the division made by the mystic Christians: body, soul, and spirit?

A. Just the same. We could easily make of the body the vehicle of the "vital Double"; of the latter the vehicle of Life or Prana; of Kamarupa,or (animal) soul, the vehicle of the higher and the lower mind, and make of this six principles, crowning the whole with the one immortal spirit. In Occultism every qualitative change in the state of our consciousness gives to man a new aspect, and if it prevails and becomes part of the living and acting Ego, it must be (and is) given a special name, to distinguish the man in that particular state from the man he is when he places himself in another state.

Q. It is just that which it is so difficult to understand.

A. It seems to me very easy, on the contrary, once that you have seized the main idea,i.e., that man acts on this or another plane of consciousness, in strict accordance with his mental and spiritual condition. But such is the materialism of the age that the more we explain the less people seem capable of understanding what we say. Divide the terrestrial being called man into three chief aspects, if you like, and unless you make of him a pure animal you cannot do less. Take his objective body; the thinking principle in him - which is only a little higher than the instinctual element in the animal - or the vital conscious soul; and that which places him so immeasurably beyond and higher than the animal - i.e.,his reasoning soul or "spirit". Well, if we take these three groups or representative entities, and subdivide them, according to the occult teaching, what do we get?

First of all, Spirit (in the sense of the Absolute, and therefore, indivisible All), or Atma. As this can neither be located nor limited in philosophy, being simply that which is in Eternity, and which cannot be absent from even the tiniest geometrical or mathematical point of the universe of matter or substance, it ought not to be called, in truth, a "human" principle at all. Rather, and at best, it is in Metaphysics, that point in space which the human Monad and its vehicle man

71

occupy for the period of every life. Now that point is as imaginary as man himself, and in reality is an illusion, a Maya ; but then for ourselves, as for other personal Egos, we are a reality during that fit of illusion called life, and we have to take ourselves into account, in our own fancy at any rate, if no one else does. To make it more conceivable to the human intellect, when first attempting the study of Occultism, and to solve the a-b-c of the mystery of man, Occultism calls this seventh principle the synthesis of the sixth, and gives it for vehicle the Spiritual Soul, Buddhi. Now the latter conceals a mystery, which is never given to any one, with the exception of irrevocably pledged Chelas, or those, at any rate, who can be safely trusted. Of course, there would be less confusion, could it only be told; but, as this is directly concerned with the power of projecting one's double consciously and at will, and as this gift, like the "ring of Gyges", would prove very fatal to man at large and to the possessor of that faculty in particular, it is carefully guarded. But let us proceed with the principles. This divine soul, or Buddhi, then, is the vehicle of the Spirit. In conjunction, these two are one, impersonal and without any attributes (on this plane, of course), and make two spiritual principles. If we pass onto the Human Soul, Manas or mens, everyone will agree that the intelligence of man is dual to say the least: e.g., the high-minded man can hardly become low-minded; the very intellectual and spiritual-minded man is separated by an abyss from the obtuse, dull, and material, if not animal-minded man.

Q. But why should not man be represented by two principles or two aspects, rather?

A. Every man has these two principles in him, one more active than the other, and in rare cases, one of these is entirely stunted in its growth, so to say, or paralysed by the strength and predominance of the other aspect, in whatever direction. These, then, are what we call the two principles or aspects of Manas, the higher and the lower; the former, the higher Manas, or the thinking, conscious Ego gravitating toward the spiritual Soul (Buddhi); and the latter, or its instinctual principle, attracted to Kama,the seat of animal desires and passions in man. Thus, we have four principles justified; the last three being (1) the "Double", which we have agreed to call Protean, or Plastic Soul; the vehicle of (2) the life principle; and (3) the physical body. Of course no physiologist or biologist will accept these principles, nor can he make head or tail of them. And this is why, perhaps, none of them understand to this day either the functions of the spleen, the physical vehicle of the Protean Double, or those of a certain organ on the right side of man, the seat of the above-mentioned desires, nor yet does he know anything of the pineal gland, which he describes as a horny gland with a little sand in it, which gland is in truth the very seat of the highest and divinest consciousness in man, his omniscient, spiritual and all-embracing mind. And this shows to you still more plainly that we have neither invented these seven principles, nor are they new in the world of philosophy, as we can easily prove.

Q. But what is it that reincarnates, in your belief?

A. The Spiritual thinking Ego, the permanent principle in man, or that which is the seat of Manas. It is not Atma, or even Atma-Buddhi, regarded as the dual Monad, which is the individual, or divine man, but Manas; for Atma is the Universal All, and becomes the Higher-Self of man only in conjunction with Buddhi, its vehicle, which links it to the individuality (or divine man). For it is the Buddhi-Manas which is called the Causal body,(the United fifth and sixth Principles) and which is Consciousness,that connects it with every personality it inhabits on earth. Therefore, Soul being a generic term, there are in men three aspects of Soul - the terrestrial, or animal; the Human Soul; and the Spiritual Soul; these, strictly speaking, are one Soul in its three aspects. Now of the first aspect, nothing remains after death; of the second (nous or Manas) only its divine essence if left unsoiled survives, while the third in addition to being immortal becomes consciously divine, by the assimilation of the higher Manas. But to make it clear, we have to say a few words first of all about Reincarnation.

Q. You will do well, as it is against this doctrine that your enemies fight the most ferociously.

A. You mean the Spiritualists? I know; and many are the absurd objections laboriously spun by them over the pages of Light. So obtuse and malicious are some of them, that they will stop at nothing. One of them found recently a contradiction, which he gravely discusses in a letter to that journal, in two statements picked out of Mr. Sinnett's lectures. He discovers that grave contradiction in these two sentences: "Premature returns to earth-life in the cases when they occur may be due to Karmic complication ... "; and "there is no accident in the supreme act of divine justice guiding evolution. .So profound a thinker would surely see a contradiction of the law of gravitation if a man stretched out his hand to stop a falling stone from crushing the head of a child!

On Reincarnation or Rebirth
What is Memory According to Theosophical Teaching?

Q. The most difficult thing for you to do, will be to explain and give reasonable grounds for such a belief. No Theosophist has ever yet succeeded in bringing forward a single valid proof to shake my skepticism. First of all, you have against this theory of reincarnation, the fact that no single man has yet been found to remember that he has lived, least of all who he was, during his previous life.

A. Your argument, I see, tends to the same old objection; the loss of memory in each of us of our previous incarnation. You think it invalidates our doctrine? My answer is that it does not, and that at any rate such an objection cannot be final.

Q. I would like to hear your arguments.

A. They are short and few. Yet when you take into consideration (a) the utter inability of the best modern psychologists to explain to the world the nature of mind; and (b) their complete ignorance of its potentialities, and higher states, you have to admit that this objection is based on an a priori conclusion drawn from prima facie and circumstantial evidence more than anything else. Now what is "memory" in your conception, pray?

Q. That which is generally accepted: the faculty in our mind of remembering and of retaining the knowledge of previous thoughts, deeds, and events.

A. Please add to it that there is a great difference between the three accepted forms of memory. Besides memory in general you have Remembrance, Recollection,and Reminiscence, have you not? Have you ever thought over the difference? Memory, remember, is a generic name.

Q. Yet, all these are only synonyms.

A. Indeed, they are not - not in philosophy, at all events. Memory is simply an innate power in thinking beings, and even in animals, of reproducing past impressions by an association of ideas principally suggested by objective things or by some action on our external sensory organs. Memory is a faculty depending entirely on the more or less healthy and normal functioning of our physical brain; and remembrance and recollection are the attributes and handmaidens of that memory. But reminiscence is an entirely different thing. Reminiscence is defined by the modern psychologist as something intermediate between remembrance and recollection,or "a conscious process of recalling past occurrences, but without that full and varied reference to particular things which characterizes recollection". Locke, speaking of recollection and remembrance, says: When an idea again recurs without the operation of the like object on the external sensory, it is remembrance;if it be sought after by the mind, and with pain and endeavor found and brought again into view, it is recollection. But even Locke leaves reminiscence without any clear definition, because it is no faculty or attribute of our physical memory, but an intuitional perception apart from and outside our physical brain; a perception which, covering as it does (being called into action by the ever-present knowledge of our spiritual Ego) all those visions in man which are regarded as abnormal - from the pictures suggested by genius to the ravings of fever and even madness - are classed by science as having no existence outside of our fancy. Occultism and Theosophy, however, regard reminiscence in an entirely different light. For us, while memory is physical and evanescent and depends on the physiological conditions of the brain - a fundamental proposition with all teachers of mnemonics, who have the researches of modern scientific psychologists to back them - we call reminiscence the memory of the soul. And it is this memory which gives the assurance to almost every human being, whether he understands it or not, of his having lived before and having to live again. Indeed, as Wordsworth has it:

> *Our birth is but a sleep and a forgetting,*
> *The soul that rises with us, our life's star,*
> *Hath elsewhere had its setting,*
> *And cometh from afar.*

Q. If it is on this kind of memory - poetry and abnormal fancies, on your own confession - that you base your doctrine, then you will convince very few, I am afraid.

A. I did not "confess" it was a fancy. I simply said that physiologists and scientists in general regard such reminiscences as hallucinations and fancy, to which learned conclusion they are welcome. We do not deny that such visions of the past and glimpses far back into the corridors of time, are not abnormal, as contrasted with our normal daily life experience and physical memory. But we do maintain with Professor W. Knight, that: The absence of memory of any action done in a previous state cannot be a conclusive argument against our having lived through it. And every fair-minded opponent must agree with what is said in Butler's *Lectures on Platonic Philosophy*: *That the feeling of extravagance with which it (preexistence) affects us has its secret source in materialistic or semi-materialistic prejudices.* Besides which we maintain that memory, as Olympiodorus called it, is simply fantasy, and the most unreliable thing in us.

Says Olympiodorus, in *Platonis Phaed.*:

The fantasy is an impediment to our intellectual conceptions; and hence, when we are agitated by the inspiring influence of the Divinity, if the fantasy intervenes, the enthusiastic energy ceases: for enthusiasm and the ecstasy are contrary to each other. Should it be asked whether the soul is able to energize without the fantasy, we reply, that its perception of universals proves that it is able. It has perceptions, therefore, independent of the fantasy; at the same time, however, the fantasy attends in its energies, just as a storm pursues him who sails on the sea.

Ammonius Saccas asserted that the only faculty in man directly opposed to prognostication, or looking into futurity, is memory. Furthermore, remember that memory is one thing and mind or thought is another; one is a recording machine, a register which very easily gets out of order; the other (thoughts) are eternal and imperishable. Would you refuse to believe in the existence of certain things or men only because your physical eyes have not seen them? Would not the collective testimony of past generations who have seen him be a sufficient guarantee that Julius Caesar once lived? Why should not the same testimony of the psychic senses of the masses be taken into consideration?

Q. But don't you think that these are too fine distinctions to be accepted by the majority of mortals?

A. Say rather by the majority of materialists. And to them we say, behold: even in the short span of ordinary existence, memory is too weak to register all the events of a lifetime. How frequently do even most important events lie dormant in our memory until awakened by some association of ideas, or aroused to function and activity by some other link. This is especially the case with people of advanced age, who are always found suffering from feebleness of recollection. When, therefore, we remember that which we know about the physical and the spiritual principles in man, it is not the fact that our memory has failed to record our precedent life and lives that ought to surprise us, but the contrary, were it to happen.

Why Do We Not Remember Our Past Lives?

Q. You have given me a bird's eye view of the seven principles; now how do they account for our complete loss of any recollection of having lived before?

A. Very easily. Since those principles which we call physical, and none of which is denied by science, though it calls them by other names - namely, the body, life, passional and animal instincts, and the astral eidolon of every man (whether perceived in thought or our mind's eye, or objectively and separate from the physical body), which principles we call Sthula-sharira, Prana, Kamarupa, and Linga-sharira (see above).

[Those principles] are disintegrated after death with their constituent elements, memory along with its brain, this vanished memory of a vanished personality, can neither remember nor record anything in the subsequent reincarnation of the Ego. Reincarnation means that this Ego will be furnished with a new body, a new brain, and a new memory. Therefore it would be as absurd to expect this memory to remember that which it has never recorded as it would be idle to examine under a microscope a shirt never worn by a murderer, and seek on it for the stains of blood which are to be found only on the clothes he wore. It is not the clean shirt that we have to question, but the clothes worn during the perpetration of the crime; and if these are burnt and destroyed, how can you get at them?

Q. Aye! How can you get at the certainty that the crime was ever committed at all, or that the "man in the clean shirt" ever lived before?

A. Not by physical processes, most assuredly; nor by relying on the testimony of that which exists no longer. But there is such a thing as circumstantial evidence, since our wise laws accept it, more, perhaps, even than they should. To get convinced of the fact of reincarnation and past lives, one must put oneself in rapport with one's real permanent Ego, not one's evanescent memory.

Q. But how can people believe in that which they do not know, nor have ever seen, far less put themselves in *rapport* with it?

A. If people, and the most learned, will believe in the Gravity, Ether, Force, and what not of Science, abstractions "and working hypotheses", which they have neither seen, touched, smelt, heard, nor tasted - why should not other people believe, on the same principle, in one's permanent Ego, a far more logical and important "working hypothesis" than any other?

Q. What is, finally, this mysterious eternal principle? Can you explain its nature so as to make it comprehensible to all?

A. The Ego which reincarnates, the individual and immortal - not personal -"I"; the vehicle, in short, of the Atma-Buddhic Monad, that which is rewarded in Devachan and punished on earth, and that, finally, to which the reflection only of the Skandhas, or attributes, of every incarnation attaches itself. There are five Skandhas or attributes in the Buddhist teachings: Rupa (form or body), material qualities;Vedana , sensation; Sanna , abstract ideas; Samkhara,tendencies of mind; Vinnana, mental powers. Of these we are formed, by them we are conscious of existence; and through them communicate with the world about us.

Q. What do you mean by *Skandhas*?

A. Just what I said: "attributes", among which is memory, all of which perish like a flower, leaving behind them only a feeble perfume. Here is another paragraph from H.S. Olcott's *Buddhist Catechism* which bears directly upon the subject. It deals with the question as follows: *The aged man remembers the incidents of his youth, despite his being physically and mentally changed. Why, then, is not the recollection of past lives brought over by us from our last birth into the present birth? Because memory is included within the Skandhas, and the Skandhas having changed with the new existence, a memory, the record of that particular existence, develops. Yet the record or reflection of all the past lives must survive, for when Prince Siddhartha became Buddha, the full sequence of His previous births were seen by Him ... and any one who attains to the state of Jñana can thus retrospectively trace the line of his lives.* This proves to you that while the undying qualities of the personality - such as love, goodness, charity, etc.- attach themselves to the immortal Ego, photographing on it, so to speak, a permanent image of the divine aspect of the man who was, his material Skandhas (those which generate the most marked Karmic effects) are as evanescent as a flash of lightning, and cannot impress the new brain of the new personality; yet their failing to do so impairs in no way the identity of the reincarnating Ego.

Q. Do you mean to infer that which survives is only the Soul-memory, as you call it, that Soul or Ego being one and the same, while nothing of the personality remains?

A. Not quite; something of each personality, unless the latter was an absolute materialist with not even a chink in his nature for a spiritual ray to pass through, must survive, as it leaves its eternal impress on the incarnating permanent Self or Spiritual Ego. (Or the Spiritual,in contradistinction to the personal Self. The student must not confuse this Spiritual Ego with the "higher self" which is Atma, the God within us, and inseparable from the Universal Spirit.)

The personality with its Skandhas is ever changing with every new birth. It is, as said before, only the part played by the actor (the true Ego) for one night. This is why we preserve no memory on the physical plane of our past lives, though the real "Ego" has lived them over and knows them all.

Q. Then how does it happen that the real or Spiritual man does not impress his new personal "I" with this knowledge?

A. How is it that the servant-girls in a poor farmhouse could speak Hebrew and play the violin in their trance or somnambular state, and knew neither when in their normal condition? Because, as every genuine psychologist of the old, not your modern, school, will tell you, the Spiritual Ego can act only when the personal Ego is paralyzed. The Spiritual "I" in man is omniscient and has every knowledge innate in it; while the personal self is the creature of its environment and the slave of the physical memory. Could the former manifest itself uninterruptedly, and without impediment, there would be no longer men on earth, but we should all be gods.

Q. Still there ought to be exceptions, and some ought to remember.

A. And so there are. But who believes in their report? Such sensitives are generally regarded as hallucinated hysteriacs, as crack-brained enthusiasts, or humbugs, by modern materialism. Let them read, however, works on this subject, preeminently Reincarnation, a Study of Forgotten Truth by E.D. Walker, F.T.S., and see in it the mass of proofs which the able author brings to bear on this vexed question. One speaks to people of soul, and some ask "What is Soul?". "Have you ever proved its existence?" Of course it is useless to argue with those who are materialists. But even to them I would put the question:

Can you remember what you were or did when a baby? Have you preserved the smallest recollection of your life, thoughts, or deeds, or that you lived at all during the first eighteen months or two years of your existence? Then why not deny that you have ever lived as a babe, on the same principle?

When to all this we add that the reincarnating Ego, or individuality, retains during the Devachanic period merely the essence of the experience of its past earth-life or personality, the whole physical experience involving into a state of in potentia, or being, so to speak, translated into spiritual formulae; when we remember further that the term between two rebirths is said to extend from ten to fifteen centuries, during which time the physical consciousness is totally and absolutely inactive, having no organs to act through, and therefore no existence, the reason for the absence of all remembrance in the purely physical memory is apparent.

Q. You just said that the Spiritual Ego was omniscient. Where, then, is that vaunted omniscience during his Devachanic life, as you call it?

A. During that time it is latent and potential, because, first of all, the Spiritual Ego (the compound of Buddhi-Manas) is not the Higher Self, which being one with the Universal Soul or Mind is alone omniscient; and, secondly, because Devachan is the idealized continuation of the terrestrial life just left behind, a period of retributive adjustment, and a reward for unmerited wrongs and sufferings undergone in that special life. It is omniscient only potentially in Devachan, and de facto exclusively in Nirvana, when the Ego is merged in the Universal Mind-Soul. Yet it rebecomes quasi omniscient during those hours on earth when certain abnormal conditions and physiological changes in the body make the Ego free from the trammels of matter. Thus the examples cited above of somnambulists, a poor servant speaking Hebrew, and another playing the violin, give you an illustration of the case in point. This does not mean that the explanations of these two facts offered us by medical science have no truth in them, for one girl had, years before, heard her master, a clergyman, read Hebrew works aloud, and the other had heard an artist playing a violin at their farm. But neither could have done so as perfectly as they did had they not been ensouled by that which, owing to the sameness of its nature with the Universal Mind, is omniscient. Here the higher principle acted on the Skandhas and moved them; in the other, the personality being paralyzed, the individuality manifested itself. Pray do not confuse the two.

On Individuality and Personality

Q. But what is the difference between the two?

A. Even Col. Olcott, forced to it by the logic of Esoteric philosophy, found himself obliged to correct the mistakes of previous Orientalists who made no such distinction, and gives the reader his reasons for it. Thus he says: *The successive appearances upon the earth, or "descents into generation", of the tanhaically coherent parts (Skandhas) of a certain being, are a succession of personalities. In each birth the personality differs from that of a previous or next succeeding birth. Karma, the deus ex machina, masks (or shall we say reflects?) itself now in the personality of a sage, again as an artisan, and so on throughout the string of births. But though personalities ever shift, the one line of life along which they are strung, like beads, runs unbroken; it is ever that particular line, never any other. It is therefore individual, an individual vital undulation, which began in Nirvana, or the subjective side of nature, as the light or heat undulation through aether, began at its dynamic source; is careering through the objective side of nature under the impulse of Karma and the creative direction of Tanha (the unsatisfied desire for existence); and leads through many cyclic changes back to Nirvana. Mr. Rhys-Davids calls that which passes from personality to personality along the individual chain character, or doing. Since character is not a mere metaphysical abstraction, but the sum of one's mental qualities and moral propensities, would it not help to dispel what Mr. Rhys-Davids calls "the desperate expedient of a mystery" if we regarded the life-undulation as individuality, and each of its series of natal manifestations as a separate personality? The perfect individual, Buddhist speaking, is a Buddha, I should say; for Buddha is but the rare flower of humanity, without the least supernatural admixture. And as countless generations ("four asankheyyas and a hundred thousand cycles") are required to develop a man into a Buddha, and the iron will to become one runs throughout all the successive births, what shall we call that which thus wills and perseveres? Character? One's individuality: an individuality but partly manifested in any one birth, but built up of fragments from all the births?*

Q. I confess that I am still in the dark. Indeed it is just that difference, then, that you cannot impress too much on our minds.

A. I try to; but alas, it is harder with some than to make them feel a reverence for childish impossibilities, only because they are orthodox,and because orthodoxy is respectable. To understand the idea well, you have to first study the dual sets of principles: the spiritual,or those which belong to the imperishable Ego; and the material,or those principles which make up the ever-changing bodies or the series of personalities of that Ego. Let us fix permanent names to these, and say that:

1. *Atma,* the "Higher Self", is neither your Spirit nor mine, but like sunlight shines on all. It is the universally diffused "divine principle", and is inseparable from its one and absolute Meta-Spirit, as the sunbeam is inseparable from sunlight.

2. *Buddhi* (the spiritual soul) is only its vehicle. Neither each separately, nor the two collectively, are of any more use to the body of man, than sunlight and its beams are for a mass of granite buried in the earth, unless the divine Duad is assimilated by, and reflected in, some consciousness .Neither Atma nor Buddhi are ever reached by Karma, because the former is the highest aspect of Karma, its working agent of itself in one aspect, and the other is unconscious on this plane. This consciousness or mind is,

3. *Manas,* the derivation or product in a reflected form of Ahankara, "the conception of I", or Ego-ship. It is, therefore, when inseparably united to the first two, called the Spiritual Ego, and Taijasi (the radiant). This is the real Individuality, or the divine man. It is this Ego which - having originally incarnated in the senseless human form animated by, but unconscious (since it had no consciousness) of, the presence in itself of the dual monad - made of that human-like form a real man.

Mahat or the "Universal Mind" is the source of Manas. The latter is Mahat, i.e., mind, in man. Manas is also called Kshetrajña, "embodied Spirit", because it is, according to our philosophy, the Manasaputras,or "Sons of the Universal Mind", who created,or rather produced, the thinking man, "manu", by incarnating in the third Race mankind in our Round. It is Manas, therefore, which is the real incarnating and permanent Spiritual Ego, the individuality, and our various and numberless personalities only its external masks.

It is that Ego, that "Causal Body", which overshadows every personality Karma forces it to incarnate into; and this Ego which is held responsible for all the sins committed through, and in, every new body or personality - he evanescent masks which hide the true Individual through the long series of rebirths.

Q. But is this just? Why should this Ego receive punishment as the result of deeds which it has forgotten?

A. It has not forgotten them; it knows and remembers its misdeeds as well as you remember what you have done yesterday. Is it because the memory of that bundle of physical compounds called "body" does not recollect what its predecessor (the personality that was) did, that you imagine that the real Ego has forgotten them?

As well say it is unjust that the new boots on the feet of a boy, who is flogged for stealing apples, should be punished for that which they know nothing of.

Q. But are there no modes of communication between the Spiritual and human consciousness or memory?

A. Of course there are; but they have never been recognized by your scientific modern psychologists. To what do you attribute intuition, the "voice of the conscience", premonitions, vague undefined reminiscences, etc., etc., if not to such communications? Would that the majority of educated men, at least, had the fine spiritual perceptions of Coleridge, who shows how intuitional he is in some of his comments. Hear what he says with respect to the probability that "all thoughts are in themselves imperishable". If the intelligent faculty (sudden 'revivals' of memory) should be rendered more comprehensive, it would require only a different and appropriate organization, the body celestial instead of the body terrestrial, to bring before every human soul the collective experience of its whole past existence(existences, rather). And this body celestial is our Manasic Ego.

On the Reward and Punishment of the Ego

Q. I have heard you say that the Ego, whatever the life of the person he incarnated in may have been on Earth, is never visited with postmortem punishment.

A. Never, save in very exceptional and rare cases of which we will not speak here, as the nature of the "punishment" in no way approaches any of your theological conceptions of damnation.

Q. But if it is punished in this life for the misdeeds committed in a previous one, then it is this Ego that ought to be rewarded also, whether here, or when disincarnated.

A. And so it is. If we do not admit of any punishment outside of this earth, it is because the only state the Spiritual Self knows of, hereafter, is that of unalloyed bliss.

Q. What do you mean?

A. Simply this: *crimes and sins committed on a plane of objectivity and in a world of matter, cannot receive punishment in a world of pure subjectivity.* We believe in no hell or paradise as localities; in no objective hell fires and worms that never die, nor in any Jerusalem with streets paved with sapphires and diamonds. What we believe in is a postmortem state or mental condition, such as we are in during a vivid dream. We believe in an immutable law of absolute Love, Justice, and Mercy. And believing in it, we say: Whatever the sin and dire

81

results of the original Karmic transgression of the now incarnated Egos no man (or the outer material and periodical form of the Spiritual Entity) can be held, with any degree of justice, responsible for the consequences of his birth. He does not ask to be born, nor can he choose the parents that will give him life. In every respect he is a victim to his environment, the child of circumstances over which he has no control; and if each of his transgressions were impartially investigated, there would be found nine out of every ten cases when he was the one sinned against, rather than the sinner.

It is on this transgression that the cruel and illogical dogma of the Fallen Angels has been built. It is explained in Vol. II of *The Secret Doctrine*. All our "Egos" are thinking and rational entities (Manasaputas) who had lived, whether under human or other forms, in the precedent life cycle (Manvantara), and whose Karma it was to incarnate in the man of this one. It was taught in the Mysteries that, having delayed to comply with this law (or having "refused to create" as Hinduism says of the Kumaras and Christian legend of the Archangel Michael), i.e., having failed to incarnate in due time, the bodies predestined for them got defiled, hence the original sin of the senseless forms and the punishment of the Egos. That which is meant by the rebellious angels being hurled down into Hell is simply explained by these pure Spirits or Egos being imprisoned in bodies of unclean matter, flesh.

Life is at best a heartless play, a stormy sea to cross, and a heavy burden often too difficult to bear. The greatest philosophers have tried in vain to fathom and find out its raison d'être, and have all failed except those who had the key to it, namely, the Eastern sages. Life is, as Shakespeare describes it:

> ... but a walking shadow - a poor player,
> That struts and frets his hour upon the stage,
> And then is heard no more. It is a tale
> Told by an idiot, full of sound and fury,
> Signifying nothing.

Nothing in its separate parts, yet of the greatest importance in its collectivity or series of lives. At any rate, almost every individual life is, in its full development, a sorrow. And are we to believe that poor, helpless man, after being tossed about like a piece of rotten timber on the angry billows of life, is, if he proves too weak to resist them, to be punished by never-ending damnation, or even a temporary punishment? Never! Whether a great or an average sinner, good or bad, guilty or innocent, once delivered of the burden of physical life, the tired and worn-out Manu ("thinking Ego") has won the right to a period of absolute rest and bliss. The same unerringly wise and just rather than merciful Law, which inflicts upon the incarnated Ego the Karmic punishment for every sin committed during the preceding life on Earth, provided for the now disembodied Entity a long lease of mental rest, i.e., the entire oblivion of every sad event, aye, to the smallest painful thought, that took place in its last life as a personality, leaving in the soul-memory but the reminiscence of that which was bliss, or led to happiness. Plotinus, who said that our body was the true river of Lethe, for "souls plunged into it forget all", meant more than he said. For, as our terrestrial body is like Lethe, so is our celestial body in Devachan, and much more.

Q. Then am I to understand that the murderer, the transgressor of law divine and human in every shape, is allowed to go unpunished?

A. Who ever said that? Our philosophy has a doctrine of punishment as stern as that of the most rigid Calvinist, only far more philosophical and consistent with absolute justice. No deed, not even a sinful thought, will go unpunished; the latter more severely even than the former, as a thought is far more potential in creating evil results than even a deed. *Verily I say unto you, that whosoever looketh at a woman to lust after her, hath committed adultery with her already in his heart.* We believe in an unerring law of Retribution, called Karma, which asserts itself in a natural concatenation of causes and their unavoidable results.

Q. And how, or where, does it act?

A. Every labourer is worthy of his hire, saith Wisdom in the Gospel; every action, good or bad, is a prolific parent, saith the Wisdom of the Ages. Put the two together, and you will find the "why". After allowing the Soul, escaped from the pangs of personal life, a sufficient, aye, a hundredfold compensation, Karma, with its army of Skandhas, waits at the threshold of Devachan, whence the Ego reemerges to assume a new incarnation. It is at this moment that the future destiny of the now-rested Ego trembles in the scales of just Retribution, as it now falls once again under the sway of active Karmic law. It is in this rebirth which is ready for it, a rebirth selected and prepared by this mysterious, inexorable, but in the equity and wisdom of its decrees infallible law, that the sins of the previous life of the Ego are punished. Only it is into no imaginary Hell, with theatrical flames and ridiculous tailed and horned devils, that the Ego is cast, but verily onto this earth, the plane and region of his sins, where he will have to atone for every bad thought and deed. As he has sown, so will he reap. Reincarnation will gather around him all those other Egos who have suffered, whether directly or indirectly, at the hands, or even through the unconscious instrumentality, of the past personality. They will be thrown by Nemesis in the way of the new man, concealing the old, the eternal Ego, and …

Q. But where is the equity you speak of, since these new "personalities" are not aware of having sinned or been sinned against?

A. Has the coat torn to shreds from the back of the man who stole it, by another man who was robbed of it and recognizes his property, to be regarded as fairly dealt with? The new "personality" is no better than a fresh suit of clothes with its specific characteristics, color, form, and qualities; but the real man who wears it is the same culprit as of old. It is the individuality who suffers through his "personality". And it is this, and this alone, that can account for the terrible, still only apparent, injustice in the distribution of lots in life to man. When your modern philosophers will have succeeded in showing to us a good reason, why so many apparently innocent and good men are born only to suffer during a whole lifetime; why so many are born poor unto starvation in the slums of great cities, abandoned by fate and men; why, while these are born in the gutter, others open their eyes to light in palaces; while a noble birth and fortune seem often given to the worst of men and only rarely to the worthy; while there are beggars whose inner selves are peers to the highest and noblest of men; when this, and much more, is satisfactorily explained by either your philosophers or theologians, then only, but not till then, you will have the right to reject the theory of reincarnation. The highest and grandest of poets have dimly perceived this truth of truths. Shelley believed in it, Shakespeare must have thought of it when writing on the worthlessness of Birth. Remember his words:

> *Why should my birth keep down my mounting spirit?*
> *Are not all creatures subject unto time?*
> *There's legions now of beggars on the earth,*
> *That their original did spring from Kings,*
> *And many monarchs now, whose fathers were*
> *The riff-raff of their age ...*

Alter the word fathers into Egos - and you will have the truth.

On the Kamaloka and Devachan
On the Fate of the Lower Principles

Q. You spoke of Kamaloka,what is it?

A. When the man dies, his lower three principles leave him forever; i.e., body, life, and the vehicle of the latter, the astral body or the double of the living man. And then, his four principles - the central or middle principle, the animal soul or Kamarupa, with what it has assimilated from the lower Manas, and the higher triad find themselves in Kamaloka. The latter is an astral locality, the limbus of scholastic theology, the Hades of the ancients, and, strictly speaking, a locality only in a relative sense. It has neither a definite area nor boundary, but exists within subjective space; i.e., is beyond our sensuous perceptions. Still it exists, and it is there that the astral eidolons of all the beings that have lived, animals included, await their second death. For the animals it comes with the disintegration and the entire fading out of their astral particles to the last. For the human eidolon it begins when the Atma-Buddhi-Manasic triad is said to "separate" itself from its lower principles, or the reflection of the ex-personality, by falling into the Devachanic state.

Q. And what happens after this?

A. Then the Kamarupic phantom, remaining bereft of its informing thinking principle, the higher Manas, and the lower aspect of the latter, the animal intelligence, no longer receiving light from the higher mind, and no longer having a physical brain to work through, collapses.

Q. In what way?

A. Well, it falls into the state of the frog when certain portions of its brain are taken out by the vivisector. It can think no more, even on the lowest animal plane. Henceforth it is no longer even the lower Manas, since this "lower" is nothing without the "higher".

Q. And is it this nonentity which we find materializing in Séance rooms with Mediums?

A. It is this nonentity. A true nonentity, however, only as to reasoning or cogitating powers, still an Entity, however astral and fluidic, as shown in certain cases when, having been magnetically and unconsciously drawn toward a medium, it is revived for a time and lives in him by proxy, so to speak. This "spook", or the Kamarupa, may be compared with the jelly-fish, which has an ethereal gelatinous appearance so long as it is in its own element, or water (the medium's specific aura), but which, no sooner is it thrown out of it, than it dissolves in the hand or on the sand, especially in sunlight. In the medium's Aura, it lives a kind of vicarious life and reasons and speaks either through the medium's brain or those of other persons present. But this would lead us too far, and upon other people's grounds, whereon I have no desire to trespass. Let us keep to the subject of reincarnation.

Q. What of the latter? How long does the incarnating Ego remain in the Devachanic state?

A. This, we are taught, depends on the degree of spirituality and the merit or demerit of the last incarnation. The average time is from ten to fifteen centuries, as I already told you.

Q. But why could not this Ego manifest and communicate with mortals as Spiritualists will have it? What is there to prevent a mother from communicating with the children she left on earth, a husband with his wife, and so on? It is a most consoling belief, I must confess; nor do I wonder that those who believe in it are so averse to give it up.

A. Nor are they forced to, unless they happen to prefer truth to fiction, however "consoling". Uncongenial our doctrines may be to Spiritualists; yet, nothing of what we believe in and teach is half as selfish and cruel as what they preach.

Q. I do not understand you. What is selfish?

A. Their doctrine of the return of Spirits, the real "personalities" as they say; and I will tell you why. If Devachan - call it "paradise" if you like, a "place of bliss and of supreme felicity". if it is anything - is such a place (or say state), logic tells us that no sorrow or even a shade of pain can be experienced therein. "God shall wipe away all the tears from the eyes" of those in paradise, we read in the book of many promises. And if the "Spirits of the dead" are enabled to return and see all that is happening on earth, and especially in their homes, what kind of bliss can be in store for them?

Why Theosophists Do Not Believe
in the Return of Pure "Spirits"

Q. What do you mean? Why should this interfere with their bliss?

A. Simply this; and here is an instance. A mother dies, leaving behind her little helpless children - orphans whom she adores - perhaps a beloved husband also. We say that her "Spirit" or Ego - that individuality which is now all impregnated, for the entire Devachanic period, with the noblest feelings held by its late personality,i.e., love for her children, pity for those who suffer, and so on - we say that it is now entirely separated from the "vale of tears", that its future bliss consists in that blessed ignorance of all the woes it left behind. Spiritualists say, on the contrary, that it is as vividly aware of them, and more so than before, for "Spirits see more than mortals in the flesh do". We say that the bliss of the Devachanee consists in its complete conviction that it has never left the earth, and that there is no such thing as death at all; that the postmortem spiritual consciousness of the mother will represent to her that she lives surrounded by her children and all those whom she loved; that no gap, no link, will be missing to make her disembodied state the most perfect and absolute happiness. The Spiritualists deny this point blank. According to their doctrine, unfortunate man is not liberated even by death from the sorrows of this life. Not a drop from the life-cup of pain and suffering will miss his lips; and whether willing or unwilling, since he sees everything now, shall he drink it to the bitter dregs. Thus, the loving wife, who during her lifetime was ready to save her husband sorrow at the price of her heart's blood, is now doomed to see, in utter helplessness, his despair, and to register every hot tear he sheds for her loss. Worse than that, she may see the tears dry too soon, and another beloved face shine on him, the father of her children; find another woman replacing her in his affections; doomed to hear her orphans giving the holy name of "mother" to one indifferent to them, and to see those little children neglected, if not ill-treated. According to this doctrine the "gentle wafting to immortal life" becomes without any transition the way into a new path of mental suffering! And yet, the columns of the Banner of Light, the veteran journal of the American Spiritualists, are filled with messages from the dead, the "dear departed ones", who all write to say how very happy they are! Is such a state of knowledge consistent with bliss? Then bliss stands in such a case for the greatest curse, and orthodox damnation must be a relief in comparison to it!

Q. But how does your theory avoid this? How can you reconcile the theory of Soul's omniscience with its blindness to that which is taking place on earth?

A. Because such is the law of love and mercy. During every Devachanic period the Ego, omniscient as it is per se, clothes itself, so to say, with the reflection of the "personality" that was. I have just told you that the ideal efflorescence of all the abstract, therefore undying and eternal qualities or attributes, such as love and

86

mercy, the love of the good, the true and the beautiful, that ever spoke in the heart of the living "personality", clung after death to the Ego, and therefore followed it to Devachan. For the time being, then, the Ego becomes the ideal reflection of the human being it was when last on earth, and that is not omniscient. Were it that, it would never be in the state we call Devachan at all.

Q. What are your reasons for it?

A. If you want an answer on the strict lines of our philosophy, then I will say that it is because everything is illusion (Maya) outside of eternal truth, which has neither form, color, nor limitation. He who has placed himself beyond the veil of Maya - and such are the highest Adepts and Initiates - can have no Devachan. As to the ordinary mortal, his bliss in it is complete. It is an absolute oblivion of all that gave it pain or sorrow in the past incarnation, and even oblivion of the fact that such things as pain or sorrow exist at all. The Devachanee lives its intermediate cycle between two incarnations surrounded by everything it had aspired to in vain, and in the companionship of everyone it loved on earth. It has reached the fulfillment of all its soul-yearnings. And thus it lives throughout long centuries an existence of unalloyed happiness, which is the reward for its sufferings in earth-life. In short, it bathes in a sea of uninterrupted felicity spanned only by events of still greater felicity in degree.

Q. But this is more than simple delusion, it is an existence of insane hallucinations!

A. From your standpoint it may be, not so from that of philosophy. Besides which, is not our whole terrestrial life filled with such delusions? Have you never met men and women living for years in a fool's paradise? And because you should happen to learn that the husband of a wife, whom she adores and believes herself as beloved by him, is untrue to her, would you go and break her heart and beautiful dream by rudely awakening her to the reality? I think not. I say it again, such oblivion and hallucination - if you call it so - are only a merciful law of nature and strict justice. At any rate, it is a far more fascinating prospect than the orthodox golden harp with a pair of wings. The assurance that

The soul that lives ascends frequently and runs familiarly through the streets of the heavenly Jerusalem, visiting the patriarchs and prophets, saluting the apostles, and admiring the army of martyrs.

- may seem of a more pious character to some. Nevertheless, it is a hallucination of a far more delusive character, since mothers love their children with an immortal love, we all know, while the personages mentioned in the "heavenly Jerusalem" are still of a rather doubtful nature. But I would, still, rather accept the "new Jerusalem", with its streets paved like the show windows of a jeweler's shop, than find consolation in the heartless doctrine of the Spiritualists. The idea alone that the intellectual conscious souls of one's father, mother, daughter, or brother find their bliss in a "Summerland" - only a little more natural, but just as ridiculous as the "New Jerusalem" in its description - would be enough to make one lose every respect for one's "departed ones". To believe that a pure spirit can feel happy while doomed to witness the sins, mistakes, treachery, and, above all, the sufferings of those from whom it is severed by death and whom it loves best, without being able to help them, would be a maddening thought.

Q. There is something in your argument. I confess to having never seen it in this light.

A. Just so, and one must be selfish to the core and utterly devoid of the sense of retributive justice, to have ever imagined such a thing. We are with those whom we have lost in material form, and far, far nearer to them now, than when they were alive. And it is not only in the fancy of the Devachanee, as some may imagine, but in reality. For pure divine love is not merely the blossom of a human heart, but has its roots in eternity. Spiritual holy love is immortal, and Karma brings sooner or later all those who loved each other with such a spiritual affection to incarnate once more in the same family group. Again we say that love beyond the grave, illusion though you may call it, has a magic and divine potency which reacts on the living. A mother's Ego filled with love for the imaginary children it sees near itself, living a life of happiness, as real to it as when on earth - that love will always be felt by the children in flesh. It will manifest in their dreams, and often in various events - in providential protection and escape, for love is a strong shield, and is not limited by space or time. As with this Devachanic "mother", so with the rest of human relationships and attachments, save the purely selfish or material. Analogy will suggest to you the rest.

Q. In no case, then, do you admit the possibility of the communication of the living with the disembodied spirit?

A. Yes, there is a case, and even two exceptions to the rule.

The first exception is during the few days that follow immediately the death of a person and before the Ego passes into the Devachanic state. Whether any living mortal, save a few exceptional cases has derived much benefit from the return of the spirit into the objective plane is another question. The spirit is dazed after death and falls very soon into what we call "pre-devachanic unconsciousness". When the intensity of the desire in the dying person to return for some purpose forced the higher consciousness to remain awake,and therefore it was really the individuality, the "Spirit" that communicated.

The second exception is found in the Nirmanakayas.

Q. What about them? And what does the name mean for you?

A. It is the name given to those who, though they have won the right to Nirvana and cyclic rest have out of pity for mankind and those they left on earth renounced the Nirvanic state. This is not "Devachan", as the latter is an illusion of our consciousness, a happy dream, and as those who are fit for Nirvana must have lost entirely every desire or possibility of the world's illusions.

Such an adept, or Saint, or whatever you may call him, believing it a selfish act to rest in bliss while mankind groans under the burden of misery produced by ignorance, renounces Nirvana, and determines to remain invisible in spirit on this earth. They have no material body, as they have left it behind; but otherwise they remain with all their principles even in astral life in our sphere. And such can and do communicate with a few elect ones, only surely not with ordinary mediums.

Q. I have put you the question about Nirmanakayas because I read in some German and other works that it was the name given to the terrestrial appearances or bodies assumed by Buddhas in the Northern Buddhist teachings.

A. So they are, only the Orientalists have confused this terrestrial body by understanding it to be objective and physical instead of purely astral and subjective.

Q. And what good can they do on earth?

A. Not much, as regards individuals, as they have no right to interfere with Karma, and can only advise and inspire mortals for the general good. Yet they do more beneficent actions than you imagine.

Q. To this Science would never subscribe, not even modern psychology. For them, no portion of intelligence can survive the physical brain. What would you answer them?

A. I would not even go to the trouble of answering, but would simply say, in the words given to "M.A. Oxon", *Intelligence is perpetuated after the body is dead. Though it is not a question of the brain only ... It is reasonable to propound the indestructibility of the human spirit from what we know.*

Q. But "M.A. Oxon" is a Spiritualist?

A. Quite so, and the only true Spiritualist I know of, though we may still disagree with him on many a minor question. Apart from this, no Spiritualist comes nearer to the occult truths than he does. Like any one of us he speaks incessantly ... *of the surface dangers that beset the ill-equipped, feather-headed muddler with the occult, who crosses the threshold without counting the cost. Some things that I do know of Spiritualism and some that I do not.* Our only disagreement rests in the question of "Spirit Identity". Otherwise, I, for one, coincide almost entirely with him, and accept the three propositions he embodied in his address of July, 1884. It is this eminent Spiritualist, rather, who disagrees with us, not we with him.

Q. What are these propositions?

A. They are:

1. That there is a life coincident with, and independent of the physical life of the body.

2. That, as a necessary corollary, this life extends beyond the life of the body. We say it extends throughout Devachan.

3. That there is communication between the denizens of that state of existence and those of the world in which we now live.

All depend, you see, on the minor and secondary aspects of these fundamental propositions. Everything depends on the views we take of Spirit and Soul, or Individuality and Personality. Spiritualists confuse the two into one. We separate them, and say that, with the exceptions above enumerated, no Spirit will revisit the earth, though the animal Soul may. But let us return once more to our direct subject, the Skandhas.

Q. I begin to understand better now. It is the Spirit, so to say, of those Skandhas which are the most ennobling, which, attaching themselves to the incarnating Ego, survive, and are added to the stock of its angelic experiences. And it is the attributes connected with the material Skandhas, with selfish and personal motives. which, disappearing from the field of action between two incarnations, reappear at the subsequent incarnation as Karmic results to be atoned for; and therefore the Spirit will not leave Devachan. Is it so?

A. Very nearly so. If you add to this that the law of retribution, or Karma, rewarding the highest and most spiritual in Devachan, never fails to reward them again on earth by giving them a further development, and furnishing the Ego with a body fitted for it, then you will be quite correct.

A Few Words About the Skandhas

Q. What becomes of the other, the lower Skandhas of the personality, after the death of the body? Are they quite destroyed?

A. They are and yet they are not - a fresh metaphysical and occult mystery for you. They are destroyed as the working stock in hand of the personality; they remain as Karmic effects, as germs, hanging in the atmosphere of the terrestrial plane, ready to come to life, as so many avenging fiends, to attach themselves to the new personality of the Ego when it reincarnates.

Q. This really passes my comprehension, and is very difficult to understand.

A. Not once that you have assimilated all the details. For then you will see that for logic, consistency, profound philosophy, divine mercy and equity, this doctrine of Reincarnation has not its equal on earth. It is a belief in a perpetual progress for each incarnating Ego, or divine soul, in an evolution from the outward into the inward, from the material to the Spiritual, arriving at the end of each stage at absolute unity with the divine Principle. From strength to strength, from the beauty and perfection of one plane to the greater beauty and perfection of another, with accessions of new glory, of fresh knowledge and power in each cycle, such is the destiny of every Ego, which thus becomes its own Savior in each world and incarnation.

Q. But Christianity teaches the same. It also preaches progression.

A. Yes, only with the addition of something else. It tells us of the impossibility of attaining Salvation without the aid of a miraculous Savior, and therefore dooms to perdition all those who will not accept the dogma. This is just the difference between Christian theology and Theosophy. The former enforces belief in the Descent of the Spiritual Ego into the Lower Self; the latter inculcates the necessity of endeavoring to elevate oneself to the Christos, or Buddhi state.

Q. By teaching the annihilation of consciousness in case of failure, however, don't you think that it amounts to the annihilation of Self, a in the opinion of the non-metaphysical?

A. From the standpoint of those who believe in the resurrection of the body literally,and insist that every bone, every artery and atom of flesh will be raised bodily on the Judgment Day - of course it does. If you still insist that it is the perishable form and finite qualities that make up immortal man, then we shall hardly understand each other. And if you do not understand that, by limiting the existence of every Ego to one life on earth, you make of Deity an ever-drunken Indra of the Puric dead letter, a cruel Moloch, a god who makes an inextricable mess on Earth, and yet claims thanks for it, then the sooner we drop the conversation the better.

Q. But let us return, now that the subject of the Skandhas is disposed of, to the question of the consciousness which survives death. This is the point which interests most people. Do we possess more knowledge in Devachan than we do in earth life?

A. In one sense, we can acquire more knowledge; that is, we can develop further any faculty which we loved and strove after during life, provided it is concerned with abstract and ideal things, such as music, painting, poetry, etc., since Devachan is merely an idealized and subjective continuation of earth-life.

Q. But if in Devachan the Spirit is free from matter, why should it not possess all knowledge?

A. Because, as I told you, the Ego is, so to say, wedded to the memory of its last incarnation. Thus, if you think over what I have said, and string all the facts together, you will realize that the Devachanic state is not one of omniscience, but a transcendental continuation of the personal life just terminated. It is the rest of the soul from the toils of life.

Q. But the scientific materialists assert that after the death of man nothing remains; that the human body simply disintegrates into its component elements; and that what we call soul is merely a temporary selfconsciousness produced as a byproduct of organic action, which will evaporate like steam. Is not theirs a strange state of mind?

A. Not strange at all, that I see. If they say that self-consciousness ceases with the body, then in their case they simply utter an unconscious prophecy, for once they are firmly convinced of what they assert, no conscious after-life is possible for them. For there are exceptions to every rule.

On Postmortem and Postnatal Consciousness

Q. But if human self-consciousness survives death as a rule, why should there be exceptions?

A. In the fundamental principles of the spiritual world no exception is possible. But there are rules for those who see, and rules for those who prefer to remain blind.

Q. Quite so, I understand. This is but an aberration of the blind man, who denies the existence of the sun because he does not see it. But after death his spiritual eyes will certainly compel him to see. Is this what you mean?

A. He will not be compelled, nor will he see anything. Having persistently denied during life the continuance of existence after death, he will be unable to see it, because his spiritual capacity having been stunted in life, it cannot develop after death, and he will remain blind. By insisting that he must see it, you evidently mean one thing and I another. You speak of the spirit from the spirit, or the flame from the flame - of Atma, in short - and you confuse it with the human soul-Manas … You do not understand me; let me try to make it clear. The whole gist of your question is to know whether, in the case of a downright materialist, the complete loss of self-consciousness and self-perception after death is possible? Isn't it so? I answer, it is possible. Because, believing firmly in our Esoteric Doctrine, which refers to the *postmortem period,* or the interval between two lives or births, as merely a transitory state, I say, whether that interval between two acts of the illusionary drama of life lasts one year or a million, that postmortem state may, without any breach of the fundamental law, prove to be just the same state as that of a man who is in a dead faint.

Q. But since you have just said that the fundamental laws of the after-death state admit of no exceptions, how can this be?

A. Nor do I say that it does admit of an exception. But the spiritual law of continuity applies only to things which are truly real. To one who has read and understood Mundakya Upanishad and Vedantasara all this becomes very clear. I will say more: it is sufficient to understand what we mean by Buddhi and the duality of Manas to gain a clear perception why the materialist may fail to have a self-conscious survival after death. Since Manas, in its lower aspect, is the seat of the terrestrial mind, it can, therefore, give only that perception of the Universe which is based on the evidence of that mind; it cannot give spiritual vision. It is said in the Eastern school, that between Buddhi and Manas (the Ego), or Isvara and Prajna [Isvara is the collective consciousness of the manifested godhead, Brahma, i.e. the collective consciousness of the host of Dhyan Chohans (see Secret Doctrine); Prajna is their individual wisdom] there is in reality no more difference than between a forest and its trees, a lake and its waters,as the Mundakya teaches. One or hundreds of trees dead from loss of vitality, or uprooted, are yet incapable of preventing the forest from being still a forest.

Q. But, as I understand it, Buddhi represents in this simile the forest, and Manas-Taijasi 2] the trees. And if Buddhi is immortal, how can that which is similar to it, i.e.,Manas-Taijasi [Taijasi means the 'radiant', as a consequence of its union with Buddhi, i.e. Manas, the human soul, enlightened by the rays of the divine soul. Hence Manas-Taijasi can be described as radiant intellect, the human reason enlightened by the light of the spirit; and Buddhi-Manas is the revelation of the divine plus the human intellect and selfconsciousness] , entirely lose its consciousness till the day of its new incarnation? I cannot understand it.

A. You cannot, because you will mix up an abstract representation of the whole with its casual changes of form. Remember that if it can be said of Buddhi-Manas that it is unconditionally immortal, the same cannot be said of the lower Manas, still less of Taijasi , which is merely an attribute. Neither of these, neither Manas nor Taijasi , can exist apart from Buddhi, the divine soul, because the first (Manas) is, in its lower aspect, a quality of the terrestrial personality, and the second (Taijasi) is identical with the first, because it is the same Manas only with the light of Buddhi reflected on it. In its turn, Buddhi would remain only an impersonal spirit without this element which it borrows from the human soul, which conditions and makes of it, in this illusive Universe, as it were something separate from the universal soul for the whole period of the cycle of incarnation. Say rather that Buddhi-Manas can neither die nor lose its compound self-consciousness in Eternity, nor the recollection of its previous incarnations in which the two - i.e., the spiritual and the human soul - had been closely linked together. But it is not so in the case of a materialist, whose human soul not only receives nothing from the divine soul, but even refuses to recognize its existence. You can hardly apply this axiom to the attributes and qualities of the human soul, for it would be like saying that because your divine soul is immortal, therefore the bloom on your cheek must also be immortal; whereas this bloom, like Taijasi , is simply a transitory phenomenon.

Q. Do I understand you to say that we must not mix in our minds the noumenon with the phenomenon, the cause with its effect?

A. I do say so, and repeat that, limited to Manas or the human soul alone, the radiance of Taijas itself becomes a mere question of time; because both immortality and consciousness after death become, for the terrestrial personality of man, simply conditioned attributes, as they depend entirely on conditions and beliefs created by the human soul itself during the life of its body. Karma acts incessantly: we reap in our after-life only the fruit of that which we have ourselves sown in this.

Q. But if my Ego can, after the destruction of my body, become plunged in a state of entire unconsciousness, then where can be the punishment for the sins of my past life?

A. Our philosophy teaches that Karmic punishment reaches the Ego only in its next incarnation. After death it receives only the reward for the unmerited sufferings endured during its past incarnation.

(Some Theosophists have taken exception to this phrase, but the words are those of Master, and the meaning attached to the word unmerited is that given above. In the T.P.S. pamphlet No. 6, a phrase, criticized subsequently in Lucifer, was used which was intended to convey the same idea. In form, however, it was awkward and open to the criticism directed against it; but the essential idea was that men often suffer from the effects of the actions done by others, effects which thus do not strictly belong to their own Karma - and for these sufferings they of course deserve compensation.)

The whole punishment after death, even for the materialist, consists, therefore, in the absence of any reward, and the utter loss of the consciousness of one's bliss and rest. Karma is the child of the terrestrial Ego, the fruit of the actions of the tree which is the objective personality visible to all, as much as the fruit of all the thoughts and even motives of the spiritual "I"; but Karma is also the tender mother, who heals the wounds inflicted by her during the preceding life, before she will begin to torture this Ego by inflicting upon him new ones. If it may be said that there is not a mental or physical suffering in the life of a mortal which is not the direct fruit and consequence of some sin in a preceding existence; on the other hand, since he does not preserve the slightest recollection of it in his actual life, and feels himself not deserving of such punishment, and therefore thinks he suffers for no guilt of his own, this alone is sufficient to entitle the human soul to the fullest consolation, rest, and bliss in his postmortem existence. Death comes to our spiritual selves ever as a deliverer and friend. For the materialist who, notwithstanding his materialism, was not a bad man, the interval between the two lives will be like the unbroken and placid sleep of a child, either entirely dreamless, or filled with pictures of which he will have no definite perception; while for the average mortal it will be a dream as vivid as life, and full of realistic bliss and visions.

Q. Then the personal man must always go on suffering blindly the Karmic penalties which the Ego has incurred?

A. Not quite so. At the solemn moment of death every man, even when death is sudden, sees the whole of his past life marshaled before him, in its minutest details. For one short instant the personal becomes one with the individual and all-knowing Ego. But this instant is enough to show to him the whole chain of causes which have been at work during his life. He sees and now understands himself as he is, unadorned by flattery or self-deception. He reads his life, remaining as a spectator looking down into the arena he is quitting; he feels and knows the justice of all the suffering that has overtaken him.

Q. Does this happen to everyone?

A. Without any exception. Very good and holy men see, we are taught, not only the life they are leaving, but even several preceding lives in which were produced the causes that made them what they were in the life just closing. They recognize the law of Karma in all its majesty and justice.

Q. Is there anything corresponding to this before rebirth?

A. There is. As the man at the moment of death has a retrospective insight into the life he has led, so, at the moment he is reborn onto earth, the Ego, awaking from the state of Devachan, has a prospective vision of the life which awaits him, and realizes all the causes that have led to it. He realizes them and sees futurity, because it is between Devachan and rebirth that the Ego regains his full manasic consciousness, and rebecomes for a short time the god he was, before, in compliance with Karmic law, he first descended into matter and incarnated in the first man of flesh. The "golden thread" sees all its "pearls" and misses not one of them.

What is Really Meant by Annihilation

Q. I have heard some Theosophists speak of a golden thread on which their lives were strung. What do they mean by this?

A. In the Hindu Sacred books it is said that the part of us which undergoes periodical incarnation is the Sutratman, which means literally the Thread Soul. It is a synonym of the reincarnating Ego-Manas conjoined with Buddhi - which absorbs the Manasic recollections of all our preceding lives. It is so called, because, like the pearls on a thread, so is the long series of human lives strung together on that one thread. In some Upanishad these recurrent rebirths are likened to the life of a mortal which oscillates periodically between sleep and waking.

Q. This, I must say, does not seem very clear, and I will tell you why. For the man who awakes, another day commences, but that man is the same in soul and body as he was the day before; whereas at every incarnation a full change takes place not only of the external envelope, sex, and personality, but even of the mental and psychic capacities. The simile does not seem to me quite correct. The man who arises from sleep remembers quite clearly what he has done yesterday, the day before, and even months and years ago. But none of us has the slightest recollection of a preceding life or of any fact or event concerning it … I may forget in the morning what I have dreamt during the night, still I know that I have slept and have the certainty that I lived during sleep; but what recollection can I have of my past incarnation until the moment of death? How do you reconcile this?

A. Some people do recollect their past incarnations during life; but these are Buddhas and Initiates. This is what the Yogis call Samma -Sambuddha, or the knowledge of the whole series of one's past incarnations.

Q. But we ordinary mortals who have not reached Samma -Sambuddha, how are we to understand this simile?

A. By studying it and trying to understand more correctly the characteristics and the three kinds of sleep. Sleep is a general and immutable law for man as for beast, but there are different kinds of sleep and still more different dreams and visions.

Q. But this takes us to another subject. Let us return to the materialist who, while not denying dreams, which he could hardly do, yet denies immortality in general and the survival of his own individuality.

A. And the materialist, without knowing it, is right. One who has no inner perception of, and faith in, the immortality of his soul, in that man the soul can never become Buddhi-Taijasi , but will remain simply Manas, and for Manas alone there is no immortality possible. In order to live in the world to come a conscious life, one has to believe first of all in that life during the terrestrial existence. On these two aphorisms of the Secret Science all the philosophy about the postmortem consciousness and the immortality of the soul is built. The Ego receives always according to its deserts. After the dissolution of the body, there commences for it a period of full awakened consciousness, or a state of chaotic dreams, or an utterly dreamless sleep undistinguishable from annihilation, and these are the three kinds of sleep. If our physiologists find the cause of dreams and visions in an unconscious preparation for them during the waking hours, why cannot the same be admitted for the postmortem dreams? I repeat it: death is sleep. After death, before the spiritual eyes of the soul, begins a performance according to a program learnt and very often unconsciously composed by ourselves: the practical carrying out of correct beliefs or of illusions which have been created by ourselves. The Methodist will be Methodist, the Muslim a Muslim, at least for some time - in a perfect fool's paradise of each man's creation and making. These are the postmortem fruits of the tree of life. Naturally, our belief or unbelief in the fact of conscious immortality is unable to influence the unconditioned reality of the fact itself, once that it exists; but the belief or unbelief in that immortality as the property of independent or separate entities, cannot fail to give color to that fact in its application to each of these entities. Now do you begin to understand it?

Q. I think I do. The materialist, disbelieving in everything that cannot be proven to him by his five senses, or by scientific reasoning, based exclusively on the data furnished by these senses in spite of their inadequacy, and rejecting every spiritual manifestation, accepts life as the only conscious existence. Therefore according to their beliefs so will it be unto them. They will lose their personal Ego, and will plunge into a dreamless sleep until a new awakening. Is it so?

A. Almost so. Remember the practically universal teaching of the two kinds of conscious existence: the terrestrial and the spiritual. The latter must be considered real from the very fact that it is inhabited by the eternal, changeless, and immortal

Monad; whereas the incarnating Ego dresses itself up in new garments entirely different from those of its previous incarnations, and in which all except its spiritual prototype is doomed to a change so radical as to leave no trace behind.

Q. How so? Can my conscious terrestrial "I" perish not only for a time, like the consciousness of the materialist, but so entirely as to leave no trace behind?

A. According to the teaching, it must so perish and in its fullness; all except the principle which, having united itself with the Monad, has thereby become a purely spiritual and indestructible essence, one with it in the Eternity. But in the case of an out-and-out materialist, in whose personal "I" no Buddhi has ever reflected itself, how can the latter carry away into the Eternity one particle of that terrestrial personality? Your spiritual "I" is immortal; but from your present self it can carry away into Eternity that only which has become worthy of immortality, namely, the aroma alone of the flower that has been mown by death.

Q. Well, and the flower, the terrestrial "I"?

A. The flower, as all past and future flowers which have blossomed and will have to blossom on the mother bough, the Sutratman, all children of one root or Buddhi - will return to dust. Your present "I", as you yourself know, is not the body now sitting before me, nor yet is it what I would call Manas-Sutratman, but Sutratman-Buddhi.

Q. But this does not explain to me, at all, why you call life after death immortal, infinite, and real, and the terrestrial life a simple phantom or illusion; since even that postmortem life has limits, however much wider they may be than those of terrestrial life.

A. No doubt. The spiritual Ego of man moves in eternity like a pendulum between the hours of birth and death. But if these hours, marking the periods of life terrestrial and life spiritual, are limited in their duration, and if the very number of such stages in Eternity between sleep and awakening, illusion and reality, has its beginning and its end, on the other hand, the spiritual pilgrim is eternal. Therefore are the hours of his postmortem life, when, disembodied, he stands face to face with truth and not the mirages of his transitory earthly existences, during the period of that pilgrimage which we call "the cycle of rebirths" - the only reality in our conception. Such intervals, their limitation notwithstanding, do not prevent the Ego, while ever perfecting itself, from following undeviatingly, though gradually and slowly, the path to its last transformation, when that Ego, having reached its goal, becomes a divine being. These intervals and stages help towards this final result instead of hindering it; and without such limited intervals the divine Ego could never reach its ultimate goal. I have given you once already a familiar illustration by comparing the Ego, or the individuality, to an actor, and its numerous and various incarnations to the parts it plays. Will you call these parts or their costumes the individuality of the actor himself? Like that actor, the Ego is forced to play during the cycle of necessity, up to the very threshold of ParaNirvana, many parts such as may be unpleasant to it. But as the bee collects its honey from every flower, leaving the rest as food for the earthly worms, so does our spiritual individuality, whether we call it Sutratman or Ego. Collecting from every terrestrial personality, into which Karma forces it to incarnate, the nectar alone of the spiritual qualities and self-consciousness, it unites all these into one whole and emerges from its chrysalis as the glorified Dhyani-Chohan. So much the worse for those terrestrial personalities from which it could collect nothing. Such personalities cannot assuredly outlive consciously their terrestrial existence.

Q. Thus, then, it seems that, for the terrestrial personality, immortality is still conditional. Is, then, immortality itself not unconditional?

A. Not at all. But immortality cannot touch the non-existent: for all that which exists as Sat, or emanates from Sat, immortality and Eternity are absolute. Matter is the opposite pole of spirit, and yet the two are one. The essence of all this, i.e., Spirit, Force, and Matter, or the three in one, is as endless as it is beginningless; but the form acquired by this triple unity during its incarnations, its externality, is certainly only the illusion of our personal conceptions. Therefore do we call Nirvana and the Universal life alone a reality, while relegating the terrestrial life, its terrestrial personality included, and even its Devachanic existence, to the phantom realm of illusion.

Q. But why in such a case call sleep the reality, and waking the illusion?

A. It is simply a comparison made to facilitate the grasping of the subject, and from the standpoint of terrestrial conceptions it is a very correct one.

Q. And still I cannot understand, if the life to come is based on justice and the merited retribution for all our terrestrial suffering, how in the case of materialists, many of whom are really honest and charitable men, there should remain of their personality nothing but the refuse of a faded flower.

A. No one ever said such a thing. No materialist, however unbelieving, can die forever in the fullness of his spiritual individuality. What was said is that consciousness can disappear either fully or partially in the case of a materialist, so that no conscious remains of his personality survive.

Q. But surely this is annihilation?

A. Certainly not. One can sleep a dead sleep and miss several stations during a long railway journey, without the slightest recollection or consciousness, and awake at another station and continue the journey past innumerable other halting-places till the end of the journey or the goal is reached. Three kinds of sleep were mentioned to you: the dreamless, the chaotic, and the one which is so real, that to the sleeping man his dreams become full realities. If you believe in the latter why can't you believe in the former; according to the after-life a man has believed in and expected, such is the life he will have. He who expected no life to come will have an absolute blank, amounting to annihilation, in the interval between the two rebirths. This is just the carrying out of the program we spoke of, a program created by the materialists themselves. But there are various kinds of materialists, as you say. A selfish, wicked Egoist, one who never shed a tear for anyone but himself, thus adding entire indifference to the whole world to his unbelief, must, at the threshold of death, drop his personality forever. This personality having no tendrils of sympathy for the world around and hence nothing to hook onto Sutratman, it follows that with the last breath every connection between the two is broken. There being no Devachan for such a materialist, the Sutratman will reincarnate almost immediately. But those materialists who erred in nothing but their disbelief will oversleep but one station. And the time will come when that ex-materialist will perceive himself in the Eternity and perhaps repent that he lost even one day, one station, from the life eternal.

Q. Still, would it not be more correct to say that death is birth into a new life, or a return once more into eternity?

A. You may if you like. Only remember that births differ, and that there are births of "still-born beings", which are failures of nature. Moreover, with your Western fixed ideas about material life, the words living and being are quite inapplicable to the pure subjective state of postmortem existence. It is just because, save in a few philosophers who are not read by the many, and who themselves are too confused to present a distinct picture of it, it is just because your Western ideas of life and death have finally become so narrow, that on the one hand they have led to crass materialism, and on the other, to the still more material conception of the other life, which the Spiritualists have formulated in their Summerland. There the souls of men eat, drink, marry, and live in a paradise quite as sensual as that of Mohammed, but even less philosophical. Nor are the average conceptions of the uneducated Christians any better, being if possible still more material. What between truncated angels, brass trumpets, golden harps, and material hell fires, the Christian heaven seems like a fairy scene at a Christmas pantomime.

It is because of these narrow conceptions that you find such difficulty in understanding. It is just because the life of the disembodied soul, while possessing all the vividness of reality, as in certain dreams, is devoid of every grossly objective form of terrestrial life, that the Eastern philosophers have compared it with visions during sleep.

Definite Words for Definite Things

Q. Don't you think it is because there are no definite and fixed terms to indicate each principle in man, that such a confusion of ideas arises in our minds with respect to the respective functions of these principles?

A. I have thought of it myself. The whole trouble has arisen from this: we have started our expositions of, and discussion about, the principles, using their Sanskrit names instead of coining immediately, for the use of Theosophists, their equivalents in English. We must try and remedy this now.

Q. You will do well, as it may avoid further confusion; no two theosophical writers, it seems to me, have hitherto agreed to call the same principle by the same name.

A. The confusion is more apparent than real, however. I have heard some of our Theosophists express surprise at, and criticize several essays speaking of these principles; but, when examined, there was no worse mistake in them than that of using the word Soul to cover the three principles without specifying the distinctions. The first, as positively the clearest of our Theosophical writers, Mr. A.P. Sinnett, has some comprehensive and admirably-written passages on the "Higher Self". His real idea has also been misconceived by some, owing to his using the word Soul in a general sense. Yet here are a few passages which will show to you how clear and comprehensive is all that he writes on the subject:

The human soul, once launched on the streams of evolution as a human individuality, passes through alternate periods of physical and relatively spiritual existence. It passes from the one plane, or stratum, or condition of nature to the other under the guidance of its Karmic affinities; living in incarnations the life which its Karma has preordained; modifying its progress within the limitations of circumstances, and - developing fresh Karma by its use or abuse of opportunities - it returns to spiritual existence (Devachan) after each physical life - through the intervening region of Kamaloka - for rest and refreshment and for the gradual absorption into its essence, as so much cosmic progress, of the life's experience gained on earth or during physical existence. This view of the matter will, moreover, have suggested many collateral inferences to anyone thinking over the subject; for instance, that the transfer of consciousness from the Kamaloka to the Devachanic stage of this progression would necessarily be gradual; that in truth, no hard-and-fast line separates the varieties of spiritual conditions, that even the spiritual and physical planes, as psychic faculties in living people show, are not so hopelessly walled off from one another as materialistic theories would suggest; that all states of nature are all around us simultaneously, and appeal to different perceptive faculties; and so on ... It is clear that during physical existence people who possess psychic faculties remain in connection with the planes of super-physical consciousness; and although most people may not be endowed with such faculties, we all, as the phenomena of sleep, even, and especially ... those of somnambulism or mesmerism, show, are capable of entering into conditions of consciousness that the five physical senses have nothing to do with. We - the souls within us - are not as it were altogether adrift in the ocean of matter. We clearly retain some surviving interest or rights in the shore from which, for a time, we have floated off. The process of incarnation, therefore, is not fully described when we speak of an alternate existence on the physical and spiritual planes, and thus picture the soul as a complete entity slipping entirely from the one state of existence to the other. The more correct definitions of the process would probably represent incarnation as taking place on this physical plane of nature by reason of an efflux emanating from the soul. The Spiritual realm would all the while be the proper habitat of the Soul, which would never entirely quit it; and that non-materializable portion of the Soul which abides permanently on the spiritual plane may fitly, perhaps, be spoken of as the Higher Self.

This "Higher Self" is Atma, and of course it is "non-materializable", as Mr. Sinnett says. Even more, it can never be "objective" under any circumstances, even to the highest spiritual perception. For Atma or the "Higher Self" is really Brahma, the Absolute, and indistinguishable from it. In hours of Samadhi, the higher spiritual consciousness of the Initiate is entirely absorbed in the one essence, which is Atma, and therefore, being one with the whole, there can be nothing objective for it. Now some of our Theosophists have got into the habit of using the words Self and Ego as synonymous, of associating the term Self with only man's higher individual or even personal "Self" or Ego,whereas this term ought never to be applied except to the One universal Self. Hence the confusion. Speaking of Manas, the "causal body", we may call it - when connecting it with the Buddhic radiance - the Higher Ego, never the Higher Self. For even Buddhi, the "Spiritual Soul", is not the Self, but the vehicle only of Self. All the other "Selves" - such as the "Individual self" and "personal self "- ought never to be spoken or written of without their qualifying and characteristic adjectives.

Thus in this most excellent essay on the Higher Self, this term is applied to the sixth principle or Buddhi; and has in consequence given rise to just such misunderstandings. The statement that *A child does not acquire its sixth principle - or become a morally responsible being capable of generating Karma - until seven years old. - proves what is meant therein by the Higher Self. Therefore, the able author is quite justified in explaining that after the Higher Self has passed into the human being and saturated the personality - in some of the finer organizations only - with its consciousness*

People with psychic faculties may indeed perceive this Higher Self through their finer senses from time to time.

But so are those, who limit the term Higher Self to the Universal Divine Principle, "justified" in misunderstanding him. For, when we read, without being prepared for this shifting of metaphysical terms, that while Fully manifesting on the physical plane ... the Higher Self still remains a conscious spiritual Ego on the corresponding plane of Nature. We are apt to see in the Higher Self of this sentence, Atma, and in the spiritual Ego, Manas,or rather Buddhi-Manas, and forthwith to criticize the whole thing as incorrect. To avoid henceforth such misapprehensions, I propose to translate literally from the Occult Eastern terms their equivalents in English, and offer these for future use.

The Higher Self is Atma, the inseparable ray of the Universal and One Self. It is the God above, more than within, us. Happy the man who succeeds in saturating his inner Ego with it! *The Spiritual divine Ego* is the Spiritual soul or Buddhi, in close union with Manas, the mind-principle, without which it is no Ego at all, but only the Atmic Vehicle. *The Inner, or Higher Ego* is Manas, the Fifth Principle, so-called, independently of Buddhi. The Mind- Principle is only the Spiritual Ego when merged into one with Buddhi - no materialist being supposed to have in him such an Ego, however great his intellectual capacities. It is the permanent Individuality or the 'Reincarnating Ego'. *The Lower, or Personal "Ego"* is the physical man in conjunction with his lower Self, i.e., animal instincts, passions, desires, etc. It is called the "false" personality, and consists of the lower Manas combined with Kamarupa, and operating through the Physical body and its phantom or double. The remaining principle *Prana, or Life,* is, strictly speaking, the radiating force or Energy of Atma - as the Universal Life and the One Self - Its lower or rather (in its effects) more physical, because manifesting, aspect. Prana or Life permeates the whole being of the objective Universe; and is called a principle only because it is an indispensable factor and the deus ex machina of the living man.

Q. This division being so much simplified in its combinations will answer better, I believe. The other is much too metaphysical.

A. If outsiders as well as Theosophists would agree to it, it would certainly make matters much more comprehensible.

On the Nature of Our Thinking Principle
The Mystery of the Ego

Q. I perceive in the quotation you brought forward a little while ago from The *Buddhist Catechism* a discrepancy that I would like to hear explained. It is there stated that the Skandhas - memory included - change with every new incarnation. And yet, it is asserted that the reflection of the past lives, which, we are told, are entirely made up of Skandhas, "must" survive. At the present moment I am not quite clear in my mind as to what it is precisely that survives, and I would like to have it explained. What is it? Is it only that "reflection", or those Skandhas, or always that same Ego, the Manas?

A. I have just explained that the reincarnating Principle, or that which we call the divine man, is indestructible throughout the life cycle: indestructible as a thinking Entity, and even as an ethereal form. The "reflection" is only the spiritualized remembrance,during the Devachanic period, of the ex-personality, Mr. A. or Mrs. B. - with which the Ego identifies itself during that period. Since the latter is but the continuation of the earth-life, so to say, the very acme and pitch, in an unbroken series, of the few happy moments in that now past existence, the Ego has to identify itself with the personal consciousness of that life, if anything shall remain of it.

Q. This means that the Ego, notwithstanding its divine nature, passes every such period between two incarnations in a state of mental obscuration, or temporary insanity.

A. You may regard it as you like. Believing that, outside the One Reality, nothing is better than a passing illusion - the whole Universe included - we do not view it as insanity, but as a very natural sequence or development of the terrestrial life. What is life? A bundle of the most varied experiences, of daily changing ideas, emotions, and opinions. In our youth we are often enthusiastically devoted to an ideal, to some hero or heroine whom we try to follow and revive; a few years later, when the freshness of our youthful feelings has faded out and sobered down, we are the first to laugh at our fancies. And yet there was a day when we had so thoroughly identified our own personality with that of the ideal in our mind - especially if it was that of a living being - that the former was entirely merged and lost in the latter. Can it be said of a man of fifty that he is the same being that he was at twenty? The inner man is the same; the outward living personality is completely transformed and changed. Would you also call these changes in the human mental states insanity?

Q. How would you name them, and especially how would you explain the permanence of one and the evanescence of the other?

A. We have our own doctrine ready, and to us it offers no difficulty. The clue lies in the double consciousness of our mind, and also, in the dual nature of the mental principle. There is a spiritual consciousness, the Manasic mind illumined by the light of Buddhi, that which subjectively perceives abstractions; and the sentient consciousness (the lower Manasic light), inseparable from our physical brain and senses. This latter consciousness is held in subjection by the brain and physical senses, and, being in its turn equally dependent on them, must of course fade out and finally die with the disappearance of the brain and physical senses. It is only the former kind of consciousness, whose root lies in eternity, which survives and lives forever, and may, therefore, be regarded as immortal. Everything else belongs to passing illusions.

Q. What do you really understand by illusion in this case?

A. It is very well described in the just-mentioned essay on The Higher Self. Says its author: *The theory we are considering (the interchange of ideas between the Higher Ego and the lower self) harmonizes very well with the treatment of this world in which we live as a phenomenal world of illusion, the spiritual plane of nature being on the other hand the noumenal world or plane of reality. That region of nature in which, so to speak, the permanent soul is rooted is more real than that in which its transitory blossoms appear for a brief space to wither and fall to pieces, while the plant recovers energy for sending forth a fresh flower. Supposing flowers only were perceptible to ordinary senses, and their roots existed in a state of Nature intangible and invisible to us, philosophers in such a world who divined that there were such things as roots in another plane of existence would be apt to say of the flowers: "These are not the real plants; they are of no relative importance, merely illusive phenomena of the moment".*

This is what I mean. The world in which blossom the transitory and evanescent flowers of personal lives is not the real permanent world; but that one in which we find the root of consciousness, that root which is beyond illusion and dwells in the eternity.

Q. What do you mean by the root dwelling in eternity?

A. I mean by this root the thinking entity, the Ego which incarnates, whether we regard it as an Angel, Spirit, or a Force. Of that which falls under our sensuous perceptions only what grows directly from, or is attached to this invisible root above, can partake of its immortal life. Hence every noble thought, idea, and aspiration of the personality it informs, proceeding from and fed by this root, must become permanent. As to the physical consciousness, as it is a quality of the sentient but lower principle, (Kamarupa or animal instinct, illuminated by the lower manasic reflection), or the human Soul - it must disappear. That which displays activity, while the body is asleep or paralyzed, is the higher consciousness, our memory registering but feebly and inaccurately - because automatically - such experiences, and often failing to be even slightly impressed by them.

Q. But how is it that Manas, although you call it Nous, a "God", is so weak during its incarnations, as to be actually conquered and fettered by its body?

A. I might retort with the same question and ask: How is it that he, whom you regard as the God of Gods and the One living God, is so weak as to allow evil (or the Devil) to have the best of him as much as of all his creatures, whether while he remains in Heaven, or during the time he was incarnated on this earth? You are sure to reply again: "This is a Mystery; and we are forbidden to pry into the mysteries of God". Not being forbidden to do so by our religious philosophy, I answer your question that, unless a God descends as an Avatara,no divine principle can be otherwise than cramped and paralyzed by turbulent, animal matter. Heterogeneity will always have the upper hand over homogeneity, on this plane of illusions, and the nearer an essence is to its root-principle, Primordial Homogeneity, the more difficult it is for the latter to assert itself on earth. Spiritual and divine powers lie dormant in every human Being; and the wider the sweep of his spiritual vision the mightier will be the God within him. But as few men can feel that God, and since, as an average rule, deity is always bound and limited in our thought by earlier conceptions, those ideas that are inculcated in us from childhood, therefore, it is so difficult for you to understand our philosophy.

Q. And is it this Ego of ours which is our God?

A. Not at all; "A God" is not the universal deity, but only a spark from the one ocean of Divine Fire. Our God within us, or "our Father in Secret" is what we call the Higher Self, Atma.Our incarnating Ego was a God in its origin, as were all the primeval emanations of the One Unknown Principle. But since its "fall" into Matter, having to incarnate throughout the cycle, in succession, from first to last, it is no longer a free and happy god, but a poor pilgrim on his way to regain that which he has lost. I can answer you more fully by repeating what is said of the Inner Man:

From the remotest antiquity mankind as a whole have always been convinced of the existence of a personal spiritual entity within the personal physical man. This inner entity was more or less divine, according to its proximity to the crown. The closer the union the more serene man's destiny, the less dangerous the external conditions. This belief is neither bigotry nor superstition, only an ever-present, instinctive feeling of the proximity of another spiritual and invisible world, which, though it be subjective to the senses of the outward man, is perfectly objective to the inner ego. Furthermore, they believed that there are external and internal conditions which affect the determination of our will upon our actions. They rejected fatalism, for fatalism implies a blind course of some still blinder power. But they believed in destiny or Karma, which from birth to death every man is weaving thread by thread around himself, as a spider does his cobweb; and this destiny is guided by that presence termed by some the guardian angel, or our more intimate astral inner man, who is but too often the evil genius of the man of flesh or the personality. Both these lead on Man, but one of them must prevail; and from the very beginning of the invisible affray the stern and implacable law of compensation and retribution steps in and takes its course, following faithfully the fluctuating of the conflict. When the last strand is woven, and man is seemingly enwrapped in the net-work of his own doing, then he finds himself completely under the empire of this self-made destiny. It then either fixes him like the inert shell against the immovable rock, or like a feather carries him away in a whirlwind raised by his own actions.

Such is the destiny of the Man - the true Ego, not the Automaton, the shell that goes by that name. It is for him to become the conqueror over matter.

The Complex Nature of Manas

Q. But you wanted to tell me something of the essential nature of Manas, and of the relation in which the Skandhas of physical man stand to it?

A. It is this nature, mysterious, Protean, beyond any grasp, and almost shadowy in its correlations with the other principles, that is most difficult to realize, and still more so to explain. Manas is a principle, and yet it is an Entity and individuality or Ego. He is a "God", and yet he is doomed to an endless cycle of incarnations, for each of which he is made responsible, and for each of which he has to suffer. All this seems as contradictory as it is puzzling; nevertheless, there are hundreds of people, even in Europe, who realize all this perfectly, for they comprehend the Ego not only in its integrity but in its many aspects. Finally, if I would make myself comprehensible, I must begin by the beginning and give you the genealogy of this Ego in a few lines.

Q. Say on.

A. Try to imagine a "Spirit", a celestial Being, whether we call it by one name or another, divine in its essential nature, yet not pure enough to be one with the All, and having, in order to achieve this, to do purify its nature as to finally gain that goal. It can do so only by passing individually and personally, i.e.,spiritually and physically, through every experience and feeling that exists in the manifold or differentiated Universe. It has, therefore, after having gained such experience in the lower kingdoms, and having ascended higher and still higher with every rung on the ladder of being, to pass through every experience on the human planes. In its very essence it is thought, and is, therefore, called in its plurality Manasaputra, "the Sons of the (Universal) mind". This individualized Thought is what we Theosophists call the real human Ego, the thinking Entity imprisoned in a case of flesh and bones. This is surely a Spiritual Entity, not Matter, and such Entities are the incarnating Egos that inform the bundle of animal matter called mankind, and whose names are Manasa or Minds. But once imprisoned, or incarnate, their essence becomes dual: that is to say, the rays of the eternal divine Mind, considered as individual entities, assume a two-fold attribute which is (a) their essential inherent characteristic, heaven-aspiring mind (higher Manas), and (b) the human quality of thinking, or animal cogitation, rationalized owing to the superiority of the human brain, the Kama-tending or lower Manas. One gravitates toward Buddhi, the other, tending downward, to the seat of passions and animal desires. The latter have no room in Devachan, nor can they associate with the divine triad which ascends as one into mental bliss. Yet it is the Ego, the Manasic Entity, which is held responsible for all the sins of the lower attributes, just as a parent is answerable for the transgressions of his child, so long as the latter remains irresponsible.

Q. Is this "child" the "personality"?

A. It is. When, therefore, it is stated that the "personality" dies with the body it does not state all. The body, which was only the objective symbol of Mr. A. or Mrs. B., fades away with all its material Skandhas, which are the visible expressions thereof. But all that which constituted during life the spiritual bundle of experiences, the noblest aspirations, undying affections, and unselfish nature of Mr. A. or Mrs. B. clings for the time of the Devachanic period to the Ego, which is identified with the spiritual portion of that terrestrial Entity, now passed away out of sight. The Actor is so imbued with the role just played by him that he dreams of it during the whole Devachanic night, which vision continues till the hour strikes for him to return to the stage of life to enact another part.

Q. But how is it that this doctrine, which you say is as old as thinking men, has found no room, say, in Christian theology?

A. You are mistaken, it has; only theology has disfigured it out of all recognition, as it has many other doctrines. Theology calls the Ego the Angel that God gives us at the moment of our birth, to take care of our Soul. Instead of holding that "Angel" responsible for the transgressions of the poor helpless Soul, it is the latter which, according to theological logic, is punished for all the sins of both flesh and mind! It is the Soul, the immaterial breath of God and his alleged creation, which, by some most amazing intellectual jugglery, is doomed to burn in a material hell without ever being consumed, while the "Angel escapes scot-free, after folding his white pinions and wetting them with a few tears. Aye, these are our "ministering Spirits", the "messengers of mercy" who are sent, Bishop Mant tells us:

> ... to fulfill
> Good for Salvation's heirs, for us they still
> Grieve when we sin, rejoice when we repent ...

Yet it becomes evident that if all the Bishops the world over were asked to define once for all what they mean by Soul and its functions, they would be as unable to do so as to show us any shadow of logic in the orthodox belief!

The Doctrine is Taught in St. John's Gospel

Q. To this the adherents to this belief might answer, that if even the orthodox dogma does promise the impenitent sinner and materialist a bad time of it in a rather too realistic Inferno, it gives them, on the other hand, a chance for repentance to the last minute. Nor do they teach annihilation, or loss of personality, which is all the same.

A. If the Church teaches nothing of the kind, on the other hand, Jesus does; and that is something to those, at least, who place Christ higher than Christianity.

Q. Does Christ teach anything of the sort?

A. He does; and every well-informed Occultist and even Cabalist will tell you so. Christ, or the fourth Gospel at any rate, teaches reincarnation as also the annihilation of the personality, if you but forget the dead letter and hold to the esoteric Spirit. Remember the parable spoken of by St. John. What does the parable speak about if not of the upper triad in man? Atma is the Husbandman - the Spiritual Ego or Buddhi (Christos) the Vine, while the animal and vital Soul, the personality, is the "branch". *I am the true vine, and my Father is the Husbandman. Every branch in me that beareth not fruit he taketh away ... As the branch cannot bear fruit of itself except it abide in the vine; no more can ye, except ye abide in me. I am the Vine - ye are the branches. If a man abide not in me he is cast forth as a branch, and is withered and cast into the fire and burned.*

Now we explain it in this way. Disbelieving in the hellfire which theology discovers as underlying the threat to the branches, we say that the "Husbandman" means Atma, the Symbol for the infinite, impersonal Principle, while the Vine stands for the Spiritual Soul, Christos, and each "branch" represents a new incarnation.

Q. But what proofs have you to support such an arbitrary interpretation?

A. Universal symbology is a warrant for its correctness and that it is not arbitrary. Hermas says of "God" that he "planted the Vineyard", i.e., he created mankind. In the Cabala, it is shown that the Aged of the Aged, or the "Long Face, plants a vineyard, the latter typifying mankind; and a vine, meaning Life. The Spirit of "King Messiah" is, therefore, shown as washing his garments in the wine from above, from the creation of the world. [Zohar XL, 10] And King Messiah is the Ego purified by *washing his garments* (i.e., his personalities in rebirth), in the wine from above, or Buddhi. Adam, or A-Dam, is blood. The Life of the flesh is in the blood (nephesh-soul). And Adam-Kadmon is the Only-Begotten. Noah also plants a vineyard - the allegorical hotbed of future humanity. As a consequence of the adoption of the same allegory, we find it reproduced in the Nazarene Codex. *Seven* vines are procreated - which seven vines are our Seven Races with their seven Saviors or Buddhas - which spring from Iukabar Zivo, and Ferho (or Parcha) Raba waters them.[Codex Nazareus, iii, pp. 60,61] When the blessed will ascend among the creatures of Light, they shall see Iavar-Xivo, Lord of Life, and the First Vine.[Cod. Naz., ii, p.281] These Cabalistic metaphors are thus naturally repeated in the Gospel according to St. John.

Let us not forget that in the human system - even according to those philosophies which ignore our septenary division - the Ego or thinking man is called the Logos, or the Son of Soul and Spirit. Manas is the *adopted Son of King and Queen* (esoteric equivalents for Atma and Buddhi), says an occult work. He is the "man-god of Plato, who crucifies himself in Space (or the duration of the life cycle) for the redemption of Matter. This he does by incarnating over and over again, thus leading mankind onward to perfection, and making thereby room for lower forms to develop into higher. Not for one life does he cease progressing himself and helping all physical nature to progress; even the occasional, very rare event of his losing one of his personalities, in the case of the latter being entirely devoid of even a spark of spirituality, helps toward his individual progress.

Q. But surely, if the Ego is held responsible for the transgressions of its personalities, it has to answer also for the loss, or rather the complete annihilation, of one of such.

A. Not at all, unless it has done nothing to avert this dire fate. But if, all its efforts notwithstanding, its voice, that of our conscience, was unable to penetrate through the wall of matter, then the obtuseness of the latter proceeding from the imperfect nature of the material is classed with other failures of nature. The Ego is sufficiently punished by the loss of Devachan, and especially by having to incarnate almost immediately.

Q. This doctrine of the possibility of losing one's soul - or personality, do you call it? - militates against the ideal theories of both Christians and Spiritualists, though Swedenborg adopts it to a certain extent, in what he calls Spiritual *death*. They will never accept it.

A. This can in no way alter a fact in nature, if it be a fact, or prevent such a thing occasionally taking place. The universe and everything in it, moral, mental, physical, psychic, or Spiritual, is built on a perfect law of equilibrium and harmony. As said before (see *Isis Unveiled*), the centripetal force could not manifest itself without the centrifugal in the harmonious revolutions of the spheres, and all forms and their progress are the products of this dual force in nature. Now the Spirit (or Buddhi) is the centrifugal and the soul (Manas) the centripetal spiritual energy; and to produce one result they have to be in perfect union and harmony. Break or damage the centripetal motion of the earthly soul tending toward the center which attracts it; arrest its progress by clogging it with a heavier weight of matter than it can bear, or than is fit for the Devachanic state, and the harmony of the whole will be destroyed. Personal life, or perhaps rather its ideal reflection, can only be continued if sustained by the two-fold force, that is by the close union of Buddhi and Manas in every rebirth or personal life. The least deviation from harmony damages it; and when it is destroyed beyond redemption the two forces separate at the moment of death. During a brief interval the personal form (called indifferently Kamarupa and Mayavirupa), the spiritual efflorescence of which, attaching itself to the Ego, follows it into Devachan and gives to the permanent individuality its personal colouring (pro tem, so to speak), is carried off to remain in Kamaloka and to be gradually annihilated. For it is after the death of the utterly depraved, the unspiritual and the wicked beyond redemption, that arrives the critical and supreme moment. If during life the ultimate and desperate effort of the Inner Self (Manas), to unite something of the personality with itself and the high glimmering ray of the divine Buddhi, is thwarted; if this ray is allowed to be more and more shut out from the everthickening crust of physical brain, the Spiritual Ego or Manas, once freed from the body, remains severed entirely from the ethereal relic of the personality; and the latter, or Kamarupa, following its earthly attractions, is drawn into and remains in Hades,which we call the Kamaloka. These are "the withered branches" mentioned by Jesus as being cut off from the Vine. Annihilation, however, is never instantaneous, and may require centuries sometimes for its accomplishment. But there the personality remains along with the remnants of other more fortunate personal Egos, and becomes with them a shell and an Elementary.As said in *Isis Unveiled*, it is these two classes of Spirits, the shells and the Elementaries, which are the leading "Stars "on the great spiritual stage of "materializations". And you may be sure of it, it is not they who incarnate; and, therefore, so few of these "dear departed ones" know anything of reincarnation, misleading thereby the Spiritualists.

Q. But does not the author of *Isis Unveiled* stand accused of having preached against reincarnation?

A. By those who have misunderstood what was said, yes. At the time that work was written, reincarnation was not believed in by any Spiritualists, either English or American, and what is said there of reincarnation was directed against the French Spiritists, whose theory is as unphilosophical and absurd as the Eastern teaching is logical and self-evident in its truth. The Reincarnationists of the Allan Kardec School believe in an arbitrary and immediate reincarnation. With them, the dead father can incarnate in his own unborn daughter, and so on. They have neither Devachan, Karma, nor any philosophy that would warrant or prove the necessity of consecutive rebirths. But how can the author of *Isis Unveiled* argue against Karmic reincarnation, at long intervals varying between 1,000 and 1,500 years, when it is the fundamental belief of both Buddhists and Hindus?

Q. Then you reject the theories of both the Spiritists and the Spiritualists, in their entirety?

A. Not in their entirety, but only with regard to their respective fundamental beliefs. Both rely on what their "Spirits" tell them; and both disagree as much with each other as we Theosophists disagree with both. Truth is one; and when we hear the French spooks preaching reincarnation, and the English spooks denying and denouncing the doctrine, we say that either the French or the English "Spirits" do not know what they are talking about. We believe with the Spiritualists and the Spiritists in the existence of "Spirits", or invisible Beings endowed with more or less intelligence. But, while in our teachings their kinds and genera are legion, our opponents admit of no other than human disembodied "Spirits", which, to our knowledge, are mostly Kamalokic Shells.

Q. You seem very bitter against Spirits. As you have given me your views and your reasons for disbelieving in the materialization of, and direct communication in séances, with the disembodied spirits - or the "spirits of the dead" - would you mind enlightening me as to one more fact? Why are some Theosophists never tired of saying how dangerous is intercourse with spirits, and mediumship? Have they any particular reason for this?

A. We must suppose so. I know I have. Owing to my familiarity for over half a century with these invisible, yet but too tangible and undeniable influences, from the conscious Elementals, semi-conscious shells, down to the utterly senseless and nondescript spooks of all kinds, I claim a certain right to my views.

Q. Can you give an instance or instances to show why these practices should be regarded as dangerous?

A. This would require more time than I can give you. Every cause must be judged by the effects it produces. Go over the history of Spiritualism for the last fifty years, ever since its reappearance in this century in America - and judge for yourself whether it has done its votaries more good or harm. Pray understand me. I do not speak against real Spiritualism, but against the modern movement which goes under that name, and the so-called philosophy invented to explain its phenomena.

Q. Don't you believe in their phenomena at all?

A. It is because I believe in them with too good reason, and (save some cases of deliberate fraud) know them to be as true as that you and I live, that all my being revolts against them. Once more I speak only of physical, not mental or even psychic phenomena. Like attracts like. There are several high-minded, pure, good men and women, known to me personally, who have passed years of their lives under the direct guidance and even protection of high Spirits, whether disembodied or planetary. But these Intelligences are not of the type of the John Kings and the Ernests who figure in séance rooms. These Intelligences guide and control mortals only in rare and exceptional cases to which they are attracted and magnetically drawn by the Karmic past of the individual. It is not enough to sit for development in order to attract them. That only opens the door to a swarm of "spooks", good, bad, and indifferent, to which the medium becomes a slave for life. It is against such promiscuous mediumship and intercourse with goblins that I raise my voice, not against spiritual mysticism. The latter is ennobling and holy; the former is of just the same nature as the phenomena of two centuries ago, for which so many witches and wizards have been made to suffer. Read Glanvil and other authors on the subject of witchcraft, and you will find recorded there the parallels of most, if not all, of the physical phenomena of nineteenth century "Spiritualism".

Q. Do you mean to suggest that it is all witchcraft and nothing more?

A. What I mean is that, whether conscious or unconscious, all this dealing with the dead is necromancy, and a most dangerous practice. For ages before Moses such raising of the dead was regarded by all the intelligent nations as sinful and cruel, inasmuch as it disturbs the rest of the souls and interferes with their evolutionary development into higher states. The collective wisdom of all past centuries has ever been loud in denouncing such practices. Finally, I say, what I have never ceased repeating orally and in print for fifteen years: While some of the so-called spirits do not know what they are talking about, repeating merely-like poll-parrots - what they find in the mediums' and other people's brains, others are most dangerous, and can only lead one to evil. These are two self-evident facts. Go into Spiritualistic circles of the Allan Kardec school, and you find spirits asserting reincarnation and speaking like Roman Catholics born. Turn to the dear departed ones in England and America, and you will hear them denying reincarnation through thick and thin, denouncing those who teach it, and holding to Protestant views. Your best, your most powerful mediums, have all suffered in health of body and mind. Think of the sad end of Charles Foster, who died in an asylum, a raving lunatic; of Slade, an epileptic; of Eglinton - the best medium now in England - subject to the same. Look back over the life of D.D. Home, a man whose mind was steeped in gall and bitterness, who never had a good word to say of anyone whom he suspected of possessing psychic powers, and who slandered every other medium to the bitter end. This Calvin of Spiritualism suffered for years from a terrible spinal disease, brought on by his intercourse with the spirits, and died a perfect wreck. Think again of the sad fate of poor Washington Irving Bishop. I knew him in New York, when he was fourteen, and he was undeniably a medium. It is true that the poor man stole a march on his spirits, and baptized them unconscious muscular action, to the great *gaudium* of all the corporations of highly learned and scientific fools, and to the replenishment of his own pocket. But d*e mortuis nil nisi bonum*; his end was a sad one. He had strenuously concealed his epileptic fits - the first and strongest symptom of genuine mediumship - and who knows whether he was dead or in a trance when the postmortem examination was performed? His relatives insist that he was alive, if we are to believe Reuter's telegrams. Finally, behold the veteran mediums, the founders and prime movers of modern spiritualism - the Fox sisters. After more than forty years of intercourse with the Angels, the latter have led them to become incurable sots, who are now denouncing, in public lectures, their own life - long work and philosophy as a fraud. What kind of spirits must they be who prompted them, I ask you?

Q. But is your inference a correct one?

A. What would you infer if the best pupils of a particular school of singing broke down from overstrained sore throats? That the method followed was a bad one. So I think the inference is equally fair with regard to Spiritualism when we see their best mediums fall a prey to such a fate. We can only say: Let those who are interested in the question judge the tree of Spiritualism by its fruits, and ponder over the lesson. We Theosophists have always regarded the Spiritualists as brothers having the same mystic tendency as ourselves, but they have always regarded us as enemies. We, being in possession of an older philosophy, have tried to help and warn them; but they have repaid us by reviling and traducing us and our motives in every possible way. Nevertheless, the best English Spiritualists say just as we do, wherever they treat of their belief seriously. Hear 'M.A. Oxon' confessing this truth: Spiritualists are too much inclined to dwell exclusively on the intervention of external spirits in this world of ours,and to ignore the powers of the incarnate Spirit. Why vilify and abuse us, then, for saying precisely the same? Henceforward, we will have nothing more to do with Spiritualism. And now let us return to Reincarnation.

On the Mysteries of Reincarnation
Periodical Rebirths

Q. You mean, then, that we have all lived on earth before, in many past incarnations, and shall go on so living?

A. I do. The life cycle, or rather the cycle of conscious life, begins with the separation of the mortal animal-man into sexes, and will end with the close of the last generation of men, in the seventh round and seventh race of mankind. Considering we are only in the fourth round and fifth race, its duration is more easily imagined than expressed.

Q. And we keep on incarnating in new personalities all the time?

A. Most assuredly so; because this life cycle or period of incarnation may be best compared to human life. As each such life is composed of days of activity separated by nights of sleep or of inaction, so, in the incarnation cycle, an active life is followed by a Devachanic rest.

Q. And it is this succession of births that is generally defined as reincarnation?

A. Just so. It is only through these births that the perpetual progress of the countless millions of Egos toward final perfection and final rest (as long as was the period of activity) can be achieved.

Q. And what is it that regulates the duration, or special qualities of these incarnations?

A. Karma, the universal law of retributive justice.

Q. Is it an intelligent law?

A. For the Materialist, who calls the law of periodicity which regulates the marshaling of the several bodies, and all the other laws in nature, blind forces and mechanical laws, no doubt Karma would be a law of chance and no more. For us, no adjective or qualification could describe that which is impersonal and no entity, but a universal operative law. If you question me about the causative intelligence in it, I must answer you I do not know. But if you ask me to define its effects and tell you what these are in our belief, I may say that the experience of thousands of ages has shown us that they are absolute and unerring equity, wisdom, and intelligence.For Karma in its effects is an unfailing redresser of human injustice, and of all the failures of nature; a stern adjuster of wrongs; a retributive law which rewards and punishes with equal impartiality. It is, in the strictest sense, 'no respecter of persons', though, on the other hand, it can neither be propitiated, nor turned aside by prayer. This is a belief common to Hindus and Buddhists, who both believe in Karma.

Q. In this Christian dogmas contradict both, and I doubt whether any Christian will accept the teaching.

A. No; and Inman gave the reason for it many years ago. As he puts it, while
... *the Christians will accept any nonsense, if promulgated by the Church as a matter of faith ... the Buddhists hold that nothing which is contradicted by sound reason can be a true doctrine of Buddha.*

They do not believe in any pardon for their sins, except after an adequate and just punishment for each evil deed or thought in a future incarnation, and a proportionate compensation to the parties injured.

Q. Where is it so stated?

A. In most of their sacred works. Consider the following Theosophical tenet: Buddhists believe that every act, word, or thought has its consequence, which will appear sooner or later in the present or in the future state. Evil acts will produce evil consequences, good acts will produce good consequences: prosperity in this world, or birth in heaven (Devachan) … in the future state.

Q. Christians believe the same thing, don't they?

A. Oh, no; they believe in the pardon and the remission of all sins. They are promised that if they only believe in the blood of Christ (an innocent victim!), in the blood offered by Him for the expiation of the sins of the whole of mankind, it will atone for every mortal sin. And we believe neither in vicarious atonement, nor in the possibility of the remission of the smallest sin by any god, not even by a 'personal Absolute' or 'Infinite', if such a thing could have any existence. What we believe in, is strict and impartial justice. Our idea of the unknown Universal Deity, represented by Karma, is that it is a Power which cannot fail, and can, therefore, have neither wrath nor mercy, only absolute Equity, which leaves every cause, great or small, to work out its inevitable effects. The saying of Jesus: "With what measure you mete it shall be measured to you again", neither by expression nor implication points to any hope of future mercy or salvation by proxy. This is why, recognizing as we do in our philosophy the justice of this statement, we cannot recommend too strongly mercy, charity, and forgiveness of mutual offenses. Resist not evil, and render good for evil, are Buddhist precepts, and were first preached in view of the implacability of Karmic law. For man to take the law into his own hands is anyhow a sacrilegious presumption. Human Law may use restrictive not punitive measures; but a man who, believing in Karma, still revenges himself and refuses to forgive every injury, thereby rendering good for evil, is a criminal and only hurts himself. As Karma is sure to punish the man who wronged him, by seeking to inflict an additional punishment on his enemy, he, who instead of leaving that punishment to the great Law adds to it his own mite, only begets thereby a cause for the future reward of his own enemy and a future punishment for himself. The unfailing Regulator affects in each incarnation the quality of its successor; and the sum of the merit or demerit in preceding ones determines it.

Q. Are we then to infer a man's past from his present?

A. Only so far as to believe that his present life is what it justly should be, to atone for the sins of the past life. Of course - seers and great adepts excepted - we cannot as average mortals know what those sins were. From our paucity of data, it is impossible for us even to determine what an old man's youth must have been; neither can we, for like reasons, draw final conclusions merely from what we see in the life of some man, as to what his past life may have been.

What is Karma?

Q. But what is Karma?

A. As I have said, we consider it as the Ultimate Law of the Universe, the source, origin, and fount of all other laws which exist throughout Nature. Karma is the unerring law which adjusts effect to cause, on the physical, mental, and spiritual planes of being. As no cause remains without its due effect from greatest to least, from a cosmic disturbance down to the movement of your hand, and as like produces like,Karma is that unseen and unknown law which adjusts wisely, intelligently, and equitably each effect to its cause, tracing the latter back to its producer. Though itself unknowable,its action is perceivable.

Q. Then it is the 'Absolute', the 'Unknowable' again, and is not of much value as an explanation of the problems of life?

A. On the contrary. For, though we do not know what Karma is per se, and in its essence, we do know how it works, and we can define and describe its mode of action with accuracy. We only do not know its ultimate Cause, just as modern philosophy universally admits that the ultimate Cause of anything is 'unknowable'.

Q. And what has Theosophy to say in regard to the solution of the more practical needs of humanity? What is the explanation which it offers in reference to the awful suffering and dire necessity prevalent among the so-called 'lower classes'.

A. To be pointed, according to our teaching all these great social evils, the distinction of classes in Society, and of the sexes in the affairs of life, the unequal distribution of capital and of labor - all are due to what we tersely but truly denominate Karma.

Q. But, surely, all these evils which seem to fall upon the masses somewhat indiscriminately are not actual merited and individual Karma?

A. No, they cannot be so strictly defined in their effects as to show that each individual environment, and the particular conditions of life in which each person finds himself, are nothing more than the retributive Karma which the individual generated in a previous life. We must not lose sight of the fact that every atom is subject to the general law governing the whole body to which it belongs, and here we come upon the wider track of the Karmic law. Do you not perceive that the aggregate of individual Karma becomes that of the nation to which those individuals belong, and further, that the sum total of National Karma is that of the World? The evils that you speak of are not peculiar to the individual or even to the Nation, they are more or less universal; and it is upon this broad line of Human interdependence that the law of Karma finds its legitimate and equable issue.

Q. Do I, then, understand the law of Karma is not necessarily an individual law?

A. That is just what I mean. It is impossible that Karma could readjust the balance of power in the world's life and progress, unless it had a broad and general line of action. It is held as a truth among Theosophists that the interdependence of Humanity is the cause of what is called Distributive Karma, and it is this law which affords the solution to the great question of collective suffering and its relief. It is an occult law, moreover, that no man can rise superior to his individual failings, without lifting, be it ever so little, the whole body of which he is an integral part. In the same way, no one can sin, nor suffer the effects of sin, alone. In reality, there is no such thing as 'Separateness'; and the nearest approach to that selfish state, which the laws of life permit, is in the intent or motive.

Q. And are there no means by which the distributive or national Karma might be concentrated or collected, so to speak, and brought to its natural and legitimate fulfillment without all this protracted suffering?

A. As a general rule, and within certain limits which define the age to which we belong, the law of Karma cannot be hastened or retarded in its fulfillment. But of this I am certain, the point of possibility in either of these directions has never yet been touched. Listen to the following recital of one phase of national suffering, and then ask yourself whether, admitting the working power of individual, relative, and distributive Karma, these evils are not capable of extensive modification and general relief. What I am about to read to you is from the pen of a National Savior, one who, having overcome Self, and being free to choose, has elected to serve Humanity, in bearing at least as much as a woman's shoulders can possibly bear of National Karma. This is what she says:

Yes, Nature always does speak, don't you think? only sometimes we make so much noise that we drown her voice. That is why it is so restful to go out of the town and nestle awhile in the Mother's arms. I am thinking of the evening on Hampstead Heath when we watched the sun go down; but oh! upon what suffering and misery that sun had set! A lady brought me yesterday a big hamper of wild flowers. I thought some of my East - end family had a better right to it than I, and so I took it down to a very poor school in Whitechapel this morning. You should have seen the pallid little faces brighten! Thence I went to pay for some dinners at a little cook shop for some children. It was in a back street, narrow, full of jostling people; stench indescribable, from fish, meat, and other food, all reeking in a sun that, in Whitechapel, festers instead of purifying. The cook shop was the quintessence of all the smells. Indescribable meat-pies at 1 d., loathsome lumps of 'food' and swarms of flies, a very altar of Beelzebub! All about, babies on the prowl for scraps, one, with the face of an angel, gathering up cherrystones as a light and nutritious form of diet. I came westward with every nerve shuddering and jarred, wondering whether anything can be done with some parts of London save swallowing them up in an earthquake and starting their inhabitants afresh, after a plunge into some purifying Lethe, out of which not a memory might emerge! And then I thought of Hampstead Heath, and -

pondered. If by any sacrifice one could win the power to save these people, the cost would not be worth counting; but, you see, they must be changed - and how can that be wrought? In the condition they now are, they would not profit by any environment in which they might be placed; and yet, in their present surroundings they must continue to putrefy. It breaks my heart, this endless, hopeless misery, and the brutish degradation that is at once its outgrowth and its root. It is like the banyan tree; every branch roots itself and sends out new shoots. What a difference between these feelings and the peaceful scene at Hampstead! and yet we, who are the brothers and sisters of these poor creatures, have only a right to use Hampstead Heaths to gain strength to save Whitechapels.

Q. That is a sad but beautiful letter, and I think it presents with painful conspicuity the terrible workings of what you have called 'Relative and Distributive Karma'. But alas! there seems no immediate hope of any relief short of an earthquake, or some such general engulfment!

A. What right have we to think so while one-half of humanity is in a position to effect an immediate relief of the privations which are suffered by their fellows? When every individual has contributed to the general good what he can of money, of labor, and of ennobling thought, then, and only then, will the balance of National Karma be struck, and until then we have no right nor any reasons for saying that there is more life on the earth than Nature can support. It is reserved for the heroic souls, the Saviors of our Race and Nation, to find out the cause of this unequal pressure of retributive Karma, and by a supreme effort to readjust the balance of power, and save the people from a moral engulfment a thousand times more disastrous and more permanently evil than the like physical catastrophe, in which you seem to see the only possible outlet for this accumulated misery.

Q. Well, then, tell me generally how you describe this law of Karma?

A. We describe Karma as that Law of readjustment which ever tends to restore disturbed equilibrium in the physical, and broken harmony in the moral world. We say that Karma does not act in this or that particular way always; but that it always does act so as to restore Harmony and preserve the balance of equilibrium, in virtue of which the Universe exists.

Q. Give me an illustration.

A. Later on I will give you a full illustration. Think now of a pond. A stone falls into the water and creates disturbing waves. These waves oscillate backwards and forwards till at last, owing to the operation of what physicists call the law of the dissipation of energy, they are brought to rest, and the water returns to its condition of calm tranquility. Similarly all action, on every plane, produces disturbance in the balanced harmony of the Universe, and the vibrations so produced will continue to roll backwards and forwards, if its area is limited, till equilibrium is restored. But since each such disturbance starts from some particular point, it is clear that equilibrium and harmony can only be restored by the reconverging to that same point of all the forces which were set in motion from it. And here you have proof that the consequences of a man's deeds, thoughts, etc. must all react upon himself with the same force with which they were set in motion.

Q. But I see nothing of a moral character about this law. It looks to me like the simple physical law that action and reaction are equal and opposite.

A. I am not surprised to hear you say that. Europeans have got so much into the ingrained habit of considering right and wrong, good and evil, as matters of an arbitrary code of law laid down either by men, or imposed upon them by a Personal God. We Theosophists, however, say that 'Good' and 'Harmony', and 'Evil' and 'Dis-harmony', are synonymous. Further we maintain that all pain and suffering are results of want of Harmony, and that the one terrible and only cause of the disturbance of Harmony is selfishness in some form or another. Hence Karma gives back to every man the actual consequences of his own actions, without any regard to their moral character; but since he receives his due for all, it is obvious that he will be made to atone for all sufferings which he has caused, just as he will reap in joy and gladness the fruits of all the happiness and harmony he had helped to produce. I can do no better than quote for your benefit certain passages from books and articles written by our Theosophists - those who have a correct idea of Karma.

Q. I wish you would, as your literature seers to be very sparing on this subject?

A. Because it is the most difficult of all our tenets. Some short time ago there appeared the following objection from a Christian pen: *Granting that the teaching in regard to Theosophy is correct, and that man must be his own savior, must overcome self and conquer the evil that is in his dual nature, to obtain the emancipation of his soul, what is man to do after he has been awakened and converted to a certain extent from evil or wickedness? How is he to get emancipation, or pardon, or the blotting out of the evil or wickedness he has already done?*

To this Mr. J.H. Conelly replies very pertinently that no one can hope to "make the theosophical engine run on the theological track". As he has it:

The possibility of shirking individual responsibility is not among the concepts of Theosophy. In this faith there is no such thing as pardoning, or 'blotting out' of evil or wickedness already done, otherwise than by the adequate punishment therefore of the wrong-doer and the restoration of the harmony in the universe that had been disturbed by his wrongful act. The evil has been his own, and while others must suffer its consequences, atonement can be made by nobody but himself.

The condition contemplated ... in which a man shall have been 'awakened' and converted to a certain extent from evil or wickedness, is that in which a man shall have realized that his deeds are evil and deserving of punishment. In that realization a sense of personal responsibility is inevitable, and just in proportion to the extent of his awakening or 'converting' must be the sense of that awful responsibility. While it is strong upon him is the time when he is urged to accept the doctrine of vicarious atonement.

He is told that he must also repent, but nothing is easier than that. It is an amiable weakness of human nature that we are quite prone to regret the evil we have done when our attention is called, and we have either suffered from it ourselves or enjoyed its fruits. Possibly, close analysis of the feeling would show us that thing which we regret is rather the necessity that seemed to require the evil as a means of attainment of our selfish ends than the evil itself.

Attractive as this prospect of casting our burden of sins 'at the foot of the cross' may be to the ordinary mind, it does not commend itself to the Theosophic student. He does not apprehend why the sinner by attaining knowledge of his evil can thereby merit any pardon for or the blotting out of his past wickedness; or why repentance and future right living entitle him to a suspension in his favor of the universal law of relation between cause and effect. The results of his evil deeds continue to exist; the suffering caused to others by his wickedness is not blotted out. The Theosophical student takes the result of wickedness upon the innocent into his problem. He considers not only the guilty person, but his victims.

Evil is an infraction of the laws of harmony governing the universe, and the penalty thereof must fall upon the violator of that law himself. Christ uttered the warning, "Sin no more, lest a worse thing come upon thee", and St. Paul said, "Work out your own salvation. Whatsoever a man soweth, that shall he also reap". That, by the way, is a fine metaphoric rendering of the sentence of the Pur as far antedating him - that "every man reaps the consequences of his own acts".

This is the principle of the law of Karma which is taught by Theosophy. Sinnett, in his *Esoteric Buddhism*, rendered Karma as "the law of ethical causation". "The law of retribution", as Mme. Blavatsky translates its meaning, is better. It is the power which

> *Just though mysterious, leads us on unerring*
> *Through ways unmarked from guilt to punishment.*

But it is more. It rewards merit as unerringly and amply as it punishes demerit. It is the outcome of every act, of thought, word, and deed, and by it men mould themselves, their lives and happenings. Eastern philosophy rejects the idea of a newly created soul for every baby born. It believes in a limited number of monads, evolving and growing more and more perfect through their assimilation of many successive personalities. Those personalities are the product of Karma and it is by Karma and reincarnation that the human monad in time returns to its source - absolute deity.

E.D. Walker, in his *Reincarnation*, offers the following explanation:

Briefly, the doctrine of Karma is that we have made ourselves what we are by former actions, and are building our future eternity by present actions. There is no destiny but what we ourselves determine. There is no salvation or condemnation except what we ourselves bring about ... Because it offers no shelter for culpable actions and necessitates a sterling manliness, it is less welcome to weak natures than the easy religious tenets of vicarious atonement, intercession, forgiveness, and deathbed conversions ... In the domain of eternal justice the offense and the punishment are inseparably connected as the same event, because there is no real distinction between the action and its outcome ... It is Karma, or our old acts, that draws us back into earthly life. The spirit's abode changes according to its Karma, and this Karma forbids any long continuance in one condition, because it is always changing. So long as action is governed by material and selfish motives, just so long must the effect of that action be manifested in physical rebirths. Only the perfectly selfless man can elude the gravitation of material life. Few have attained this, but it is the goal of mankind. And then the writer quotes from *The Secret Doctrine*:

"Those who believe in Karma have to believe in destiny, which, from birth to death, every man is weaving, thread by thread, around himself, as a spider does his cobweb, and this destiny is guided either by the heavenly voice of the invisible prototype outside of us, or by our more intimate astral or inner man, who is but too often the evil genius of the embodied entity called man. Both these lead on the outward man, but one of them must prevail; and from the very beginning of the invisible affray the stern and implacable law of compensation steps in and takes its course, faithfully following the fluctuations. When the last strand is woven, and man is seemingly enwrapped in the network of his own doing, then he finds himself completely under the empire of this self-made destiny ... An Occultist or a philosopher will not speak of the goodness or cruelty of Providence; but, identifying it with Karma-Nemesis, he will teach that, nevertheless, it guards the good and watches over them in this as in future lives; and that it punishes the evil-doer - aye, even to his seventh rebirth - so long, in short, as the effect of his having thrown into perturbation even the smallest atom in the infinite world of harmony has not been finally readjusted. For the only decree of Karma - an eternal and immutable decree - is absolute harmony in the world of matter as it is in the world of spirit. It is not, therefore, Karma that rewards or punishes, but it is we who reward or punish ourselves according to whether we work with, through and along with nature, abiding by the laws on which that harmony depends, or - break them. Nor would the ways of Karma be inscrutable were men to work in union and harmony, instead of disunion and strife. For our ignorance of those ways - which one portion of mankind calls the ways of Providence, dark and intricate; while another sees in them the action of blind fatalism; and a third simple chance, with neither gods nor devils to guide them - would surely disappear if we would but attribute all these to their correct cause ... We stand bewildered before the mystery of our own making and the riddles of life that we will not solve, and then accuse the great Sphinx of devouring us. But verily there is not an accident of our lives, not a misshapen day, or a misfortune, that could not be traced back to our own doings in this or in another life ... The law of Karma is inextricably interwoven with that of reincarnation ... It is only this doctrine that can explain to us the mysterious problem of good and evil, and reconcile man to the terrible and apparent injustice of life. Nothing but such certainty can quiet our revolted sense of justice. For, when one unacquainted with the noble doctrine looks around him and observes the inequalities of birth and fortune, of intellect and capacities; when one sees honor paid to fools and wastrels, on whom fortune has heaped her favours by mere privilege of birth, and their nearest neighbor, with all his intellect and noble virtues - far more deserving in every way - perishing for want and for lack of sympathy - when one sees all this and has to turn away, helpless to relieve the undeserved suffering, one's ears ringing and heart aching with the cries of pain around him - that blessed knowledge of Karma alone prevents him from cursing life and men as well as their supposed Creator ... This law, whether conscious or unconscious, predestines nothing and no one. It exists from and in eternity truly, for it is eternity itself; and as such, since no act can be coequal with eternity, it cannot be said to act, for it is action itself. It is not the wave which drowns the man, but the personal action of the wretch who goes deliberately and places himself under the impersonal action of the laws that govern the ocean's motion. Karma creates nothing, nor does it design. It is man who plants and creates causes, and Karmic law adjusts the effects, which adjustment is not an act but universal harmony, tending ever to resume its original position, like a bough, which, bent down too forcibly, rebounds with corresponding vigor. If it happen to dislocate the arm that tried to bend it out of its natural position, shall we say it is the bough which broke our arm or that our own folly has brought us to grief? Karma has never sought to destroy intellectual and individual liberty, like the god invented by the Monotheists. It has not involved its decrees in darkness purposely to perplex man, nor shall it punish him who dares to scrutinize its mysteries. On the contrary, he who unveils through study and meditation its intricate paths, and throws light on those dark ways, in the windings of which so many men perish owing to their ignorance of the labyrinth of life, is working for the good of his fellowmen. Karma is an absolute and eternal law in the world of manifestation; and as there can only be one Absolute, as one Eternal, ever - present Cause, believers in Karma cannot be regarded as atheists or materialists, still less as fatalists, for Karma is one with the Unknowable, of which it is an aspect, in its effects in the phenomenal world."

Another able Theosophic writer says:

Every individual is making Karma either good or bad in each action and thought of his daily round, and is at the same time working out in this life the Karma brought about by the acts and desires of the last. When we see people afflicted by congenital ailments it may be safely assumed that these ailments are the inevitable results of causes started by themselves in a previous birth. It may be argued that, as these afflictions are hereditary, they can have nothing to do with a past incarnation; but it must be remembered that the Ego, the real man, the individuality, has no spiritual origin in the parentage by which it is reembodied, but it is drawn by the affinities which its previous mode of life attracted round it into the current that carries it, when the time comes for rebirth, to the home best fitted for the development of those tendencies ... This doctrine of Karma, when properly understood, is well calculated to guide and assist those who realize its truth to a higher and better mode of life, for it must not be forgotten that not only our actions but our thoughts also are most assuredly followed by a crowd of circumstances that will influence for good or for evil our own future, and, what is still more important, the future of many of our fellowcreatures. If sins of omission and commission could in any case be only self-regarding, the fact on the sinner's Karma would be a matter of minor consequence. The effect that every thought and act through life carries with it for good or evil a corresponding influence on other members of the human family renders a strict sense of justice, morality, and unselfishness so necessary to future happiness or progress. A crime once committed, an evil thought sent out from the mind, are past recall - no amount of repentance can wipe out their results in the future. Repentance, if sincere, will deter a man from repeating errors; it cannot save him or others from the effects of those already produced, which will most unerringly overtake him either in this life or in the next rebirth.

Mr. J.H. Conelly proceeds - The believers in a religion based upon such doctrine are willing it should be compared with one in which man's destiny for eternity is determined by the accidents of a single, brief earthly existence, during which he is cheered by the promise that "as the tree falls so shall it lie"; in which his brightest hope, when he wakes up to a knowledge of his wickedness, is the doctrine of vicarious atonement, and in which even that is handicapped, according to the Presbyterian Confession of Faith. By the decree of God, for the manifestation of his glory, some men and angels are predestinated unto everlasting life and others foreordained to everlasting death. These angels and men thus predestinated and foreordained are particularly and unchangeably designed; and their number is so certain and definite that it cannot be either increased or diminished ... As God hath appointed the elect unto glory ... Neither are any other redeemed by Christ effectually called, justified, adopted, sanctified, and saved, but the elect only. The rest of mankind God was pleased, according to the unsearchable counsel of his own will, whereby he extendeth or withholdeth mercy as he pleaseth, for the glory of his sovereign power over his creatures, to pass by and to ordain them to dishonour and wrath for their sin to the praise of his glorious justice.

This is what the able defender says. Nor can we do any better than wind up the subject as he does, by a quotation from a magnificent poem. As he says: The exquisite beauty of Edwin Arnold's exposition of Karma in The *Light of Asia* tempts to its reproduction here, but it is too long for quotation in full. Here is a portion of it:

> *Karma - all that total of a soul*
> *Which is the things it did, the thoughts it had,*
> *The 'self' it wove with woof of viewless time*
> *Crossed on the warp invisible of acts.*
> *Before beginning and without an end,*
> *As space eternal and as surety sure,*
> *Is fixed a Power divine which moves to good,*
> *Only its laws endure. It will not be despised of anyone;*
> *Who thwarts it loses, and who serves it gains;*
> *The hidden good it pays with peace and bliss,*
> *The hidden ill with pains.*
> *It seeth everywhere and marketh all;*
> *Do right - it recompenseth!*

Do one wrong - The equal retribution must be made,
Though Dharma tarry long.
It knows not wrath nor pardon; utter-true,
Its measures mete, its faultless balance weighs;
Times are as naught, tomorrow it will judge
Or after many days. . . . .

Such is the law which moves to righteousness, Which none at last can turn aside or stay; The heart of it is love, the end of it Is peace and consummation sweet. Obey. And now I advise you to compare our Theosophic views upon Karma, the law of Retribution, and say whether they are not both more philosophical and just than this cruel and idiotic dogma which makes of 'God' a senseless fiend; the tenet, namely, that the 'elect' only will be saved, and the rest doomed to eternal perdition!

Q. Yes, I see what you mean generally; but I wish you could give some concrete example of the action of Karma?

A. That I cannot do. We can only feel sure, as I said before, that our present lives and circumstances are the direct results of our own deeds and thoughts in lives that are past. But we, who are not Seers or Initiates, cannot know anything about the details of the working of the law of Karma.

Q. Can anyone, even an Adept or Seer, follow out this Karmic process of readjustment in detail?

A. Certainly: Those who know can do so by the exercise of powers which are latent even in all men.

Who Are Those Who Know?

Q. Does this hold equally of ourselves as of others?

A. Equally. As just said, the same limited vision exists for all, save those who have reached in the present incarnation the acme of spiritual vision and clairvoyance. We can only perceive that, if things with us ought to have been different, they would have been different; that we are what we have made ourselves, and have only what we have earned for ourselves.

Q. I am afraid such a conception would only embitter us.

A. I believe it is precisely the reverse. It is disbelief in the just law of retribution that is more likely to awaken every combative feeling in man. A child, as much as a man, resents a punishment, or even a reproof he believes to be unmerited, far more than he does a more severe punishment, if he feels that it is merited. Belief in Karma is the highest reason for reconcilement to one's lot in this life, and the very strongest incentive towards effort to better the succeeding rebirth. Both of these, indeed, would be destroyed if we supposed that our lot was the result of anything but strict Law, or that destiny was in any other hands than our own.

Q. You have just asserted that this system of Reincarnation under Karmic law commended itself to reason, justice, and the moral sense. But, if so, is it not at some sacrifice of the gentler qualities of sympathy and pity, and thus a hardening of the finer instincts of human nature?

A. Only apparently, not really. No man can receive more or less than his deserts without a corresponding injustice or partiality to others; and a law which could be averted through compassion would bring about more misery than it saved, more irritation and curses than thanks. Remember also, that we do not administer the law, if we do create causes for its effects; it administers itself; and again, that the most copious provision for the manifestation of just compassion and mercy is shown in the state of Devachan.

Q. You speak of Adepts as being an exception to the rule of our general ignorance. Do they really know more than we do of Reincarnation and after states?

A. They do, indeed. By the training of faculties we all possess, but which they alone have developed to perfection, they have entered in spirit these various planes and states we have been discussing. For long ages, one generation of Adepts after another has studied the mysteries of being, of life, death, and rebirth, and all have taught in their turn some of the facts so learned.

Q. And is the production of Adepts the aim of Theosophy?

A. Theosophy considers humanity as an emanation from divinity on its return path thereto. At an advanced point upon the path, Adeptship is reached by those who have devoted several incarnations to its achievement. For, remember well, no man has ever reached Adeptship in the Secret Sciences in one life; but many incarnations are necessary for it after the formation of a conscious purpose and the beginning of the needful training. Many may be the men and women in the very midst of our Society who have begun this uphill work toward illumination several incarnations ago, and who yet, owing to the personal illusions of the present life, are either ignorant of the fact, or on the road to losing every chance in this existence of progressing any farther. They feel an irresistible attraction toward occultism and the Higher Life, and yet are too personal and self-opinionated, too much in love with the deceptive allurements of mundane life and the world's ephemeral pleasures, to give them up; and so lose their chance in their present birth. But, for ordinary men, for the practical duties of daily life, such a far-off result is inappropriate as an aim and quite ineffective as a motive.

Q. What, then, may be their object or distinct purpose in joining the Theosophical Society?

A. Many are interested in our doctrines and feel instinctively that they are truer than those of any dogmatic religion. Others have formed a fixed resolve to attain the highest ideal of man's duty.

The Difference Between Faith and Knowledge,
Or Blind and Reasoned Faith

Q. You say that they accept and believe in the doctrines of Theosophy. But, as they do not belong to those Adepts you have just mentioned, then they must accept your teachings on blind faith. In what does this differ from that of conventional religions?

A. As it differs on almost all the other points, so it differs on this one. What you call 'faith', and that which is blind faith, in reality, and with regard to the dogmas of the Christian religions, becomes with us 'knowledge', the logical sequence of things we know, about facts in nature. Your Doctrines are based upon interpretation, therefore, upon the secondhand testimony of Seers; ours upon the invariable and unvarying testimony of Seers. The ordinary Christian theology, for instance, holds that man is a creature of God, of three component parts - body, soul, and spirit - all essential to his integrity, and all, either in the gross form of physical earthly existence or in the etherealized form of post-resurrection experience, needed to so constitute him forever, each man having thus a permanent existence separate from other men, and from the Divine. Theosophy, on the other hand, holds that man, being an emanation from the Unknown, yet ever present and infinite Divine Essence, his body and everything else is impermanent, hence an illusion; Spirit alone in him being the one enduring substance, and even that losing its separated individuality at the moment of its complete reunion with the Universal Spirit.

Q. If we lose even our individuality, then it becomes simply annihilation.

A. I say it does not,since I speak of separate, not of universal individuality. The latter becomes as a part transformed into the whole; the dewdrop is not evaporated, but becomes the sea. Is physical man annihilated,when from a fetus he becomes an old man? What kind of Satanic pride must be ours if we place our infinitesimally small consciousness and individuality higher than the universal and infinite consciousness!

Q. It follows, then, that there is, de facto, no man, but all is Spirit?

A. You are mistaken. It thus follows that the union of Spirit with matter is but temporary; or, to put it more clearly, since Spirit and matter are one, being the two opposite poles of the universal manifested substance - that Spirit loses its right to the name so long as the smallest particle and atom of its manifesting substance still clings to any form, the result of differentiation. To believe otherwise is blind faith.

Q. Thus it is on knowledge,not on faith, that you assert that the permanent principle, the Spirit, simply makes a transit through matter?

A. I would put it otherwise and say - we assert that the appearance of the permanent and one principle, Spirit, as matter is transient, and, therefore, no better than an illusion.

Q. Very well; and this, given out on knowledge not faith?

A. Just so. But as I see very well what you are driving at, I may just as well tell you that we hold faith, such as you advocate, to be a mental disease, and real faith, i.e., the *pistis* of the Greeks, as 'belief' based on knowledge, whether supplied by the evidence of physical or spiritual senses."

Q. What do you mean?

A. I mean, if it is the difference between the two that you want to know, then I can tell you that between faith on authority and faith on one's spiritual intuition, there is a very great difference.

Q. What is it?

A. One is human credulity and superstition, the other human belief and intuition. As Professor Alexander Wilder says in his "Introduction to the Eleusinian Mysteries": *It is ignorance which leads to profanation. Men ridicule what they do not properly understand ... The undercurrent of this world is set towards one goal; and inside of human credulity ... is a power almost infinite, a holy faith capable of apprehending the most supreme truths of all existence.*

Those who limit that 'credulity' to human authoritative dogmas alone, will never fathom that power nor even perceive it in their natures. It is stuck fast to the external plane and is unable to bring forth into play the essence that rules it; for to do this they have to claim their right of private judgment, and this they never dare to do.

Q. And is it that 'intuition' which forces you to reject God as a personal Father, Ruler, and Governor of the Universe?

A. Precisely. We believe in an ever unknowable Principle, because blind aberration alone can make one maintain that the Universe, thinking man, and all the marvels contained even in the world of matter, could have grown without some intelligent powers to bring about the extraordinarily wise arrangement of all its parts. Nature may err, and often does, in its details and the external manifestations of its materials, never in its inner causes and results. Ancient pagans held on this question far more philosophical views than modern philosophers, whether Agnostics, Materialists, or Christians; and no pagan writer has ever yet advanced the proposition that cruelty and mercy are not finite feelings, and can therefore be made the attributes of an infinite god. Their gods, therefore, were all finite. The Siamese author of the Wheel of the Law, expresses the same idea about your personal god as we do; he says:

A Buddhist might believe in the existence of a god, sublime above all human qualities and attributes - a perfect god, above love, and hatred, and jealousy, calmly resting in a quietude that nothing could disturb, and of such a god he would speak no disparagement not from a desire to please him or fear to offend him, but from natural veneration; but he cannot understand a god with the attributes and qualities of men, a god who loves and hates, and shows anger; a Deity who, whether described as by Christian Missionaries or by Mohammedans or Brahmins, or Jews, falls below his standard of even an ordinary good man.

Q. Faith for faith, is not the faith of the Christian who believes, in his human helplessness and humility, that there is a merciful Father in Heaven who will protect him from temptation, help him in life, and forgive him his transgressions, better than the cold and proud, almost fatalistic faith of the Buddhists, Vedantins, and Theosophists?

A. Persist in calling our belief 'faith' if you will. But once we are again on this ever-recurring question, I ask in my turn: faith for faith, is not the one based on strict logic and reason better than the one which is based simply on human authority or - hero-worship? Our 'faith' has all the logical force of the arithmetical truism that two and two will produce four. Your faith is like the logic of some emotional women, of whom Tourgenyeff said that for them two and two were generally five, and a tallow candle into the bargain. Yours is a faith, moreover, which clashes not only with every conceivable view of justice and logic, but which, if analyzed, leads man to his moral perdition, checks the progress of mankind, and positively making of might, right - transforms every second man into a Cain to his brother Abel.

Has God the Right to Forgive?

Q. What do you allude to?

A. To the Doctrine of Atonement; I allude to that dangerous dogma in which you believe, and which teaches us that no matter how enormous our crimes against the laws of God and of man, we have but to believe in the self-sacrifice of Jesus for the salvation of mankind, and his blood will wash out every stain. It is twenty years that I preach against it, and I may now draw your attention to a paragraph from *Isis Unveiled*, written in 1875. This is what Christianity teaches, and what we combat:

God's mercy is boundless and unfathomable. It is impossible to conceive of a human sin so damnable that the price paid in advance for the redemption of the sinner would not wipe it out if a thousandfold worse. And furthermore, it is never too late to repent. Though the offender wait until the last minute of the last hour of the last day of his mortal life, before his blanched lips utter the confession of faith, he may go to Paradise; the dying thief did it, and so may all others as vile. These are the assumptions of the Church, and of the Clergy; assumptions banged at the heads of your countrymen by England's favorite preachers, right in the "light" of the nineteenth century, …

- this most paradoxical age of all. Now to what does it lead?

Q. Does it not make the Christian happier than the Buddhist or Brahmin?

A. No; not the educated man, at any rate, since the majority of these have long since virtually lost all belief in this cruel dogma. But it leads those who still believe in it more easily to the threshold of every conceivable crime, than any other I know of. Let me quote to you once more: If we step outside the little circle of creed and consider the universe as a whole balanced by the exquisite adjustment of parts, how all sound logic, how the faintest glimmering sense of Justice, revolts against this Vicarious Atonement! If the criminal sinned only against himself, and wronged no one but himself; if by sincere repentance he could cause the obliteration of past events, not only from the memory of man, but also from that imperishable record, which no deity - not even the most Supreme of the Supreme - can cause to disappear, then this dogma might not be incomprehensible. But to maintain that one may wrong his fellowman, kill, disturb the equilibrium of society and the natural order of things, and then - through cowardice, hope, or compulsion, it matters not - be forgiven by believing that the spilling of one blood washes out the other blood spilt - this is preposterous! Can the results of a crime be obliterated even though the crime itself should be pardoned? The effects of a cause are never limited to the boundaries of the cause, nor can the results of crime be confined to the offender and his victim. Every good as well as evil action has its effects, as palpably as the stone flung into calm water. The simile is trite, but it is the best ever conceived, so let us use it. The eddying circles are greater and swifter as the disturbing object is greater or smaller, but the smallest pebble, nay, the tiniest speck, makes its ripples. And this disturbance is not alone visible and on the surface. Below, unseen, in every direction - outward and downward - drop pushes drop until the sides and bottom are touched by the force. More, the air above the water is agitated, and this disturbance passes, as the physicists tell us, from stratum to stratum out into space forever and ever; an impulse has been given to matter, and that is never lost, can never be recalled! ...

So with crime, and so with its opposite. The action may be instantaneous, the effects are eternal. When, after the stone is once flung into the pond, we can recall it to the hand, roll back the ripples, obliterate the force expended, restore the etheric waves to their previous state of non-being, and wipe out every trace of the act of throwing the missile, so that Time's record shall not show that it ever happened, then, then we may patiently hear Christians argue for the efficacy of this Atonement, - and cease to believe in Karmic Law. As it now stands, we call upon the whole world to decide, which of our two doctrines is the most appreciative of deific justice, and which is more reasonable, even on simple human evidence and logic.

Q. Yet millions believe in the Christian dogma and are happy.

A. Pure sentimentalism overpowering their thinking faculties, which no true philanthropist or Altruist will ever accept. It is not even a dream of selfishness, but a nightmare of the human intellect. Look where it leads to, and tell me the name of that pagan country where crimes are more easily committed or more numerous than in Christian lands. Look at the long and ghastly annual records of crimes committed in European countries; and behold Protestant and Biblical America. There, conversions effected in prisons are more numerous than those made by public revivals and preaching. See how the ledger-balance of Christian justice (!) stands: Red-handed murderers, urged on by the demons of lust, revene, cupidity, fanaticism, or mere brutal thirst for blood, who kill their victims, in most cases, without giving them time to repent or call on Jesus. These, perhaps, died sinful, and, of course - consistently with theological logic - met the reward of their greater or lesser of fences. But the murderer, overtaken by human justice, is imprisoned, wept over by sentimentalists, prayed with and at, pronounces the charmed words of conversion, and goes to the scaffold a redeemed child of Jesus! Except for the murder, he would not have been prayed with, redeemed, pardoned. Clearly this man did well to murder, for thus he gained eternal happiness! And how about the victim, and his, or her family, relatives, dependents, social relations; has justice no recompense for them? Must they suffer in this world and the next, while he who wronged them sits beside the 'holy thief' of Calvary, and is forever blessed? On this question the clergy keep a prudent silence. (*Isis Unveiled*) And now you know why Theosophists - whose fundamental belief and hope is justice for all, in Heaven as on earth, and in Karma - reject this dogma.

Q. The ultimate destiny of man, then, is not a Heaven presided over by God, but the gradual transformation of matter into its primordial element, Spirit?

A. It is to that final goal to which all tends in nature.

Q. Do not some of you regard this association or 'fall' of spirit into matter as evil, and rebirth as a sorrow?

A. Some do, and therefore strive to shorten their period of probation on earth. It is not an unmixed evil, however, since it ensures the experience upon which we mount to knowledge and wisdom. I mean that experience which teaches that the needs of our spiritual nature can never be met by other than spiritual happiness. As long as we are in the body, we are subjected to pain, suffering and all the disappointing incidents occurring during life. Therefore, and to palliate this, we finally acquire knowledge which alone can afford us relief and hope of a better future.

What is Practical Theosophy? Duty

Q. Why, then, the need for rebirths, since all alike fail to secure a permanent peace?

A. Because the final goal cannot be reached in any way but through life experiences, and because the bulk of these consist in pain and suffering. It is only through the latter that we can learn. Joys and pleasures teach us nothing; they are evanescent, and can only bring in the long run satiety. Moreover, our constant failure to find any permanent satisfaction in life which would meet the wants of our higher nature, shows us plainly that those wants can be met only on their own plane, to wit - the spiritual.

Q. Is the natural result of this a desire to quit life by one means or another?

A. If you mean by such desire "suicide", then I say, most decidedly not. Such a result can never be a "natural" one, but is ever due to a morbid brain disease, or to most decided and strong materialistic views. It is the worst of crimes and dire in its results. But if by desire, you mean simply aspiration to reach spiritual existence, not a wish to quit the earth, then I would call it a very natural desire indeed. Otherwise voluntary death would be an abandonment of our present post and of the duties incumbent on us, as well as an attempt to shirk Karmic responsibilities, and thus involve the creation of new Karma.

Q. But if actions on the material plane are unsatisfying, why should duties, which are such actions, be imperative?

A. First of all, because our philosophy teaches us that the object of doing our duties to all men and to ourselves the last, is not the attainment of personal happiness, but of the happiness of others; the fulfillment of right for the sake of right, not for what it may bring us. Happiness, or rather contentment, may indeed follow the performance of duty, but is not and must not be the motive for it.

Q. What do you understand precisely by "duty" in Theosophy? It cannot be the Christian duties preached by Jesus and his Apostles, since you recognize neither?

A. You are once more mistaken. What you call "Christian duties" were inculcated by every great moral and religious Reformer ages before the Christian era. All that was great, generous, heroic, was, in days of old, not only talked about and preached from pulpits as in our own time, but acted upon sometimes by whole nations. The history of the Buddhist reform is full of the most noble and most heroically unselfish acts.

Be ye all of one mind, having compassion one of another; love as brethren, be pitiful, be courteous; not rendering evil for evil, or railing for railing; but contrariwise, blessing ...- was practically carried out by the followers of Buddha, several centuries before Peter. The Ethics of Christianity are grand, no doubt; but as undeniably they are not new, and have originated as "Pagan duties".

Q. And how would you define these duties, or "duty" in general, as you understand the term?

A. Duty is that which is due to Humanity, to our fellowmen, neighbors, family, and especially that which we owe to all those who are poorer and more helpless than we are ourselves. This is a debt which, if left unpaid during life, leaves us spiritually insolvent and morally bankrupt in our next incarnation. Theosophy is the quintessence of duty.

Q. So is Christianity when rightly understood and carried out.

A. No doubt it is; but then, were it not a lip-religion in practice, Theosophy would have little to do amidst Christians. Unfortunately it is but such lip-ethics. Those who practice their duty towards all, and for duty's own sake, are few; and fewer still are those who perform that duty, remaining content with the satisfaction of their own secret consciousness. It is - ... the public voice

Of praise that honors virtue and rewards it, - which is ever uppermost in the minds of the "world" renowned philanthropists. Modern ethics are beautiful to read about and hear discussed; but what are words unless converted into actions? Finally: if you ask me how we understand Theosophical duty practically and in view of Karma, I may answer you that our duty is to drink without a murmur to the last drop, whatever contents the cup of life may have in store for us, to pluck the roses of life only for the fragrance they may shed on others, and to be ourselves content but with the thorns, if that fragrance cannot be enjoyed without depriving someone else of it.

Q. All this is very vague. What do you do more than Christians do?

A. It is not what we members of the Theosophical Society do - though some of us try our best - but how much farther Theosophy leads to good than modern Christianity does. I say - action, enforced action, instead of mere intention and talk. A man may be what he likes, the most worldly, selfish and hard-hearted of men, even a deep-dyed rascal, and it will not prevent him from calling himself a Christian, or others from so regarding him. But no Theosophist has the right to this name, unless he is thoroughly imbued with the correctness of Carlyle's truism: "The end of man is an action and not a thought,though it were the noblest - and unless he sets and models his daily life upon this truth. The profession of a truth is not yet the enactment of it; and the more beautiful and grand it sounds, the more loudly virtue or duty is talked about instead of being acted upon, the more forcibly it will always remind one of the Dead Sea fruit. Cant is the most loathsome of all vices; and cant is the most prominent feature of the greatest Protestant country of this century - England".

Q. What do you consider as due to humanity at large?

A. Full recognition of equal rights and privileges for all, and without distinction of race, color, social position, or birth.

Q. When would you consider such due not given?

A. When there is the slightest invasion of another's right - be that other a man or a nation; when there is any failure to show him the same justice, kindness, consideration, or mercy which we desire for ourselves. The whole present system of politics is built on the oblivion of such rights, and the most fierce assertion of national selfishness. The French say: "Like master, like man". They ought to add, "Like national policy, like citizen".

Q. Do you take any part in politics?

A. As a Society, we carefully avoid them, for the reasons given below. To seek to achieve political reforms before we have effected a reform in human nature, is like putting new wine into old bottles. Make men feel and recognize in their innermost hearts what is their real, true duty to all men, and every old abuse of power, every iniquitous law in the national policy, based on human, social, or political selfishness, will disappear of itself. Foolish is the gardener who seeks to weed his flowerbed of poisonous plants by cutting them off from the surface of the soil, instead of tearing them out by the roots. No lasting political reform can be ever achieved with the same selfish men at the head of affairs as of old.

The Relations of the T.S. to Political Reforms

Q. The Theosophical Society is not, then, a political organization?

A. Certainly not. It is international in the highest sense in that its members comprise men and women of all races, creeds, and forms of thought, who work together for one object, the improvement of humanity; but as a society it takes absolutely no part in any national or party politics.

Q. Why is this?

A. Just for the reasons I have mentioned. Moreover, political action must necessarily vary with the circumstances of the time and with the idiosyncrasies of individuals. While from the very nature of their position as Theosophists the members of the T.S. are agreed on the principles of Theosophy, or they would not belong to the society at all, it does not thereby follow that they agree on every other subject. As a society they can only act together in matters which are common to all - that is, in Theosophy itself; as individuals, each is left perfectly free to follow out his or her particular line of political thought and action, so long as this does not conflict with Theosophical principles or hurt the Theosophical Society.

Q. But surely the T.S. does not stand altogether aloof from the social questions which are now so fast coming to the front?

A. The very principles of the T.S. are a proof that it does not - or, rather, that most of its members do not - so stand aloof. If humanity can only be developed mentally and spiritually by the enforcement, first of all, of the soundest and most scientific physiological laws, it is the bounden duty of all who strive for this development to do their utmost to see that those laws shall be generally carried out. All Theosophists are only too sadly aware that, in Occidental countries especially, the social condition of large masses of the people renders it impossible for either their bodies or their spirits to be properly trained, so that the development of both is thereby arrested. As this training and development is one of the express objects of Theosophy, the T.S. is in thorough sympathy and harmony with all true efforts in this direction.

Q. But what do you mean by "true efforts"? Each social reformer has his own panacea, and each believes his to be the one and only thing which can improve and save humanity?

A. Perfectly true, and this is the real reason why so little satisfactory social work is accomplished. In most of these panaceas there is no really guiding principle, and there is certainly no one principle which connects them all. Valuable time and energy are thus wasted; for men, instead of cooperating, strive one against the other, often, it is to be feared, for the sake of fame and reward rather than for the great cause which they profess to have at heart, and which should be supreme in their lives.

Q. How, then, should Theosophical principles be applied so that social cooperation may be promoted and true efforts for social amelioration be carried on?

A. Let me briefly remind you what these principles are - universal Unity and Causation; Human Solidarity; the Law of Karma; Reincarnation. These are the four links of the golden chain which should bind humanity into one family, one universal Brotherhood.

Q. How?

A. In the present state of society, especially in so-called civilized countries, we are continually brought face to face with the fact that large numbers of people are suffering from misery, poverty, and disease. Their physical condition is wretched, and their mental and spiritual faculties are often almost dormant. On the other hand, many persons at the opposite end of the social scale are leading lives of careless indifference, material luxury, and selfish indulgence. Neither of these forms of existence is mere chance. Both are the effects of the conditions which surround those who are subject to them, and the neglect of social duty on the one side is most closely connected with the stunted and arrested development on the other. In sociology, as in all branches of true science, the law of universal causation holds good. But this causation necessarily implies, as its logical outcome, that human solidarity on which Theosophy so strongly insists. If the action of one reacts on the lives of all, and this is the true scientific idea, then it is only by all men becoming brothers and all women sisters, and by all practicing in their daily lives true brotherhood and true sisterhood, that the real human solidarity, which lies at the root of the elevation of the race, can ever be attained. It is this action and interaction, this true brotherhood and sisterhood, in which each shall live for all and all for each, which is one of the fundamental Theosophical principles that every Theosophist should be bound, not only to teach, but to carry out in his or her individual life.

Q. All this is very well as a general principle, but how would you apply it in a concrete way?

A. Look for a moment at what you would call the concrete facts of human society. Contrast the lives not only of the masses of the people, but of many of those who are called the middle and upper classes, with what they might be under healthier and nobler conditions, where justice, kindness, and love were paramount, instead of the selfishness, indifference, and brutality which now too often seem to reign supreme. All good and evil things in humanity have their roots in human character, and this character is, and has been, conditioned by the endless chain of cause and effect. But this conditioning applies to the future as well as to the present and the past. Selfishness, indifference, and brutality can never be the normal state of the race - to believe so would be to despair of humanity - and that no Theosophist can do. Progress can be attained, and only attained, by the development of the nobler qualities. Now, true evolution teaches us that by altering the surroundings of the organism we can alter and improve the organism; and in the strictest sense this is true with regard to man. Every Theosophist, therefore, is bound to do his utmost to help on, by all the means in his power, every wise and well-considered social effort which has for its object the amelioration of the condition of the poor. Such efforts should be made with a view to their ultimate social emancipation, or the development of the sense of duty in those who now so often neglect it in nearly every relation of life.

Q. Agreed. But who is to decide whether social efforts are wise or unwise?

A. No one person and no society can lay down a hard-and-fast rule in this respect. Much must necessarily be left to the individual judgment. One general test may, however, be given. Will the proposed action tend to promote that true brotherhood which it is the aim of Theosophy to bring about? No real Theosophist will have much difficulty in applying such a test; once he is satisfied of this, his duty will lie in the direction of forming public opinion. And this can be attained only by inculcating those higher and nobler conceptions of public and private duties which lie at the root of all spiritual and material improvement. In every conceivable case he himself must be a center of spiritual action, and from him and his own daily individual life must radiate those higher spiritual forces which alone can regenerate his fellowmen.

Q. But why should he do this? Are not he and all, as you teach, conditioned by their Karma, and must not Karma necessarily work itself out on certain lines?

A. It is this very law of Karma which gives strength to all that I have said. The individual cannot separate himself from the race, nor the race from the individual. The law of Karma applies equally to all, although all are not equally developed. In helping on the development of others, the Theosophist believes that he is not only helping them to fulfill their Karma, but that he is also, in the strictest sense, fulfilling his own. It is the development of humanity, of which both he and they are integral parts, that he has always in view, and he knows that any failure on his part to respond to the highest within him retards not only himself but all, in their progressive march. By his actions, he can make it either more difficult or more easy for humanity to attain the next higher plane of being.

Q. How does this bear on the fourth of the principles you mentioned, viz., Reincarnation?

A. The connection is most intimate. If our present lives depend upon the development of certain principles which are a growth from the germs left by a previous existence, the law holds good as regards the future. Once grasp the idea that universal causation is not merely present, but past, present, and future, and every action on our present plane falls naturally and easily into its true place, and is seen in its true relation to ourselves and to others. Every mean and selfish action sends us backward and not forward, while every noble thought and every unselfish deed are stepping-stones to the higher and more glorious planes of being. If this life were all, then in many respects it would indeed be poor and mean; but regarded as a preparation for the next sphere of existence, it may be used as the golden gate through which we may pass, not selfishly and alone, but in company with our fellows, to the palaces which lie beyond.

On Self-Sacrifice

Q. Is equal justice to all and love to every creature the highest standard of Theosophy?

A. No; there is an even far higher one.

Q. What can it be?

A. The giving to others more than to oneself - self-sacrifice. Such was the standard and abounding measure which marked so preeminently the greatest Teachers and Masters of Humanity - e.g., Gautama Buddha in History, and Jesus of Nazareth as in the Gospels. This trait alone was enough to secure to them the perpetual reverence and gratitude of the generations of men that come after them. We say, however, that self-sacrifice has to be performed with discrimination; and such a self- abandonment, if made without justice, or blindly, regardless of subsequent results, may often prove not only made in vain, but harmful. One of the fundamental rules of Theosophy is, justice to oneself - viewed as a unit of collective humanity, not as a personal self-justice, not more but not less than to others; unless, indeed, by the sacrifice of the oneself we can benefit the many.

Q. Could you make your idea clearer by giving an instance?

A. There are many instances to illustrate it in history. Self-sacrifice for practical good to save many, or several people, Theosophy holds as far higher than self-abnegation for a sectarian idea, such as that of "saving" the heathen from damnation, for instance. In our opinion, Father Damien, the young man of thirty who offered his whole life in sacrifice for the benefit and alleviation of the sufferings of the lepers at Molokai, and who went to live for eighteen years alone with them, to finally catch the loathsome disease and die, has not died in vain. He has given relief and relative happiness to thousands of miserable wretches. He has brought to them consolation, mental and physical. He threw a streak of light into the black and dreary night of an existence, the hopelessness of which is unparalleled in the records of human suffering. He was a true Theosophist, and his memory will live forever in our annals. In our sight this poor Belgian priest stands immeasurably higher than - for instance - all those sincere but vainglorious fools, the Missionaries who have sacrificed their lives in the South Sea Islands or China. What good have they done? They went in one case to those who are not yet ripe for any truth; and in the other to a nation whose systems of religious philosophy are as grand as any, if only the men who have them would live up to the standard of Confucius and their other sages. And they died victims of irresponsible cannibals and savages, and of popular fanaticism and hatred. Whereas, by going to the slums of Whitechapel or some other such locality of those that stagnate right under the blazing sun of our civilization, full of Christian savages and mental leprosy, they might have done real good, and preserved their lives for a better and worthier cause.

135

Q. But the Christians do not think so?

A. Of course not, because they act on an erroneous belief. They think that by baptizing the body of an irresponsible savage they save his soul from damnation. One church forgets her martyrs, the other beatifies and raises statues to such men as Labro, who sacrificed his body for forty years only to benefit the vermin which it bred. Had we the means to do so, we would raise a statue to Father Damien, the true, practical saint, and perpetuate his memory forever as a living exemplar of Theosophical heroism and of Buddha - and Christ-like mercy and self-sacrifice.

Q. Then you regard self-sacrifice as a duty?

A. We do; and explain it by showing that altruism is an integral part of self-development. But we have to discriminate. A man has no right to starve himself to death that another man may have food, unless the life of that man is obviously more useful to the many than is his own life. But it is his duty to sacrifice his own comfort, and to work for others if they are unable to work for themselves. It is his duty to give all that which is wholly his own and can benefit no one but himself if he selfishly keeps it from others. Theosophy teaches self-abnegation, but does not teach rash and useless self-sacrifice, nor does it justify fanaticism.

Q. But how are we to reach such an elevated status?

A. By the enlightened application of our precepts to practice. By the use of our higher reason, spiritual intuition, and moral sense, and by following the dictates of what we call "the still small voice" of our conscience, which is that of our Ego, and which speaks louder in us than the earthquakes and the thunders of Jehovah, wherein the Lord is not.

Q. If such are our duties to humanity at large, what do you understand by our duties to our immediate surroundings?

A. Just the same, plus those that arise from special obligations with regard to family ties.

Q. Then it is not true, as it is said, that no sooner does a man enter into the Theosophical Society than he begins to be gradually severed from his wife, children, and family duties?

A. It is a groundless slander, like so many others. The first of the Theosophical duties is to do one's duty by all men, and especially by those to whom one's specific responsibilities are due, because one has either voluntarily undertaken them, such as marriage ties, or because one's destiny has allied one to them; I mean those we owe to parents or next of kin.

Q. And what may be the duty of a Theosophist to himself?

A. To control and conquer, *through the Higher, the lower self.* To purify himself inwardly and morally; to fear no one, and nought, save the tribunal of his own conscience. Never to do a thing by halves; i.e., if he thinks it the right thing to do, let him do it openly and boldly, and if wrong, never touch it at all. It is the duty of a Theosophist to lighten his burden by thinking of the wise aphorism of Epictetus, who says: *Be not diverted from your duty by any idle reflection the silly world may make upon you, for their censures are not in your power, and consequently should not be any part of your concern.*

Q. But suppose a member of your Society should plead inability to practice altruism by other people, on the ground that "charity begins at home", urging that he is too busy, or too poor, to benefit mankind or even any of its units - what are your rules in such a case?

A. No man has a right to say that he can do nothing for others, on any pretext whatever. By doing the proper duty in the proper place, a man may make the world his debtor, says an English writer. A cup of cold water given in time to a thirsty wayfarer is a nobler duty and more worth, than a dozen of dinners given away, out of season, to men who can afford to pay for them. No man who has not got it in him will ever become a Theosophist; but he may remain a member of our Society all the same. We have no rules by which we could force any man to become a practical Theosophist, if he does not desire to be one.

Q. Then why does he enter the Society at all?

A. That is best known to him who does so. For, here again, we have no right to prejudge a person, not even if the voice of a whole community should be against him, and I may tell you why. In our day, vox populi(so far as regards the voice of the educated, at any rate) is no longer vox dei, but ever that of prejudice, of selfish motives, and often simply that of unpopularity. Our duty is to sow seeds broadcast for the future, and see they are good; not to stop to enquire why we should do so, and how and wherefore we are obliged to lose our time, since those who will reap the harvest in days to come will never be ourselves.

On Charity

Q. How do you Theosophists regard the Christian duty of charity?

A. What charity do you mean? Charity of mind, or practical charity in the physical plane?

Q. I mean practical charity, as your idea of Universal brotherhood would include, of course, charity of mind.

A. Then you have in your mind the practical carrying out of the commandments given by Jesus in the Sermon on the Mount?

Q. Precisely so.

A. Then why call them "Christian"? Because, although your Savior preached and practiced them, the last thing the Christians of today think of is to carry them out in their lives.

Q. And yet many are those who pass their lives in dispensing charity?

A. Yes, out of the surplus of their great fortunes. But point out to me that Christian, among the most philanthropic, who would give to the shivering and starving thief, who would steal his coat, his cloak also; or offer his right cheek to him who smote him on the left, and never think of resenting it?

Q. Ah, but you must remember that these precepts have not to be taken literally. Times and circumstances have changed since Christ's day. Moreover, He spoke in Parables.

A. Then why don't your Churches teach that the doctrine of damnation and hellfire is to be understood as a parable too? Why do some of your most popular preachers, while virtually allowing these "parables" to be understood as you take them, insist on the literal meaning of the fires of Hell and the physical tortures of an "Asbestos-like" soul? If one is a "parable", then the other is. If Hellfire is a literal truth, then Christ's commandments in the Sermon on the Mount have to be obeyed to the very letter. And I tell you that many who do not believe in the Divinity of Christ-like Count Leo Tolstoi and more than one Theosophist - do carry out these noble, because universal, precepts literally; and many more good men and women would do so, were they not more than certain that such a walk in life would very probably land them in a lunatic asylum - so Christian are your laws!

Q. But surely everyone knows that millions and millions are spent annually on private and public charities?

A. Oh, yes; half of which sticks to the hands it passes through before getting to the needy; while a good portion or remainder gets into the hands of professional beggars, those who are too lazy to work, thus doing no good whatever to those who are really in misery and suffering. Haven't you heard that the first result of the great outflow of charity towards the East-end of London was to raise the rents in Whitechapel by some twenty percent?

Q. What would you do, then?

A. Act individually and not collectively; follow the Northern Buddhist precepts:
Never put food into the mouth of the hungry by the hand of another.

Never let the shadow of thy neighbor (a third person) come between thyself and the object of thy bounty.

Never give to the Sun time to dry a tear before thou hast wiped it.
Again
Never give money to the needy, or food to the priest, who begs at thy door, through thy servants, lest thy money should diminish gratitude, and thy food turn to gall.

Q. But how can this be applied practically?

A. The Theosophical ideas of charity mean personal exertion for others; personal mercy and kindness; personal interest in the welfare of those who suffer; personal sympathy, forethought and assistance in their troubles or needs. It is important to note that we Theosophists do not believe in giving money, if we had it, through other people's hands or organizations. We believe in giving to the money a thousandfold greater power and effectiveness by our personal contact and sympathy with those who need it. We believe in relieving the starvation of the soul, as much if not more than the emptiness of the stomach; for gratitude does more good to the man who feels it, than to him for whom it is felt. Where's the gratitude which your millions of pounds should have called forth, or the good feelings provoked by them? Is it shown in the hatred of the East-End poor for the rich? In the growth of the party of anarchy and disorder? Or by those thousands of unfortunate working girls, victims to the "sweating" system, driven daily to eke out a living by going on the streets? Do your helpless old men and women thank you for the workhouses; or your poor for the poisonously unhealthy dwellings in which they are allowed to breed new generations of diseased, and rickety children, only to put money into the pockets of the insatiable Shylocks who own houses? Therefore it is that every sovereign of all those "millions", contributed by good and would-be charitable people, falls like a burning curse instead of a blessing on the poor whom it should relieve. We call this *generating national Karma,* and terrible will be its results on the day of reckoning.

Theosophy for the Masses

Q. And you think that Theosophy would, by stepping in, help to remove these evils, under the practical and adverse conditions of our modern life?

A. Had we more money, and had not most of the Theosophists to work for their daily bread, I firmly believe we could.

Q. How? Do you expect that your doctrines could ever take hold of the uneducated masses, when they are so abstruse and difficult that well-educated people can hardly understand them?

A. You forget one thing, which is that your much-boasted modern education is precisely that which makes it difficult for you to understand Theosophy. Your mind is so full of intellectual subtleties and preconceptions that your natural intuition and perception of the truth cannot act. It does not require metaphysics or education to make a man understand the broad truths of Karma and Reincarnation. Look at the millions of poor and uneducated Buddhists and Hindus, to whom Karma and reincarnation are solid realities, simply because their minds have never been cramped and distorted by being forced into an unnatural groove. They have never had the innate human sense of justice perverted in them by being told to believe that their sins would be forgiven because another man had been put to death for their sakes. And the Buddhists, note well, live up to their beliefs without a murmur against Karma, or what they regard as a just punishment; whereas the Christian populace neither lives up to its moral ideal, nor accepts its lot contentedly. Hence murmuring and dissatisfaction, and the intensity of the struggle for existence in Western lands.

Q. But this contentedness, which you praise so much, would do away with all motive for exertion and bring progress to a stand-still.

A. And we, Theosophists, say that your vaunted progress and civilization are no better than a host of willo'- the-wisps, flickering over a marsh which exhales a poisonous and deadly miasma. This, because we see selfishness, crime, immorality, and all the evils imaginable, pouncing upon unfortunate mankind from this Pandora's box which you call an age of progress, and increasing pari passu with the growth of your material civilization. At such a price, better the inertia and inactivity of Buddhist countries, which have arisen only as a consequence of ages of political slavery.

Q. Then is all this metaphysics and mysticism with which you occupy yourself so much, of no importance?

A. To the masses, who need only practical guidance and support, they are not of much consequence; but for the educated, the natural leaders of the masses, those whose modes of thought and action will sooner or later be adopted by those masses, they are of the greatest importance. It is only by means of the philosophy that an intelligent and educated man can avoid the intellectual suicide of believing on blind faith; and it is only by assimilating the strict continuity and logical coherence of the Eastern, if not esoteric, doctrines, that he can realize their truth. Conviction breeds enthusiasm, and "Enthusiasm", says Bulwer Lytton, "is the genius of sincerity, and truth accomplishes no victories without it", while Emerson most truly remarks that "every great and commanding movement in the annals of the world is the triumph of enthusiasm". And what is more calculated to produce such a feeling than a philosophy so grand, so consistent, so logical, and so all-embracing as our Eastern Doctrines?

Q. And yet its enemies are very numerous, and every day Theosophy acquires new opponents.

A. And this is precisely that which proves its intrinsic excellence and value. People hate only the things they fear, and no one goes out of his way to overthrow that which neither threatens nor rises beyond mediocrity.

Q. Do you hope to impart this enthusiasm, one day, to the masses?

A. Why not? Since history tells us that the masses adopted Buddhism with enthusiasm, while, as said before, the practical effect upon them of this philosophy of ethics is still shown by the smallness of the percentage of crime amongst Buddhist populations as compared with every other religion. The chief point is, to uproot that most fertile source of all crime and immorality - the belief that it is possible for them to escape the consequences of their own actions. Once teach them that greatest of all laws, Karma and Reincarnation,and besides feeling in themselves the true dignity of human nature, they will turn from evil and eschew it as they would a physical danger.

How Members Can Help the Society

Q. How do you expect the Fellows of your Society to help in the work?

A. First by studying and comprehending the theosophical doctrines, so that they may teach others, especially the young people. Secondly, by taking every opportunity of talking to others and explaining to them what Theosophy is, and what it is not; by removing misconceptions and spreading an interest in the subject. Thirdly, by assisting in circulating our literature, by buying books when they have the means, by lending and giving them and by inducing their friends to do so. Fourthly, by defending the Society from the unjust aspersions cast upon it, by every legitimate device in their power. Fifth, and most important of all, by the example of their own lives.

Q. But all this literature, to the spread of which you attach so much importance, does not seem to me of much practical use in helping mankind. This is not practical charity.

A. We think otherwise. We hold that a good book which gives people food for thought, which strengthens and clears their minds, and enables them to grasp truths which they have dimly felt but could not formulate - we hold that such a book does a real, substantial good. As to what you call practical deeds of charity, to benefit the bodies of our fellowmen, we do what little we can; but, as I have already told you, most of us are poor, whilst the Society itself has not even the money to pay a staff of workers. All of us who toil for it, give our labor gratis, and in most cases money as well. The few who have the means of doing what are usually called charitable actions, follow the Buddhist precepts and do their work themselves, not by proxy or by subscribing publicly to charitable funds. What the Theosophist has to do above all is to forget his personality.

What a Theosophist Ought Not to Do

Q. Have you any prohibitory laws or clauses for Theosophists in your Society?

A. Many, but - alas! - none of them are enforced. They express the ideal of our organization, but the practical application of such things we are compelled to leave to the discretion of the Fellows themselves. Unfortunately, the state of men's minds in the present century is such that, unless we allow these clauses to remain, so to speak, obsolete, no man or woman would dare to risk joining the Theosophical Society. This is precisely why I feel forced to lay such a stress on the difference between true Theosophy and its hard-struggling and well-intentioned, but still unworthy vehicle, the Theosophical Society.

Q. May I be told what are these perilous reefs in the open sea of Theosophy?

A. Well may you call them reefs, as more than one otherwise sincere and well-meaning F.T.S. has had his Theosophical canoe shattered into splinters on them! And yet to avoid certain things seems the easiest thing in the world to do. For instance, here is a series of such negatives, screening positive Theosophical duties:

No Theosophist should be silent when he hears evil reports or slanders spread about the Society, or innocent persons, whether they be his colleagues or outsiders.

Q. But suppose what one hears is the truth, or may be true without one knowing it?

A. Then you must demand good proofs of the assertion, and hear both sides impartially before you permit the accusation to go uncontradicted. You have no right to believe in evil, until you get undeniable proof of the correctness of the statement.

Q. And what should you do then?

A. Pity and forbearance, charity and long-suffering, ought to be always there to prompt us to excuse our sinning brethren, and to pass the gentlest sentence possible upon those who err. A Theosophist ought never to forget what is due to the shortcomings and infirmities of human nature.

Q. Ought he to forgive entirely in such cases?

A. In every case, especially he who is sinned against.

Q. But if by so doing, he risks to injure, or allow others to be injured? What ought he to do then?

A. His duty; that which his conscience and higher nature suggests to him; but only after mature deliberation. Justice consists in doing no injury to any living being; but justice commands us also never to allow injury to be done to the many, or even to one innocent person, by allowing the guilty one to go unchecked.

Q. What are the other negative clauses?

A. No Theosophist ought to be contented with an idle or frivolous life, doing no real good to himself and still less to others. He should work for the benefit of the few who need his help if he is unable to toil for Humanity, and thus work for the advancement of the Theosophical cause.

Q. This demands an exceptional nature, and would come rather hard upon some persons.

A. Then they had better remain outside the T.S. instead of sailing under false colors. No one is asked to give more than he can afford, whether in devotion, time, work, or money.

Q. What comes next?

A. No working member should set too great value on his personal progress or proficiency in Theosophic studies; but must be prepared rather to do as much altruistic work as lies in his power. He should not leave the whole of the heavy burden and responsibility of the Theosophical Movement on the shoulders of the few devoted workers. Each member ought to feel it his duty to take what share he can in the common work, and help it by every means in his power.

Q. This is but just. What comes next?

A. No Theosophist should place his personal vanity, or feelings, above those of his Society as a body. He who sacrifices the latter, or other people's reputations on the altar of his personal vanity, worldly benefit, or pride, ought not to be allowed to remain a member. One cancerous limb diseases the whole body.

Q. Is it the duty of every member to teach others and preach Theosophy?

A. It is indeed. No fellow has a right to remain idle, on the excuse that he knows too little to teach. For he may always be sure that he will find others who know still less than himself. And also it is not until a man begins to try to teach others, that he discovers his own ignorance and tries to remove it. But this is a minor clause.

Q. What do you consider, then, to be the chief of these negative Theosophical duties?

A. To be ever prepared to recognize and confess one's faults. To rather sin through exaggerated praise than through too little appreciation of one's neighbor's efforts. Never to backbite or slander another person. Always to say openly and direct to his face anything you have against him. Never to make yourself the echo of anything you may hear against another, nor harbor revenge against those who happen to injure you.

Q. But it is often dangerous to tell people the truth to their faces. Don't you think so? I know one of your members who was bitterly offended, left the Society, and became its greatest enemy, only because he was told some unpleasant truths to his face, and was blamed for them.

A. Of such we have had many. No member, whether prominent or insignificant, has ever left us without becoming our bitter enemy.

Q. How do you account for it?

A. It is simply this. Having been, in most cases, intensely devoted to the Society at first, and having lavished upon it the most exaggerated praises, the only possible excuse such a backslider can make for his subsequent behavior and past short-sightedness, is to pose as an innocent and deceived victim, thus casting the blame from his own shoulders onto those of the Society in general, and its leaders especially. Such persons remind one of the old fable about the man with a distorted face, who broke his lookingglass on the ground that it reflected his countenance crookedly.

Q. But what makes these people turn against the Society?

A. Wounded vanity in some form or other, almost in every case. Generally, because their dicta and advice are not taken as final and authoritative; or else, because they are of those who would rather reign in Hell than serve in Heaven. Because, in short, they cannot bear to stand second to anybody in anything. So, for instance, one member - a true "Sir Oracle" - criticized, and almost defamed every member in the T.S. to outsiders as much as to Theosophists, under the pretext that they were all untheosophical, blaming them precisely for what he was himself doing all the time. Finally, he left the Society, giving as his reason a profound conviction that we were all (the Founders especially) - Frauds! Another one, after intriguing in every possible way to be placed at the head of a large Section of the Society, finding that the members would not have him, turned against the Founders of the T.S., and became their bitterest enemy, denouncing one of them whenever he could, simply because the latter could not, and would not, force him upon the Members. This was simply a case of an outrageous wounded vanity. Still another wanted to, and virtually did, practice black-magic - i.e., undue personal psychological influence on certain Fellows, while pretending devotion and every Theosophical virtue. When this was put a stop to, the Member broke with Theosophy, and now slanders and lies against the same hapless leaders in the most virulent manner, endeavoring to break up the society by blackening the reputation of those whom that worthy Fellow was unable to deceive.

Q. What would you do with such characters?

A. Leave them to their Karma. Because one person does evil that is no reason for others to do so.

Q. But, to return to slander, where is the line of demarcation between backbiting and just criticism to be drawn? Is it not one's duty to warn one's friends and neighbors against those whom one knows to be dangerous associates?

A. If by allowing them to go on unchecked other persons may be thereby injured, it is certainly our duty to obviate the danger by warning them privately. But true or false, no accusation against another person should ever be spread abroad. If true, and the fault hurts no one but the sinner, then leave him to his Karma. If false, then you will have avoided adding to the injustice in the world. Therefore, keep silent about such things with everyone not directly concerned. But if your discretion and silence are likely to hurt or endanger others, then I add: Speak the truth at all costs, and say, with Annesly: "Consult duty, not events". There are cases when one is forced to exclaim, "Perish discretion, rather than allow it to interfere with duty".

Q. Methinks, if you carry out these maxims, you are likely to reap a nice crop of troubles!

A. And so we do. We have to admit that we are now open to the same taunt as the early Christians were. "See, how these Theosophists love one another!" may now be said of us without a shadow of injustice.

Q. Admitting yourself that there is at least as much, if not more, backbiting, slandering, and quarreling in the T.S. as in the Christian Churches, let alone Scientific Societies - What kind of Brotherhood is this? I may ask.

A. A very poor specimen, indeed, as at present, and, until carefully sifted and reorganized,no better than all others. Remember, however, that human nature is the same in the Theosophical Society as out of it. Its members are no saints: they are at best sinners trying to do better, and liable to fall back owing to personal weakness. Add to this that our "Brotherhood" is no "recognized" or established body, and stands, so to speak, outside of the pale of jurisdiction. Besides which, it is in a chaotic condition, and as unjustly unpopular as is no other body. What wonder, then, that those members who fail to carry out its ideal should turn, after leaving the Society, for sympathetic protection to our enemies, and pour all their gall and bitterness into their too willing ears! Knowing that they will find support, sympathy, and ready credence for every accusation, however absurd, that it may please them to launch against the Theosophical Society, they hasten to do so, and vent their wrath on the innocent looking-glass, which reflected too faithfully their faces. People never forgive those whom they have wronged. The sense of kindness received, and repaid by them with ingratitude, drives them into a madness of self-justification before the world and their own consciences. The former is but too ready to believe in anything said against a society it hates. The latter - but I will say no more, fearing I have already said too much.

Q. Your position does not seem to me a very enviable one.

A. It is not. But don't you think that there must be something very noble, very exalted, very true, behind the Society and its philosophy, when the leaders and the founders of the Movement still continue to work for it with all their strength? They sacrifice to it all comfort, all worldly prosperity, and success, even to their good name and reputation - aye, even their honor - to receive in return incessant and ceaseless obloquy, relentless persecution, untiring slander, constant ingratitude, and misunderstanding of their best efforts, blows, and buffets from all sides - when by simply dropping their work they would find themselves immediately released from every responsibility, shielded from every further attack.

Q. I confess, such a perseverance seems to me very astounding, and I wondered why you did all this.

A. Believe me for no self-gratification; only in the hope of training a few individuals to carry on our work for humanity by its original program when the Founders are dead and gone. They have already found a few such noble and devoted souls to replace them. The coming generations, thanks to these few, will find the path to peace a little less thorny, and the way a little widened, and thus all this suffering will have produced good results, and their self-sacrifice will not have been in vain. At present, the main, fundamental object of the Society is to sow germs in the hearts of men, which may in time sprout, and under more propitious circumstances lead to a healthy reform, conducive of more happiness to the masses than they have hitherto enjoyed.

On the Misconceptions About the T.S.
Theosophy and Asceticism

Q. I have heard people say that your rules require all members to be vegetarians, celibates, and rigid ascetics; but you have not told me anything of the sort yet. Can you tell me the truth once for all about this?

A. The truth is that our rules require nothing of the kind. The Theosophical Society does not even expect, far less require of any of its members that they should be ascetics in any way, except - if you call that asceticism - that they should try and benefit other people and be unselfish in their own lives.

Q. But still many of your members are strict vegetarians, and openly avow their intention of remaining unmarried. This, too, is most often the case with those who take a prominent part in connection with the work of your Society.

A. That is only natural, because most of our really earnest workers are members of the Inner Section of the Society, which I told you about before.

Q. Oh! Then you do require ascetic practices in that Inner Section?

A. No; we do not require or enjoin them even there; but I see that I had better give you an explanation of our views on the subject of asceticism in general, and then you will understand about vegetarianism and so on.

Q. Please proceed.

A. As I have already told you, most people who become really earnest students of Theosophy, and active workers in our Society, wish to do more than study theoretically the truths we teach. They wish to know the truth by their own direct personal experience, and to study Occultism with the object of acquiring the wisdom and power, which they feel that they need in order to help others, effectually and judiciously, instead of blindly and at haphazard. Therefore, sooner or later, they join the Inner Section.

Q. But you said that ascetic practices are not obligatory even in that Inner Section?

A. No more they are; but the first thing which the members learn there is a true conception of the relation of the body, or physical sheath, to the inner, the true man. The relation and mutual interaction between these two aspects of human nature are explained and demonstrated to them, so that they soon become imbued with the supreme importance of the inner man over the outer case or body. They are taught that blind unintelligent asceticism is mere folly; that such conduct as that of St. Labro which I spoke of before, or that of the Indian Fakirs and jungle ascetics, who cut, burn, and macerate their bodies in the most cruel and horrible manner, is simply self-torture for selfish ends, i.e., to develop will-power, but is perfectly useless for the purpose of assisting true spiritual, or Theosophic, development.

Q. I see, you regard only moral asceticism as necessary. It is as a means to an end, that end being the perfect equilibrium of the inner nature of man, and the attainment of complete mastery over the body with all its passions and desires?

A. Just so. But these means must be used intelligently and wisely, not blindly and foolishly; like an athlete who is training and preparing for a great contest, not like the miser who starves himself into illness that he may gratify his passion for gold.

Q. I understand now your general idea; but let us see how you apply it in practice. How about vegetarianism, for instance?

A. One of the great German scientists has shown that every kind of animal tissue, however you may cook it, still retains certain marked characteristics of the animal which it belonged to, which characteristics can be recognized. And apart from that, everyone knows by the taste what meat he is eating. We go a step farther, and prove that when the flesh of animals is assimilated by man as food, it imparts to him, physiologically, some of the characteristics of the animal it came from. Moreover, occult science teaches and proves this to its students by ocular demonstration, showing also that this "coarsening" or "animalizing" effect on man is greatest from the flesh of the larger animals, less for birds, still less for fish and other cold-blooded animals, and least of all when he eats only vegetables.

Q. Then he had better not eat at all?

A. If he could live without eating, of course it would. But as the matter stands, he must eat to live, and so we advise really earnest students to eat such food as will least clog and weight their brains and bodies, and will have the smallest effect in hampering and retarding the development of their intuition, their inner faculties, and powers.

Q. Then you do not adopt all the arguments which vegetarians in general are in the habit of using?

A. Certainly not. Some of their arguments are very weak, and often based on assumptions which are quite false. But, on the other hand, many of the things they say are quite true. For instance, we believe that much disease, and especially the great predisposition to disease which is becoming so marked a feature in our time, is very largely due to the eating of meat, and especially of tinned meats. But it would take too long to go thoroughly into this question of vegetarianism on its merits; so please pass onto something else.

Q. One question more. What are your members of the Inner Section to do with regard to their food when they are ill?

A. Follow the best practical advice they can get, of course. Don't you grasp yet that we never impose any hard-and-fast obligations in this respect? Remember once for all that in all such questions we take a rational, and never a fanatical, view of things. If from illness or long habit a man cannot go without meat, why, by all means let him eat it. It is no crime; it will only retard his progress a little; for after all is said and done, the purely bodily actions and functions are of far less importance than what a man thinks and feels,what desires he encourages in his mind, and allows to take root and grow there.

Q. Then with regard to the use of wine and spirits, I suppose you do not advise people to drink them?

A. They are worse for his moral and spiritual growth than meat, for alcohol in all its forms has a direct, marked, and very deleterious influence on man's psychic condition. Wine and spirit drinking is only less destructive to the development of the inner powers, than the habitual use of hashish, opium, and similar drugs.

Theosophy and Marriage

Q. Now to another question; must a man marry or remain a celibate?

A. It depends on the kind of man you mean. If you refer to one who intends to live in the world, one who, even though a good, earnest Theosophist, and an ardent worker for our cause, still has ties and wishes which bind him to the world, who, in short, does not feel that he has done forever with what men call life, and that he desires one thing and one thing only - to know the truth, and to be able to help others - then for such a one I say there is no reason why he should not marry, if he likes to take the risks of that lottery where there are so many more blanks than prizes. Surely you cannot believe us so absurd and fanatical as to preach against marriage altogether? On the contrary, save in a few exceptional cases of practical Occultism, marriage is the only remedy against immorality.

Q. But why cannot one acquire this knowledge and power when living a married life?

A. My dear sir, I cannot go into physiological questions with you; but I can give you an obvious and, I think, a sufficient answer, which will explain to you the moral reasons we give for it. Can a man serve two masters? No! Then it is equally impossible for him to divide his attention between the pursuit of Occultism and a wife. If he tries to, he will assuredly fail in doing either properly; and, let me remind you, practical Occultism is far too serious and dangerous a study for a man to take up, unless he is in the most deadly earnest, and ready to sacrifice all, himself first of all, to gain his end. But this does not apply to the members of our Inner Section. I am only referring to those who are determined to tread that path of discipleship which leads to the highest goal. Most, if not all of those who join our Inner Section, are only beginners, preparing themselves in this life to enter in reality upon that path in lives to come.

Theosophy and Education

Q. One of your strongest arguments for the inadequacy of the existing forms of religion in the West, as also to some extent the materialistic philosophy which is now so popular, but which you seem to consider as an abomination of desolation, is the large amount of misery and wretchedness which undeniably exists, especially in our great cities. But surely you must recognize how much has been, and is being done to remedy this state of things by the spread of education and the diffusion of intelligence.

A. The future generations will hardly thank you for such a diffusion of intelligence, nor will your present education do much good to the poor starving masses.

Q. Ah! But you must give us time. It is only a few years since we began to educate the people.

A. And what, pray, has your Christian religion been doing ever since the fifteenth century, once you acknowledge that the education of the masses has not been attempted till now - the very work, if ever there could be one, which a Christian, i.e., a Christ-following church and people, ought to perform?

Q. Well, you may be right; but now -

A. Just let us consider this question of education from a broad standpoint, and I will prove to you that you are doing harm not good, with many of your boasted improvements. The schools for the poorer children, though far less useful than they ought to be, are good in contrast with the vile surroundings to which they are doomed by your modern Society. The infusion of a little practical Theosophy would help a hundred times more in life the poor suffering masses than all this infusion of (useless) intelligence.

Q. But, really -

A. Let me finish, please. You have opened a subject on which we Theosophists feel deeply, and I must have my say. I quite agree that there is a great advantage to a small child bred in the slums, having the gutter for playground, and living amid continued coarseness of gesture and word, in being placed daily in a bright, clean schoolroom hung with pictures, and often gay with flowers. There it is taught to be clean, gentle, orderly; there it learns to sing and to play; has toys that awaken its intelligence; learns to use its fingers deftly; is spoken to with a smile instead of a frown; is gently rebuked or coaxed instead of cursed. All this humanizes the children, arouses their brains, and renders them susceptible to intellectual and moral influences. The schools are not all they might be and ought to be; but, compared with the homes, they are paradises; and they slowly are reacting on the homes. But while this is true of many of the Board schools, your system deserves the worst one can say of it.

Q. So be it; go on.

A. What is the real object of modern education? Is it to cultivate and develop the mind in the right direction; to teach the disinherited and hapless people to carry with fortitude the burden of life (allotted them by Karma); to strengthen their will; to inculcate in them the love of one's neighbor and the feeling of mutual interdependence and brotherhood; and thus to train and form the character for practical life? Not a bit of it. And yet, these are undeniably the objects of all true education. No one denies it; all your educators admit it, and talk very big indeed on the subject. But what is the practical result of their action? Every young man and boy, nay, every one of the younger generation of schoolmasters will answer: "The object of modern education is to pass examinations, a system not to develop right emulation, but to generate and breed jealousy, envy, hatred almost, in young people for one another, and thus train them for a life of ferocious selfishness and struggle for honors and emoluments instead of kindly feeling".

Q. I must admit you are right there.

A. And what are these examinations - the terror of modern boyhood and youth? They are simply a method of classification by which the results of your school teaching are tabulated. In other words, they form the practical application of the modern science method to the genus Homo, *qua* intellection. Now "science" teaches that intellect is a result of the mechanical interaction of the brain-stuff; therefore it is only logical that modern education should be almost entirely mechanical - a sort of automatic machine for the fabrication of intellect by the ton. Very little experience of examinations is enough to show that the education they produce is simply a training of the physical memory, and, sooner or later, all your schools will sink to this level. As to any real, sound cultivation of the thinking and reasoning power, it is simply impossible while everything has to be judged by the results as tested by competitive examinations. Again, school training is of the very greatest importance in forming character, especially in its moral bearing. Now, from first to last, your modern system is based on the so-called scientific revelations: "The struggle for existence" and the "survival of the fittest". All through his early life, every man has these driven into him by practical example and experience, as well as by direct teaching, till it is impossible to eradicate from his mind the idea that "self", the lower, personal, animal self, is the end-all, and be-all, of life. Here you get the great source of all the after-misery, crime, and heartless selfishness, which you admit as much as I do. Selfishness, as said over and over again, is the curse of humanity, and the prolific parent of all the evils and crimes in this life; and it is your schools which are the hotbeds of such selfishness.

Q. That is all very fine as generalities, but I should like a few facts, and to learn also how this can be remedied.

A. Very well, I will try and satisfy you. There are three great divisions of scholastic establishments, board, middle-class and public schools, running up the scale from the most grossly commercial to the idealistic classical, with many permutations and combinations. The practical commercial begets the modern side, and the ancient and orthodox classical reflects its heavy respectability even as far as the School Board pupil teacher's establishments. Here we plainly see the scientific and material commercial supplanting the effete orthodox and classical. Neither is the reason very far to seek. The objects of this branch of education are, then, pounds, shillings, and pence, the summum bonum of the nineteenth century. Thus, the energies generated by the brain molecules of its adherents are all concentrated on one point, and are, therefore, to some extent, an organized army of educated and speculative intellects of the minority of men, trained against the hosts of the ignorant, simple-minded masses doomed to be vampirized, lived, and sat upon by their intellectually stronger brethren. Such training is not only un-theosophical, it is simply unchristian. Result: The direct outcome of this branch of education is an overflooding of the market with money-making machines, with heartless selfish men-animals - who have been most carefully trained to prey on their fellows and take advantage of the ignorance of their weaker brethren!

Q. Well, but you cannot assert that of our great public schools, at any rate?

A. Not exactly, it is true. But though the form is different, the animating spirit is the same: un-theosophical and unchristian, whether Eton and Harrow turn out scientists or divines and theologians.

Q. Surely you don't mean to call Eton and Harrow "commercial"?

A. No. Of course the Classical system is above all things respectable, and in the present day is productive of some good. It does still remain the favorite at our great public schools, where not only an intellectual, but also a social education is obtainable. It is, therefore, of prime importance that the dull boys of aristocratic and wealthy parents should go to such schools to meet the rest of the young life of the "blood" and money classes. But unfortunately there is a huge competition even for entrance; for the moneyed classes are increasing, and poor but clever boys seek to enter the public schools by the rich scholarships, both at the schools themselves and from them to the Universities.

Q. According to this view, the wealthier "dullards" have to work even harder than their poorer fellows?

A. It is so. But, strange to say, the faithful of the cult of the "Survival of the fittest" do not practice their creed; for their whole exertion is to make the naturally unfit supplant the fit. Thus, by bribes of large sums of money, they allure the best teachers from their natural pupils to mechanicalize their naturally unfit progeny into professions which they uselessly overcrowd.

Q. And you attribute all this to what?

A. All this is owing to the perniciousness of a system which turns out goods to order, irrespective of the natural proclivities and talents of the youth. The poor little candidate for this progressive paradise of learning, comes almost straight from the nursery to the treadmill of a preparatory school for sons of gentlemen. Here he is immediately seized upon by the workmen of the materio-intellectual factory, and crammed with Latin, French, and Greek Accidence, Dates, and

Tables, so that if he have any natural genius it is rapidly squeezed out of him by the rollers of what Carlyle has so well called "dead vocables".

Q. But surely he is taught something besides "dead vocables", and much of that which may lead him direct to Theosophy, if not entirely into the Theosophical Society?

A. Not much. For of history, he will attain only sufficient knowledge of his own particular nation to fit him with a steel armor of prejudice against all other peoples, and be steeped in the foul cesspools of chronicled national hate and bloodthirstiness; and surely, you would not call that -Theosophy?

Q. What are your further objections?

A. Added to this is a smattering of selected, so-called, Biblical facts, from the study of which all intellect is eliminated. It is simply a memory lesson, the "Why" of the teacher being a "Why" of circumstances and not of reason.

Q. Yes; but I have heard you congratulate yourself at the ever-increasing number of the Agnostics and Atheists in our day, so that it appears that even people trained in the system you abuse so heartily do learn to think and reason for themselves.

A. Yes; but it is rather owing to a healthy reaction from that system than due to it. We prefer immeasurably more in our Society Agnostics, and even rank Atheists, to bigots of whatever religion. An Agnostic's mind is ever opened to the truth; whereas the latter blinds the bigot like the sun does an owl. The best - i.e., the most truth-loving, philanthropic, and honest - of our Fellows were, and are, Agnostics and Atheists (disbelievers in a personal God). But there are no free-thinking boys and girls, and generally early training will leave its mark behind in the shape of a cramped and distorted mind. A proper and sane system of education should produce the most vigorous and liberal mind, strictly trained in logical and accurate thought, and not in blind faith. How can you ever expect good results, while you pervert the reasoning faculty of your children by bidding them believe in the miracles of the Bible on Sunday, while for the six other days of the week you teach them that such things are scientifically impossible?

Q. What would you have, then?

A. If we had money, we would found schools which would turn out something else than reading and writing candidates for starvation. Children should above all be taught self-reliance, love for all men, altruism, mutual charity, and more than anything else, to think and reason for themselves. We would reduce the purely mechanical work of the memory to an absolute minimum, and devote the time to the development and training of the inner senses, faculties, and latent capacities. We would endeavor to deal with each child as a unit, and to educate it so as to produce the most harmonious and equal unfoldment of its powers, in order that its special aptitudes should find their full natural development. We should aim at creating freemen and women, free intellectually, free morally, unprejudiced in all respects, and above all things, unselfish. And we believe that much if not all of this could be obtained by proper and truly theosophical education.

Why Then is There So Much Prejudice Against the T.S.?

Q. If Theosophy is even half of what you say, why should there exist such a terrible ill-feeling against it? This is even more of a problem than anything else.

A. It is; but you must bear in mind how many powerful adversaries we have aroused ever since the formation of our Society. As I just said, if the Theosophical Movement were one of those numerous modern crazes, as harmless at the end as they are evanescent, it would be simply laughed at - as it is now by those who still do not understand its real purport - and left severely alone. But it is nothing of the kind. Intrinsically, Theosophy is the most serious Movement of this age; and one, moreover, which threatens the very life of most of the time-honored humbugs, prejudices, and social evils of the day - those evils which fatten and make happy the upper ten and their imitators and sycophants, the wealthy dozens of the middle classes, while they positively crush and starve out of existence the millions of the poor. Think of this, and you will easily understand the reason of such a relentless persecution by those others who, more observant and clear-sighted, do see the true nature of Theosophy, and therefore dread it.

Q. Do you mean to tell me that it is because a few have understood what Theosophy leads to, that they try to crush the Movement? But if Theosophy leads only to good, surely you cannot be prepared to utter such a terrible accusation of faithlessness, heartlessness, and treachery even against those few?

A. I am so prepared, on the contrary. I do not call the enemies we have had to battle with during the first nine or ten years of the Society's existence either powerful or "dangerous"; but only those who have arisen against us in the last three or four years. And these neither speak, write, nor preach against Theosophy, but work in silence and behind the backs of the foolish puppets who act as their visible marionettes. Yet, if invisible to most of the members of our Society, they are well known to the true "Founders" and the protectors of our Society. But they must remain for certain reasons unnamed at present.

Q. And are they known to many of you, or to yourself alone?

A. I never said I knew them. I may or may not know them - but I know of them,and this is sufficient; and I defy them to do their worst.They may achieve great mischief and throw confusion into our ranks, especially among the faint-hearted, and those who can judge only by appearances. They will not crush the Society, do what they may. Apart from these truly dangerous enemies - dangerous, however, only to those Theosophists who are unworthy of the name, and whose place is rather outside than within the T.S. - the number of our opponents is more than considerable.

Q. Can you name these, at least, if you will not speak of the others?

A. Of course I can. We have to contend against:-

1. The hatred of the Spiritualists, American, English, and French;

2. The constant opposition of the clergy of all denominations;

3. Especially the relentless hatred and persecution of the missionaries in India;

4. This led to the famous and infamous attack on our Theosophical Society by the Society for Psychical Research, an attack which was stirred up by a regular conspiracy organized by the missionaries in India.

5. We must count the defection of various prominent (?) members, for reasons I have already explained, all of whom have contributed their utmost to increase the prejudice against us.

Q. Cannot you give me more details about these, so that I may know what to answer when asked - a brief history of the Society, in short; and why the world believes all this?

A. The reason is simple. Most outsiders knew absolutely nothing of the Society itself, its motives, objects, or beliefs. From its very beginning the world has seen in Theosophy nothing but certain marvelous phenomena, in which two-thirds of the non-Spiritualists do not believe. Very soon the Society came to be regarded as a body pretending to the possession of miraculous powers. The world never realized that the Society taught absolute disbelief in miracle or even the possibility of such; that in the Society there were only a few people who possessed such psychic powers and but few who cared for them. Nor did it understand that the phenomena were never produced publicly, but only privately for friends, and merely given as an accessory, to prove by direct demonstration that such things could be produced without dark rooms, spirits, mediums, or any of the usual paraphernalia. Unfortunately, this misconception was greatly strengthened and exaggerated by the first book on the subject which excited much attention in Europe - Mr. Sinnett's The Occult World. If this work did much to bring the Society into prominence, it attracted still more obloquy, derision, and misrepresentation upon the hapless heroes and heroine thereof. Of this the author was more than warned in The Occult World, but did not pay attention to the prophecy-for such it was, though half-veiled.

Q. For what, and since when, do the Spiritualists hate you?

A. From the first day of the Society's existence. No sooner the fact became known that, as a body, the T.S. did not believe in communications with the spirits of the dead, but regarded the so-called "spirits" as, for the most part, astral reflections of disembodied personalities, shells, etc., than the Spiritualists conceived a violent hatred to us and especially to the Founders. This hatred found expression in every kind of slander, uncharitable personal remarks, and absurd misrepresentations of the Theosophical teachings in all the American Spiritualistic organs. For years we were persecuted, denounced, and abused. This began in 1875 and continues to the present day. In 1819, the headquarters of the T.S. were transferred from New York to Bombay, India, and then permanently to Madras. When the first branch of our Society, the British T.S., was founded in

London, the English Spiritualists came out in arms against us, as the Americans had done; and the French Spiritists followed suit.

Q. But why should the clergy be hostile to you, when, after all, the main tendency of the Theosophical doctrines is opposed to Materialism, the great enemy of all forms of religion in our day?

A. The Clergy opposed us on the general principle that "He who is not with me is against me". Since Theosophy does not agree with any one Sect or Creed, it is considered the enemy of all alike, because it teaches that they are all, more or less, mistaken. The missionaries in India hated and tried to crush us because they saw the flower of the educated Indian youth and the Brahmins, who are almost inaccessible to them, joining the Society in large numbers. And yet, apart from this general class hatred, the T.S. counts in its ranks' many clergymen, and even one or two bishops.

Q. And what led the S.P.R. to take the field against you? You were both pursuing the same line of study, in some respects, and several of the psychic researchers belonged to your society.

A. First of all we were very good friends with the leaders of the S.P.R.; but when the attack on the phenomena appeared in the Christian College Magazine,supported by the pretended revelations of a menial, the S.P.R. found that they had compromised themselves by publishing in their "Proceedings" too many of the phenomena which had occurred in connection with the T.S. Their ambition is to pose as an authoritative and strictly scientific body; so that they had to choose between retaining that position by throwing overboard the T.S. and even trying to destroy it, and seeing themselves merged, in the opinion of the Sadducees of the grand monde, with the credulous Theosophists and Spiritualists. There was no way for them out of it, no two choices, and they chose to throw us overboard. It was a matter of dire necessity for them. But so hard pressed were they to find any apparently reasonable motive for the life of devotion and ceaseless labor led by the two Founders, and for the complete absence of any pecuniary profit or other advantage to them, that our enemies were obliged to resort to the thrice-absurd, eminently ridiculous, and now famous Russian spy theory, to explain this devotion. But the old saying, "The blood of the martyrs is the seed of the Church", proved once more correct. After the first shock of this attack, the T.S. doubled and tripled its numbers, but the bad impression produced still remains. A French author was right in saying, "*Calomniez, calomniez toujours et encore, il en restera toujours quelque chose*". Therefore it is, that unjust prejudices are current, and that everything connected with the T.S., and especially with its Founders, is so falsely distorted, because based on malicious hearsay alone.

Q, Yet in the 14 years during which the Society has existed, you must have had ample time and opportunity to show yourselves and your work in their true light?

A. How, or when, have we been given such an opportunity? Our most prominent members had an aversion to anything that looked like publicly justifying themselves. Their policy has ever been: "We must live it down"; and "What does it matter what the newspapers say, or people think?" The Society was too poor to send out public lecturers, and therefore the expositions of our views and doctrines were confined to a few Theosophical works that met with success, but which people often misunderstood, or only knew of through hearsay. Our journals were, and still are, boycotted; our literary works ignored; and to this day no one seems even to feel quite certain whether the Theosophists are a kind of Serpent-and-Devil worshipers, or simply "Esoteric Buddhists" - whatever that may mean. It was useless for us to go on denying, day after day and year after year, every kind of inconceivable cock-and-bull stories about us; for, no sooner was one disposed of, than another, a still more absurd and malicious one, was born out of the ashes of the first. Unfortunately, human nature is so constituted that any good said of a person is immediately forgotten and never repeated. But one has only to utter a slander, or to start a story - no matter how absurd, false, or incredible it may be, if only it is connected with some unpopular character - for it to be successful and forthwith accepted as a historical fact. Like Don Basilio's Calumnia, the rumour springs up, at first, as a soft gentle breeze hardly stirring the grass under your feet, and arising no one knows whence; then, in the shortest space of time, it is transformed into a strong wind, begins to blow a gale, and forthwith becomes a roaring storm! A slander among news, is what an octopus is among fishes; it sucks into one's mind, fastens upon our memory, which feeds upon it, leaving indelible marks even after the slander has been bodily destroyed. A slanderous lie is the only master-key that will open any and every brain. It is sure to receive welcome and hospitality in every human mind, the highest as the lowest, if only a little prejudiced, and no matter from however base a quarter and motive it has started.

Q. Don't you think your assertion altogether too sweeping? The Englishman has never been over-ready to believe in anything said, and our nation is proverbially known for its love of fair play. A lie has no legs to stand upon for long, and -

A. The Englishman is as ready to believe evil as a man of any other nation; for it is human nature, and not a national feature. As to lies, if they have no legs to stand upon, according to the proverb, they have exceedingly rapid wings; and they can and do fly farther and wider than any other kind of news, in England as elsewhere. Remember lies and slander are the only kind of literature we can always get gratis, and without paying any subscription. We can make the experiment if you like. Will you, who are so interested in Theosophical matters, and have heard so much about us, will you put me questions on as many of these rumors and "hearses" as you can think of? I will answer you the truth, and nothing but the truth, subject to the strictest verification.

Q. Before we change the subject, let us have the whole truth on this one. Now, some writers have called your teachings immoral and pernicious. Others, on the ground that many so-called authorities and Orientalists find in the Indian religions nothing but sex-worship in its many forms, accuse you of teaching nothing better than Phallic worship. They say that since modern Theosophy is so closely allied with Eastern, and particularly Indian, thought, it cannot be free from this taint. Occasionally, even, they go so far as to accuse European Theosophists of reviving the practices connected with this cult. How about this?

A. I have heard and read about this before; and I answer that no more utterly baseless and lying slander has ever been invented and circulated. Silly people can see but silly dreams, says a Russian proverb. It makes one's blood boil to hear such vile accusations made without the slightest foundation, and on the strength of mere inferences. Ask the hundreds of honourable English men and women who have been members of the Theosophical Society for years whether an immoral precept or a pernicious doctrine was ever taught to them. Open *The Secret Doctrine*, and you will find page after page denouncing the Jews and other nations precisely on account of this devotion to Phallic rites, due to the dead letter interpretation of nature symbolism, and the grossly materialistic conceptions of her dualism in all the exoteric creeds. Such ceaseless and malicious misrepresentation of our teachings and beliefs is really disgraceful.

Q. But you cannot deny that the Phallic element does exist in the religions of the East?

A. Nor do I deny it; only I maintain that this proves no more than does its presence in Christianity, the religion of the West. Read Hargrave Jenning's *Rosicrucians*, if you would assure yourself of it. In the East, the Phallic symbolism is, perhaps, more crude, because more true to nature, or, I would rather say, more naive and sincere than in the West. But it is not more licentious, nor does it suggest to the Oriental mind the same gross and coarse ideas as to the Western, with, perhaps, one or two exceptions, such as the shameful sect known as the Maharaja, or *Vallabhacharya* sect.

Q. A writer in the Agnostic journal - one of your accusers - has just hinted that the followers of this disgraceful sect are Theosophists, and claim true Theosophic insight.

A. He wrote a falsehood, and that's all. There never was, nor is there at present, one single Vallabhacharya in our Society. As to their having, or claiming Theosophic insight, that is another fib, based on crass ignorance about the Indian Sects. Their Maharaja only claims a right to the money, wives, and daughters of his foolish followers and no more. This sect is despised by all the other Hindus. But you will find the whole subject dealt with at length in *The Secret Doctrine,* to which I must again refer you for detailed explanations. To conclude, the very soul of Theosophy is dead against Phallic worship; and its occult or esoteric section more so even than the exoteric teachings. There never was a more lying statement made than the above. And now ask me some other questions.

157

Is the Theosophical Society A Money-Making Concern?

Q. Agreed. Well, have either of the Founders, Colonel H.S. Olcott or H.P. Blavatsky, ever made any money, profit, or derived any worldly benefit from the T.S., as some papers say?

A. Not one penny. The papers lie. On the contrary, they have both given all they had, and literally beggared themselves. As for worldly benefits, think of the slanders and vilification they have been subjected to, and then ask the question!

Q. Yet I have read in a good many missionary organs that the entrance fees and subscriptions much more than covered all expenses; and one said that the Founders were making twenty thousand pounds a year!

A. This is a fib, like many others. In the published accounts of January, 1889, you will find an exact statement of all the money ever received from any source since 1879. The total received from all sources (entrance fees, donations, etc., etc.) during these ten years is under six thousand pounds, and of this a large part was contributed by the Founders themselves from the proceeds of their private resources and their literary work. All this has been openly and officially admitted, even by our enemies, the Society for Psychical Research. And now both the Founders are penniless: one, too old and ill to work as she did before, unable to spare time for outside literary work to help the Society in money, can only write for the Theosophical cause; the other keeps laboring for it as before, and receives as little thanks for it.

Q. But surely they need money to live?

A. Not at all. So long as they have food and lodging, even though they owe it to the devotion of a few friends, they need little more.

Q. But could not Madame Blavatsky, especially, make more than enough to live upon by her writings?

A. When in India she received on the average some thousand rupees a year for articles contributed to Russian and other papers, but gave it all away to the Society.

Q. Political articles?

A. Never. Everything she has written throughout the seven years of her stay in India is all there in print. It deals only with the religions, ethnology, and customs of India, and with Theosophy - never with politics, of which she knows nothing and cares less. Again, two years ago she refused several contracts amounting together to about 1,200 rubles in gold per month; for she could not accept them without abandoning her work for the Society, which needed all her time and strength. She has documents to prove it.

Q. But why could not both she and Colonel Olcott do as others - notably many Theosophists - do: follow out their respective professions and devote the surplus of their time to the work of the Society?

A. Because by serving two masters, either the professional or the philanthropic work would have had to suffer. Every true Theosophist is morally bound to sacrifice the personal to the impersonal, his own present good to the future benefit of other people. If the Founders do not set the example, who will?

Q. And are there many who follow it?

A. I am bound to answer you the truth. In Europe about half-a-dozen in all, out of more than that number of Branches.

Q. Then it is not true that the Theosophical Society has a large capital or endowment of its own?

A. It is false, for it has none at all. Now that the entrance fee of £1 and the small annual due have been abolished, it is even a doubtful question whether the staff at the headquarters in India will not soon be starved to death.

Q. Then why not raise subscriptions?

A. We are not the Salvation Army; we cannot and have never begged; nor have we ever followed the example of the Churches and sects and taken up collections. That which is occasionally sent for the support of the Society, the small sums contributed by some devoted Fellows, are all voluntary donations.

Q. But I have heard of large sums of money given to Mme. Blavatsky. It was said four years ago that she got £5,000 from one rich, young Fellow, who went out to join them in India, and £10,000 from another wealthy and well-known American gentleman, one of your members who died in Europe four years ago.

A. Say to those who told you this, that they either themselves utter, or repeat, a gross falsehood. Never has Madame Blavatsky asked or received one penny from the two above-named gentlemen, nor anything like that from anyone else, since the Theosophical Society was founded. Let any man living try to substantiate this slander, and it will be easier for him to prove that the Bank of England is bankrupt than that the said "Founder" has ever made any money out of Theosophy. These two slanders have been started by two high-born ladies, belonging to the London aristocracy, and have been immediately traced and disproved. They are the dead bodies, the carcasses of two inventions, which, after having been buried in the sea of oblivion, are once more raised on the surface of the stagnant waters of slander.

Q. Then I have been told of several large legacies left to the T.S. One - some £8,000 - was left to it by some eccentric Englishman, who did not even belong to the Society. The other - £3,000 or £4,000 - were testated by an Australian F.T.S. Is this true?

A. I heard of the first; and I also know that, whether legally left or not, the T.S. has never profited by it, nor have the Founders ever been officially notified of it. For, as our Society was not then a chartered body, and thus had no legal existence, the Judge at the Court of Probate, as we were told, paid no attention to such legacy and turned over the sum to the heirs. So much for the first. As for the second, it is quite true. The testator was one of our devoted Fellows, and willed all he had to the T.S. But when the President, Colonel Olcott, came to look into the matter, he found that the testator had children whom he had disinherited for some family reasons. Therefore, he called a council, and it was decided that the legacy should be refused, and the moneys passed to the legal heirs. The Theosophical Society would be untrue to its name were it to profit by money to which others are entitled virtually, at any rate on Theosophical principles, if not legally.

Q. Again, and I say this on the authority of your own Journal, The Theosophist,there's a Raja of India who donated to the Society 25,000 rupees. Have you not thanked him for his great bounty in the January Theosophist for 1888?

A. We have, in these words, "That the thanks of the Convention be conveyed to H.H. the Maharaja ... for his promised generous gift of Rupees 25,000 to the Society's Fund". The thanks were duly conveyed, but the money is still a "promise", and has never reached the Headquarters.

Q. But surely, if the Maharaja promised and received thanks for his gift publicly and in print, he will be as good as his promise?

A. He may, though the promise is 18 months old. I speak of the present and not of the future.

Q. Then how do you propose to go on?

A. So long as the T.S. has a few devoted members willing to work for it without reward and thanks, so long as a few good Theosophists support it with occasional donations, so long will it exist, and nothing can crush it.

Q. I have heard many Theosophists speak of a "power" behind the Society and of certain "Mahatmas", mentioned also in Mr. Sinnett's works, that are said to have founded the Society, to watch over and protect it.

A. You may laugh, but it is so.

The Working Staff of the T.S.

Q. These men, I have heard, are great Adepts, Alchemists, and what not. If, then, they can change lead into gold and make as much money as they like, besides doing all kinds of miracles at will, as related in Mr. Sinnett's The Occult World, why do not they find you money, and support the Founders and the Society in comfort?

A. Because they did not found a "miracle club". Because the Society is intended to help men to develop the powers latent in them through their own exertions and merit. Because whatever they may or may not produce in the way of phenomena, they are not false coiners;nor would they throw an additional and very strong temptation on the path of members and candidates: Theosophy is not to be bought. Hitherto, for the past 14 years, not a single working member has ever received pay or salary from either the Masters or the Society.

Q. Then are none of your workers paid at all?

A. Till now, not one. But as everyone has to eat, drink, and clothe himself, all those who are without any means of their own, and devote their whole time to the work of the Society, are provided with the necessaries of life at the Headquarters at Madras, India, though these "necessaries" are humble enough, in truth! But now that the Society's work has increased so greatly and still goes on increasing (owing to slanders) in Europe, we need more working hands. We hope to have a few members who will henceforth be remunerated - if the word can be used in the cases in question. For every one of these Fellows, who are preparing to give all their time to the Society, are quitting good official situations with excellent prospects, to work for us at less than half their former salary.

Q. And who will provide the funds for this?

A. Some of our Fellows who are just a little richer than the rest. The man who would speculate or make money on Theosophy would be unworthy to remain in our ranks.

Q. But you must surely make money by your books, magazines, and other publications?

A. The Theosophist of Madras, alone among the magazines, pays a profit, and this has regularly been turned over to the Society, year by year, as the published accounts show. Lucifer is slowly but steadily engulfing money, never yet having paid its expenses - thanks to its being boycotted by the pious booksellers and railway stalls.The Lotus, in France - started on the private and not very large means of a Theosophist, who has devoted to it his whole time and labor - has ceased to exist, owing to the same causes, alas! Nor does the New York Path pay its way, while the Revue Théosophique of Paris has only just been started, also from the private means of a lady-member. Moreover, whenever any of the works issued by the Theosophical Publishing Company in London do pay, the proceeds will be devoted to the service of the Society.

Q. And now please tell me all you can about the Mahatmas. So many absurd and contradictory things are said about them, that one does not know what to believe, and all sorts of ridiculous stories become current.

A. Well may you call them ridiculous!

The 'Theosophical Mahatmas'
Are They 'Spirits of Light' or 'Goblins Damned?'

Q. Who are they, finally, those whom you call your "Masters"? Some say they are "Spirits", or some other kind of supernatural beings, while others call them "myths.

A. They are neither. I once heard one outsider say to another that they were a sort of male mermaids, whatever such a creature may be. But if you listen to what people say, you will never have a true conception of them. In the first place they are living men, born as we are born, and doomed to die like every other mortal.

Q. Yes, but it is rumoured that some of them are a thousand years old. Is this true?

A. As true as the miraculous growth of hair on the head of Meredith's Shagpat. Truly, like the "Identical", no Theosophical shaving has hitherto been able to crop it. The more we deny them, the more we try to set people right, the more absurd do the inventions become. I have heard of Methuselah being 969 years old; but, not being forced to believe in it, have laughed at the statement, for which I was forthwith regarded by many as a blasphemous heretic.

Q. Seriously, though, do they outlive the ordinary age of men?

A. What do you call the ordinary age? I remember reading in The Lancet of a Mexican who was almost 190 years old; but I have never heard of mortal man, layman, or Adept, who could live even half the years allotted to Methuselah. Some Adepts do exceed, by a good deal, what you would call the ordinary age; yet there is nothing miraculous in it, and very few of them care to live very long.

Q. But what does the word Mahatma really mean?

A. Simply a "great soul", great through moral elevation and intellectual attainment. If the title of "Great" is given to a drunken soldier like Alexander, why should we not call those "Great" who have achieved far greater conquests in Nature's secrets, than Alexander ever did on the field of battle? Besides, the term is an Indian and a very old word.

Q. And why do you call them "Masters"?

A. We call them Masters because they are our teachers; and because from them we have derived all the Theosophical truths, however inadequately some of us may have expressed, and others understood, them. They are men of great learning, whom we term Initiates, and still greater holiness of life. They are not ascetics in the ordinary sense, though they certainly remain apart from the turmoil and strife of your western world.

Q. But is it not selfish thus to isolate themselves?

A. Where is the selfishness? Does not the fate of the Theosophical Society sufficiently prove that the world is neither ready to recognize them nor to profit by their teaching? Of what use would Professor Clerk Maxwell have been to instruct a class of little boys in their multiplication table? Besides, they isolate themselves only from the West. In their own country they go about as publicly as other people do.

Q. Don't you ascribe to them supernatural powers?

A. We believe in nothing supernatural, as I have told you already. Had Edison lived and invented his phonograph two hundred years ago, he would most probably have been burnt along with it, and the whole attributed to the devil. The powers which they exercise are simply the development of potencies lying latent in every man and woman, and the existence of which even official science begins to recognize.

Q. Is it true that these men inspire some of your writers, and that many, if not all, of your Theosophical works were written under their dictation?

A. Some have. There are passages entirely dictated by them verbatim, but in most cases they only inspire the ideas and leave the literary form to the writers.

Q. But this in itself is miraculous; is, in fact, a miracle. How can they do it?

A. My dear Sir, you are laboring under a great mistake, and it is science itself that will refute your arguments at no distant day. Why should it be a "miracle", as you call it? A miracle is supposed to mean some operation which is supernatural, whereas there is really nothing above or beyond Nature and Nature's laws. Among the many forms of the "miracle" which have come under modern scientific recognition, there is Hypnotism, and one phase of its power is known as Suggestion, a form of thought transference, which has been successfully used in combating particular physical diseases, etc. The time is not far distant when the World of Science will be forced to acknowledge that there exists as much interaction between one mind and another, no matter at what distance, as between one body and another in closest contact. When two minds are sympathetically related, and the instruments through which they function are tuned to respond magnetically and electrically to one another, there is nothing which will prevent the transmission of thoughts from one to the other, at will; for since the mind is not of a tangible nature, that distance can divide it from the subject of its contemplation, it follows that the only difference that can exist between two minds is a difference of state. So if this latter hindrance is overcome, where is the miracle of thought transference, at whatever distance?

Q. But you will admit that Hypnotism does nothing so miraculous or wonderful as that?

A. On the contrary, it is a well-established fact that a Hypnotist can affect the brain of his subject so far as to produce an expression of his own thoughts, and even his words, through the organism of his subject; and although the phenomena attaching to this method of actual thought transference are as yet few in number, no one, I presume, will undertake to say how far their action may extend in the future, when the laws that govern their production are more scientifically established. And so, if such results can be produced by the knowledge of the mere rudiments of Hypnotism, what can prevent the Adept in Psychic and Spiritual powers from producing results which, with your present limited knowledge of their laws, you are inclined to call "miraculous"?

Q..Then why do not our physicians experiment and try if they could not do as much? (Like e.g. prof. Bernheim and Dr. C. Lloyd Tuckey in England, profs. Beaunis and Ligeois in Nancy, Delboeuf in Lie`ge, Burot en Bourru in Rochefort, Fontain and Sigard in Bordeaux, Forel in Zurich, and the physicians Despine in Marseille, Van Renterghem and Van Eeden in Amsterdam, Wetterstrand in Stockholm, Schrenck-Notzing in Leipzig and many other respected physicians and writers.)

A. Because, first of all, they are not Adepts with a thorough understanding of the secrets and laws of psychic and spiritual realms, but materialists, afraid to step outside the narrow groove of matter; and, secondly, because they must fail at present, and indeed until they are brought to acknowledge that such powers are attainable.

Q. And could they be taught?

A. Not unless they were first of all prepared, by having the materialistic dross they have accumulated in their brains swept away to the very last atom.

Q. This is very interesting. Tell me, have the Adepts thus inspired or dictated to many of your Theosophists?

A. No, on the contrary, to very few. Such operations require special conditions. An unscrupulous but skilled Adept of the Black Brotherhood ("Brothers of the Shadow", and *Dugpas*, we call them) has far less difficulties to labor under. For, having no laws of the Spiritual kind to trammel his actions, such a Dugpa "sorcerer will most unceremoniously obtain control over any mind, and subject it entirely to his evil powers. But our Masters will never do that. They have no right, except by falling into Black Magic, to obtain full mastery over anyone's immortal Ego, and can therefore act only on the physical and psychic nature of the subject, leaving thereby the free will of the latter wholly undisturbed. Hence, unless a person has been brought into psychic relationship with the Masters, and is assisted by virtue of his full faith in, and devotion to, his Teachers, the latter, whenever transmitting their thoughts to one with whom these conditions are not fulfilled, experience great difficulties in penetrating into the cloudy chaos of that person's sphere. But this is no place to treat of a subject of this nature. Suffice it to say, that if the power exists, then there are Intelligences (embodied or disembodied) which guide this power, and living conscious instruments through whom it is transmitted and by whom it is received. We have only to beware of black magic.

Q. But what do you really mean by "black magic"?

A. Simply abuse of psychic powers, or of any secret of nature; the fact of applying to selfish and sinful ends the powers of Occultism. A hypnotist, who, taking advantage of his powers of 'suggestion', forces a subject to steal or murder, would be called a black magician by us. The famous 'rejuvenating system' of Dr. Brown-Sequard, of Paris, through a loathsome animal injection into human blood - a discovery all the medical papers of Europe are now discussing - if true, is *unconscious* black magic.

Q. But this is medieval belief in witchcraft and sorcery! Even Law itself has ceased to believe in such things?

A. So much the worse for law, as it has been led, through such a lack of discrimination, into committing more than one judiciary mistake and crime. It is the term alone that frightens you with its "superstitious" ring in it. Would not law punish an abuse of hypnotic powers, as I just mentioned? Nay, it has so punished it already in France and Germany; yet it would indignantly deny that it applied punishment to a crime of evident sorcery. You cannot believe in the efficacy and reality of the powers of suggestion by physicians and mesmerizers (or hypnotists), and then refuse to believe in the same powers when used for evil motives. And if you do, then you believe in Sorcery. You cannot believe in good and disbelieve in evil, accept genuine money and refuse to credit such a thing as false coin. Nothing can exist without its contrast, and no day, no light, no good could have any representation as such in your consciousness, were there no night, darkness, nor evil to offset and contrast them.

Q. Indeed, I have known men, who, while thoroughly believing in that which you call great psychic, or magic powers, laughed at the very mention of Witchcraft and Sorcery.

A. What does it prove? Simply that they are illogical. So much the worse for them, again. And we, knowing as we do of the existence of good and holy Adepts, believe as thoroughly in the existence of bad and unholy Adepts, or - *Dugpas*.

Q. But if the Masters exist, why don't they come out before all men and refute once for all the many charges which are made against Mme. Blavatsky and the Society?

A. What charges?

Q. That they do not exist, and that she has invented them. That they are men of straw, "Mahatmas of muslin and bladders". Does not all this injure her reputation?

A. In what way can such an accusation injure her in reality? Did she ever make money on their presumed existence, or derive benefit, or fame, therefrom? I answer that she has gained only insults, abuse, and slanders, which would have been very painful had she not learned long ago to remain perfectly indifferent to such false charges. For what does it amount to, after all? Why, to an implied compliment,which, if the fools, her accusers, were not carried away by their blind hatred, they would have thought twice before uttering. To say that she has invented the Masters comes to this: She must have invented every bit of philosophy that has ever been given out in Theosophical literature. She must be the author of the letters from which *Esoteric Buddhism* was written; the sole inventor of every tenet found in *The Secret Doctrine*, which, if the world were just, would be recognized as supplying many of the missing links of science, as will be discovered a hundred years hence. By saying what they do, they are also giving her the credit of being far cleverer than the hundreds of men - many very clever and not a few scientific men - who believe in what she says, inasmuch as she must have fooled them all! If they speak the truth, then she must be several Mahatmas rolled into one like a nest of Chinese boxes; since among the so-called "Mahatma letters" are many in totally different and distinct styles, all of which her accusers declare that she has written.

Q. It is just what they say. But is it not very painful to her to be publicly denounced as "the most accomplished impostor of the age", whose name deserves to pass to posterity, as is done in the Report of the Society for Psychical Research?

A. It might be painful if it were true, or came from people less rabidly materialistic and prejudiced. As it is, personally she treats the whole matter with contempt, while the Mahatmas simply laugh at it. In truth, it is the greatest compliment that could be paid to her. I say so, again.

Q. But her enemies claim to have proved their case.

A. Aye, it is easy enough to make such a claim when you have constituted yourself judge, jury, and prosecuting counsel at once, as they did. But who, except their direct followers and our enemies, believe in it?

Q. But they sent a representative to India to investigate the matter, didn't they?

A. They did, and their final conclusion rests entirely on the unchecked statements and unverified assertions of this young gentleman. A lawyer who read through his report told a friend of mine that in all his experience he had never seen "such a ridiculous and self-condemnatory document". It was found to be full of suppositions and "working hypotheses" which mutually destroyed each other. Is this a serious charge?

Q. Yet it has done the Society great harm. Why, then, did she not vindicate her own character, at least, before a Court of Law?

A. Because:-

1. As a Theosophist, it is her duty to leave unheeded all personal insults.

2. Neither the Society nor Mme. Blavatsky had any money to waste over such a lawsuit.

3. It would have been ridiculous for both to be untrue to their principles, because of an attack made on them by a flock of stupid old British wethers, who had been led to butt at them by an over-frolicsome lambkin from Australia.

Q. This is complimentary. But do you not think that it would have done real good to the cause of Theosophy, if she had authoritatively disproved the whole thing once for all?

A. Perhaps. But do you believe that any English jury or judge would have ever admitted the reality of psychic phenomena, even if entirely unprejudiced beforehand? And when you remember that they would have been set against us already by the "Russian Spy" scare, the charge of Atheism and infidelity, and all the other slanders that have been circulated against us, you cannot fail to see that such an attempt to obtain justice in a Court of Law would have been worse than fruitless! All this the psychic researchers knew well, and they took a base and mean advantage of their position to raise themselves above our heads and save themselves at our expense.

Q. The S.P.R. now denies completely the existence of the Mahatmas. They say that from beginning to end they were a romance which Madame Blavatsky has woven from her own brain?

A. Well, she might have done many things less clever than this. At any rate, we have not the slightest objection to this theory. As she always says now, she almost prefers that people should not believe in the Masters. She declares openly that she would rather people should seriously think that the only Mahatmaland is the grey matter of her brain, and that, in short, she has evolved them out of the depths of her own inner consciousness, than that their names and grand ideal should be so infamously desecrated as they are at present. At first she used to protest indignantly against any doubts as to their existence. Now she never goes out of her way to prove or disprove it. Let people think what they like.

Q. But, of course, these Masters do exist?

A. We affirm they do. Nevertheless, this does not help much. Many people, even some Theosophists and ex-Theosophists, say that they have never had any proof of their existence. Very well; then Mme. Blavatsky replies with this alternative: If she has invented them, then she has also invented their philosophy and the practical knowledge which some few have acquired; and if so, what does it matter whether they do exist or not, since she herself is here, and her own existence, at any rate, can hardly be denied? If the knowledge supposed to have been imparted by them is good intrinsically, and it is accepted as such by many persons of more than average intelligence, why should there be such a hullabaloo made over that question? The fact of her being an impostor has never been proved, and will always remain sub judice;whereas it is a certain and undeniable fact that, by whomsoever invented, the philosophy preached by the "Masters" is one of the grandest and most beneficent philosophies once it is properly understood. Thus the slanderers, while moved by the lowest and meanest feelings - those of hatred, revenge, malice, wounded vanity, or disappointed ambition - seem quite unaware that they are paying the greatest tribute to her intellectual powers. So be it, if the poor fools will have it so. Really, Mme. Blavatsky has not the slightest objection to being represented by her enemies as a triple Adept, and a "Mahatma" to boot. It is only her unwillingness to pose in her own sight as a crow parading in peacock's feathers that compels her to this day to insist upon the truth.

Q. But if you have such wise and good men to guide the Society, how is it that so many mistakes have been made?

A. The Masters do not guide the Society, not even the Founders; and no one has ever asserted that they did: they only watch over, and protect it. This is amply proved by the fact that no mistakes have been able to cripple it, and no scandals from within, nor the most damaging attacks from without, have been able to overthrow it. The Masters look at the future, not at the present, and every mistake is so much more accumulated wisdom for days to come. That other "Master" who sent the man with the five talents did not tell him how to double them, nor did he prevent the foolish servant from burying his one talent in the earth. Each must acquire wisdom by his own experience and merits. The Christian Churches, who claim a far higher "Master", the very Holy Ghost itself, have ever been and are still guilty not only of mistakes, but of a series of bloody crimes throughout the ages. Yet, no Christian would deny, for all that, his belief in that Master - I suppose? - although his existence is far more hypothetical than that of the Mahatmas; as no one has ever seen the Holy Ghost, and his guidance of the Church, moreover, their own ecclesiastical history distinctly contradicts. Errare humanum est. Let us return to our subject.

The Abuse of Sacred Names and Terms

Q. Then, what I have heard, namely, that many of your Theosophical writers claim to have been inspired by these Masters, or to have seen and conversed with them, is not true?

A. It may or it may not be true. How can I tell? The burden of proof rests with them. Some of them, a few - very few, indeed - have distinctly either lied or were hallucinated when boasting of such inspiration; others were truly inspired by great Adepts. The tree is known by its fruits; and as all Theosophists have to be judged by their deeds and not by what they write or say, so all Theosophical books must be accepted on their merits, and not according to any claim to authority which they may put forward.

Q. But would Mme. Blavatsky apply this to her own works -*The Secret Doctrine*, for instance?

A. Certainly; she says expressly in the Preface that she gives out the doctrines that she has learnt from the Masters, but claims no inspiration whatever for what she has lately written. As for our best Theosophists, they would also in this case far rather that the names of the Masters had never been mixed up with our books in any way. With few exceptions, most of such works are not only imperfect, but positively erroneous and misleading. Great are the desecrations to which the names of two of the Masters have been subjected. There is hardly a medium who has not claimed to have seen them. Every bogus swindling Society, for commercial purposes, now claims to be guided and directed by Masters, often supposed to be far higher than ours! Many and heavy are the sins of those who advanced these claims, prompted either by desire for material gain, vanity, or irresponsible mediumship. Many persons have been plundered of their money by such societies, which offer to sell the secrets of power, knowledge, and spiritual truth for worthless gold. Worst of all, the sacred names of Occultism and the holy keepers thereof have been dragged in this filthy mire, polluted by being associated with sordid motives and immoral practices, while thousands of men have been held back from the path of truth and light through the discredit and evil report which such shams, swindles, and frauds have brought upon the whole subject. I say again, every earnest Theosophist regrets today, from the bottom of his heart, that these sacred names and things have ever been mentioned before the public, and fervently wishes that they had been kept secret within a small circle of trusted and devoted friends.

Q. The names certainly do occur very frequently now-a-days, and I never remember hearing of such persons as Masters till quite recently.

A. It is so; and had we acted on the wise principle of silence, instead of rushing into notoriety and publishing all we knew and heard, such desecration would never have occurred. Behold, only fourteen years ago, before the Theosophical Society was founded, all the talk was of "Spirits". They were everywhere, in everyone's mouth; and no one by any chance even dreamt of talking about living "Adepts", "Mahatmas", or "Masters". One hardly heard even the name of the Rosicrucians, while the existence of such a thing as "Occultism" was suspected even but by very few. Now all that is changed. We Theosophists were, unfortunately, the first to talk of these things, to make the fact of the existence in the East of Adepts and Masters and Occult knowledge known; and now the name has become common property. It is on us, now, that the Karma, the consequences of the resulting desecration of holy names and things, has fallen. All that you now find about such matters in current literature - and there is not a little of it - all is to be traced back to the impulse given in this direction by the Theosophical Society and its Founders. Our enemies profit to this day by our mistake. The most recent book directed against our teachings is alleged to have been written by an Adept of twenty years' standing.Now, it is a *palpable lie*. We know the amanuensis and his inspirers (as he is himself too ignorant to have written anything of the sort). These "inspirers are living persons, revengeful and unscrupulous in proportion to their intellectual powers"; and these bogus Adepts are not one, but several. The cycle of "Adepts", used as sledgehammers to break the theosophical heads with, began twelve years ago, with Mrs. Emma Hardinge Britten's 'Louis' of *Art Magic* and *Ghostland*, and now ends with the 'Adept' and 'Author' of *The Light of Egypt,* a work written by Spiritualists against Theosophy and its teachings. But it is useless to grieve over what is done, and we can only suffer in the hope that our indiscretions may have made it a little easier for others to find the way to these Masters, whose names are now everywhere taken in vain, and under cover of which so many iniquities have already been perpetrated.

Q. Do you reject "Louis" as an Adept?

A. We denounce no one, leaving this noble task to our enemies. The Spiritualistic author of *Art Magic*, etc., may or may not have been acquainted with such an Adept - and saying this, I say far less than what that lady has said and written about us and Theosophy for the last several years - that is her own business. Only when, in a solemn scene of mystic vision, an alleged "Adept" sees "spirits" presumably at Greenwich, England, through Lord Rosse's telescope, which was built in, and never moved from, Parsonstown, Ireland, I may well be permitted to wonder at the ignorance of that "Adept" in matters of science. This beats all the mistakes and blunders committed at times by the *Chelas* of our Teachers! And it is this "Adept" that is used now to break the teachings of our Masters!

Q. I quite understand your feeling in this matter, and think it only natural. And now, in view of all that you have said and explained to me, there is one subject on which I should like to ask you a few questions.

A. If I can answer them I will. What is that?

Conclusion
The Future of the Theosophical Society

Q. Tell me, what do you expect for Theosophy in the future?

A. If you speak of Theosophy, I answer that, as it has existed eternally throughout the endless cycles upon cycles of the Past, so it will ever exist throughout the infinitude of the Future, because Theosophy is synonymous with everlasting truth.

Q. Pardon me; I meant to ask you rather about the prospects of the Theosophical Society.

A. Its future will depend almost entirely upon the degree of selflessness, earnestness, devotion, and last, but not least, on the amount of knowledge and wisdom possessed by those members, on whom it will fall to carry on the work, and to direct the Society after the death of the Founders.

Q. I quite see the importance of their being selfless and devoted, but I do not quite grasp how their knowledge can be as vital a factor in the question as these other qualities. Surely the literature which already exists, and to which constant additions are still being made, ought to be sufficient?

A. I do not refer to technical knowledge of the esoteric doctrine, though that is most important; I spoke rather of the great need which our successors in the guidance of the Society will have of unbiased and clear judgment. Every such attempt as the Theosophical Society has hitherto ended in failure, because, sooner or later, it has degenerated into a sect, set up hard-and-fast dogmas of its own, and so lost by imperceptible degrees that vitality which living truth alone can impart. You must remember that all our members have been bred and born in some creed or religion, that all are more or less of their generation both physically and mentally, and consequently that their judgment is but too likely to be warped and unconsciously biased by some or all of these influences. If, then, they cannot be freed from such inherent bias, or at least taught to recognize it instantly and so avoid being led away by it, the result can only be that the Society will drift off onto some sandbank of thought or another, and there remain a stranded carcass to molder and die.

Q. But if this danger be averted?

A. Then the Society will live on into and through the twentieth century. It will gradually leaven and permeate the great mass of thinking and intelligent people with its large-minded and noble ideas of Religion, Duty, and Philanthropy. Slowly but surely it will burst asunder the iron fetters of creeds and dogmas, of social and caste prejudices; it will break down racial and national antipathies and barriers, and will open the way to the practical realization of the Brotherhood of all men. Through its teaching, through the philosophy which it has rendered accessible and intelligible to the modern mind, the West will learn to understand and appreciate the East at its true value. Further, the development of the psychic powers and faculties, the premonitory symptoms of which are already visible in America, will proceed healthily and normally. Mankind will be saved from the terrible dangers, both mental and bodily, which are inevitable when that unfolding takes place, as it threatens to do, in a hotbed of selfishness and all evil passions. Man's mental and psychic growth will proceed in harmony with his moral improvement, while his material surroundings will reflect the peace and fraternal goodwill which will reign in his mind, instead of the discord and strife which is everywhere apparent around us today.

Q. A truly delightful picture! But tell me, do you really expect all this to be accomplished in one short century?

A. Scarcely. But I must tell you that during the last quarter of every hundred years an attempt is made by those "Masters", of whom I have spoken, to help on the spiritual progress of Humanity in a marked and definite way. Towards the close of each century you will invariably find that an outpouring or upheaval of spirituality - or call it mysticism if you prefer - has taken place. Some one or more persons have appeared in the world as their agents, and a greater or less amount of occult knowledge and teaching has been given out. If you care to do so, you can trace these movements back, century by century, as far as our detailed historical records extend.

Q. But how does this bear on the future of the Theosophical Society?

A. If the present attempt, in the form of our Society, succeeds better than its predecessors have done, then it will be in existence as an organized, living, and healthy body when the time comes for the effort of the twentieth century.

The general condition of men's minds and hearts will have been improved and purified by the spread of its teachings, and, as I have said, their prejudices and dogmatic illusions will have been, to some extent at least, removed. Not only so, but besides a large and accessible literature ready to men's hands, the next impulse will find a numerous and united body of people ready to welcome the new torch - bearer of Truth. He will find the minds of men prepared for his message, a language ready for him in which to clothe the new truths he brings, an organization awaiting his arrival, which will remove the merely mechanical, material obstacles and difficulties from his path. Think how much one, to whom such an opportunity is given, could accomplish. Measure it by comparison with what the Theosophical Society actually has achieved in the last fourteen years, without any of these advantages and surrounded by hosts of hindrances which would not hamper the new leader. Consider all this, and then tell me whether I am too sanguine when I say that if the Theosophical Society survives and lives true to its mission, to its original impulses through the next hundred years - tell me, I say, if I go too far in asserting that earth will be a heaven in the twenty-first century in comparison with what it is now!

ANNOTATED GLOSSARY

A.

Absoluteness. When predicated of the UNIVERSAL PRINCIPLE, it denotes an abstraction, which is more correct and logical than to apply the adjective "absolute" to that which can have neither attributes nor limitations.

Adam Kadmon (Heb.) "Archetypal man", Humanity. The "Heavenly man" not fallen into sin. Kabalists refer it to the Ten Sephiroth on the plane of human perception." In the Kabala Adam Kadmon is the manifested Logos corresponding to our third Logos, the unmanifested being the first paradigmic ideal man, and symbolizing the universe in abscondito, or in its "privation" in the Aristotelean sense. The first Logos is "the light of the World," the second and the third, its gradually deepening shadows.

Adept (Lat. adeptus). In Occultism, one who has reached the stage of initiation and become a master in the Science of Esoteric Philosophy.

Aether (Gr.) With the Ancients, the Divine luminiferous substance which pervades the whole universe; the "garment" of the Supreme Deity, Zeus, or Jupiter. With the Moderns, Ether, for the meaning of which, in physics and chemistry, see Webster's Dictionary, or some other. In Esotericism, AEther is the third principle of the Kosmic Septenary, matter (earth) being the lowest, and Akasa, the highest.

Agathon (Gr.) Plato's Supreme Deity, lit. "the good." Our ALAYA or the Soul of the World.

Agnostic. A word first used by Professor Huxley, to indicate one who believes nothing which cannot be demonstrated by the senses.

Ahankara (Sans.) The conception of "I," self-consciousness or self-identity; the "I," or egoistical and mayavic principle in man, due to our ignorance which separates our "I" from the Universal ONE-Self. Personality, egoism also.

Ain-Soph (Heb.) The "Boundless" or "Limitless" Deity emanating and extending. Ain-Soph is also written En-Soph and Ain-Suph, for no one, not even the Rabbis, are quite sure of their vowels. In the religious metaphysics of the old Hebrew philosophers, the ONE Principle was an abstraction like Parabrahm, though modern Kabalists have succeeded by mere dint of sophistry and paradoxes in making a "Supreme God" of it, and nothing higher. But with the early Chaldean Kabalists Ain-Soph was "without form or being" with "no likeness with anything else." (Franck's Die Kabbala, p. 126.) That Ain-Soph has never been considered as the "Creator" is proved conclusively by the fact that such an orthodox Jew as Philo calls "creator" the Logos, who stands next the "Limitless One," and is "the SECOND God." "The Second God is in its (Ain-Soph's) wisdom," says Philo in *Quaest et Solut*. Deity is NO-THING; it is nameless, and therefore called Ain-Soph - the word Ain meaning nothing. (See also Franck's Kabbala, p. 153.)

Alchemy, in Arabic Ul-Khemi, is as the name suggests, the chemistry of nature. Ul-Khemi or Al-Kimia, however, is really an Arabianized word, taken from the Greek chemeia from chumos "juice," extracted from a plant. Alchemy deals with the finer forces of nature and the various conditions of matter in which they are found to operate. Seeking under the veil of language, more or less artificial, to convey to the uninitiated so much of the Mysterium Magnum as is safe in the hands of a selfish world, the Alchemist postulates as his first principle, the existence of a certain Universal Solvent in the homogeneous substance from which the elements were evolved; which substance he calls pure gold, or summum materiae. This solvent, also called menstruum universale, possesses the power of removing all the seeds of disease out of the human body, of renewing youth, and prolonging life. Such is the lapis philosophorum (philosopher's stone). Alchemy first penetrated into Europe through Geber, the great Arabian sage and philosopher, in the eighth century of our era; but it was known and practised long ages ago in China and Egypt. Numerous papyri on Alchemy, and other proofs that it was the favourite study of Kings and Priests, have been exhumed and preserved under the generic name of Hermetic treatises (see Tabula Smaragdina). Alchemy is studied under three distinct aspects, which admit of many different interpretations, viz.: the Cosmic, the Human, and the Terrestrial.

These three methods were typified under the three alchemical properties - sulphur, mercury, and salt. Different writers have stated that these are three, seven, ten and twelve processes respectively; but they are all agreed there is but one object in Alchemy, which is to transmute gross metals into pure gold. But what that gold really is, very few people understand correctly. No doubt there is such a thing in Nature as transmutation of the baser metal into the nobler; but this is only one aspect of Alchemy, the terrestrial, or purely material, for we see logically the same process taking place in the bowels of the earth. Yet, besides and beyond this interpretation, there is in Alchemy a symbolical meaning, purely psychic and spiritual.

While the Kabalist-Alchemist seeks for the realization of the former, the Occultist-Alchemist, spurning the gold of the earth, gives all his attention to and directs his efforts only towards the transmutation of the baser quaternary into the divine upper trinity of man, which when finally blended, is one. The spiritual, mental, psychic, and physical planes of human existence are in Alchemy compared to the four elements - fire, air, water, and earth, and are each capable of a three-fold constitution, i. e., fixed, unstable, and volatile. Little or nothing is known by the world concerning the origin of this archaic branch of philosophy; but it is certain that it antedates the construction of any known Zodiac, and as dealing with the personified forces of nature, probably also any of the mythologies of the world. Nor is there any doubt that the true secrets of transmutation (on the physical plane) were known in the days of old, and lost before the dawn of the so-called historical period. Modern chemistry owes its best fundamental discoveries to Alchemy, but regardless of the undeniable truism of the latter, that there is but one element in the universe, chemistry placed metals in the class of elements, and is only now beginning to find out its gross mistake. Even some encyclopedists are forced to confess that if most of the accounts of transmutation are fraud or delusion, "yet some of them are accompanied by testimony which renders them probable. By means of the galvanic battery even the alkalis have been discovered to have a metallic basis. The possibility of obtaining metal from other substances which contain the ingredients composing it, of changing one metal into another . . . must therefore be left undecided. Nor are all Alchemists to be considered impostors. Many have laboured under the conviction of obtaining their object, with indefatigable patience and purity of heart, which is soundly recommended by Alchemists as the principal requisite for the success of their labours." (*Pop. Encyclop.*)

Alexandrian Philosophers (or School). This famous school arose in Alexandria, Egypt, which city was for long ages the seat of learning and philosophy. It was famous for its library, founded by Ptolemy Soter at the very beginning of his reign (Ptolemy died in 283 B. C.) - a library which once boasted 700,000 rolls, or volumes (Aulus Gellius), for its museum, the first real Academy of Sciences and Arts, for world-renowned scholars, such as Euclid, the father of scientific geometry; Apollonius of Perga, the author of the still extant work on conic sections; Nicomachus, the arithmetician: for astronomers, natural philosophers, anatomists such as Herophilus and Erasistratus; physicians, musicians, artists, etc. But it became still more famous for its eclectic, or new Platonic school, founded by Ammonius Saccas in 173 A. D., whose disciples were Origen, Plotinus, and many other men now famous in history. The most celebrated schools of the Gnostics had their origin in Alexandria. Philo-Judaeus, Josephus, Iamblichus, Porphyry, Clement of Alexandria, Eratosthenes the astronomer, Hypatia, the virgin philosopher, and numberless other stars of second magnitude, all belonged at various times to these great schools, and helped to make of Alexandria one of the most justly renowned seats of learning that the world has ever produced. Altruism, from Alter, other. A quality opposed to Egoism. Actions tending to do good to others, regardless of self.

Ammonius Saccas. A great and good philosopher who lived in Alexandria between the 2nd and 3rd centuries of our Era, the founder of the Neo-Platonic School of the Philalethians or "lovers of truth." He was of poor birth and born of Christian parents, but endowed with such prominent, almost divine goodness as to be called Theodidaktos, the "God-taught." He honoured that which was good in Christianity, but broke with it and the Churches at an early age, being unable to find in Christianity any superiority over the old religions. Analogeticists. The disciples of Ammonius Saccas (vide supra) so called because of their practice of interpreting all sacred legends, myths, and mysteries by a principle of analogy and correspondence, which rule is now found in the Kabalistic system, and pre-eminently so in the schools of Esoteric philosophy in the East. (Vide "The Twelve Signs of the Zodiac," by T. Subba Row in "Five years of Theosophy.")

Ananda (Sans.) Bliss, joy, felicity, happiness. A name of a favourite disciple of Gautama, the Lord Buddha.

Anaxagoras. A famous Ionian philosopher, who lived 500 B. C., studied philosophy under

Anaximenes of Miletus, and settled in the days of Pericles, at Athens. Socrates, Euripides,

Archelaus, and other distinguished men and philosophers were among his disciples and pupils. He was a most learned astronomer, and was one of the first to explain openly that which was taught by Pythagoras secretly - viz., the movements of the planets, the eclipses of the sun and moon, etc. It was he who taught the theory of chaos, on the principle that "nothing comes from nothing," ex nihilo nihil fit - and of atoms, as the underlying essence and substance of all bodies, "of the same nature as the bodies which they formed." These atoms, he taught, were primarily put in motion by nous (universal intelligence, the Mahat of the Hindus), which nous is an immaterial, eternal, spiritual entity; by this combination the world was formed, the material gross bodies sinking down, and the ethereal atoms (or fiery ether) rising and spreading in the upper celestial regions. Ante-dating modern science by over 2,000 years, he taught that the stars were of the same material as our earth, and the sun a glowing mass; that the moon was a dark uninhabitable body, receiving its light from the sun; and beyond the aforesaid science he confessed himself thoroughly convinced that the real existence of things, perceived by our senses, could not be demonstrably proved. He died in exile at Lampsacus, at the age of seventy-two.

Anima Mundi (Lat.) The "Soul of the World," the same as Alaya of the Northern Buddhists; the divine Essence which pervades, permeates, animates, and informs all things, from the smallest atom of matter to man and god. It is in a sense "the seven-skinned Mother"

of the stanzas in the Secret Doctrine; the essence of seven planes of sentiency, consciousness, and differentiation, both moral and physical. In its highest aspect it is Nirvana; in its lowest, the Astral Light. It was feminine with the Gnostics, the early Christians, and the Nazarenes; bisexual with other sects, who considered it only in its four lower planes, of igneous and ethereal nature in the objective world of forms, and divine and spiritual in its three higher planes. When it is said that every human soul was born by detaching itself from the Anima Mundi, it is meant, esoterically, that our higher Egos are of an essence identical with It, and Mahat is a radiation of the ever unknown Universal ABSOLUTE.

Anoia (Gr.) is "want of understanding folly"; and is the name applied by Plato and others to the lower Manas when too closely allied with Kama, which is characterised by irrationality (agnoia). The Greek agnoia is evidently a derivative of the Sanskrit ajnana (phonetically agnyana), or ignorance, irrationality, and absence of knowledge.

Anthropomorphism. From the Greek Anthropos, man. The act of endowing God or the gods with a human form and human attributes or qualities. Anugita (Sans.) One of the Upanishads. A very occult treatise. (Vide Clarendon Press series "The Sacred Books of the East.")

Apollo Belvidere. Of all the ancient statues of Apollo, the son of Jupiter and Latona, called Phoebus, Helios, the radiant, and the Sun - the best and most perfect is the one of this name, which is in the Belvidere Gallery in the Vatican, at Rome. It is called the Pythian Apollo, as the god is represented in the moment of his victory over the serpent Python. The statue was found in the ruins of Antium in 1503.

Apollonius of Tyana. A wonderful philosopher born in Cappadocia about the beginning of the first century; an ardent Pythagorean, who studied the Phoenician sciences under Euthydemus, and Pythagorean philosophy and other subjects under Euxenus of Heraclea. According to the tenets of the Pythagorean school he remained a vegetarian the whole of his long life, ate only fruit and herbs, drank no wine, wore vestments made only of plant fibres, walked barefooted and let his hair grow to the full length, as all the Initiates have done before and after him. He was initiated by the priests of the temple of AEculapius (Asclepios) at AEgae, and learnt many of the "miracles" for healing the sick wrought by the God of medicine. Having prepared himself for a higher initiation by a silence of five years, and by travel - visiting Antioch, Ephesus, and Pamphylia and other parts - he repaired via Babylon to India, alone, all his disciples having abandoned him as they feared to go to the "land of enchantments." A casual disciple, Damis, whom he met on his way, accompanied him, however, on his travels. At Babylon he got initiated by the Chaldees and Magi, according to Damis, whose narrative was copied by one named Philostratus one hundred years later. After his return from India, he showed himself a true Initiate in that the pestilence, earthquakes, deaths of kings and other events, which he prophesied, duly happened.

At Lesbos, the priests of Orpheus got jealous of him, and refused to initiate him into their peculiar mysteries, though they did so several years later. He preached to the people of Athens and other States the purest and noblest ethics, and the phenomena he produced were as wonderful as they were numerous, and well authenticated. "How is it," inquires Justin Martyr, in dismay, "how is it that the talismans (telesmata) of Apollonius have power, for they prevent, as we see, the fury of the waves, and the violence of the winds, and the attacks of wild beasts; and whilst our Lord's miracles are preserved by tradition alone, those of Apollonius are most numerous, and actually manifested in present facts?" (Quest. XXIV.) But an answer is easily found to this, in the fact that, after crossing the Hindu

Koosh, Apollonius had been directed by a king to the abode of the Sages, whose abode it may be to this day, and who taught him their unsurpassed knowledge. His dialogues, with the Corinthian Menippus, give to us truly the esoteric catechism, and disclose (when understood) many an important mystery of nature. Apollonius was the friend, correspondent, and guest of kings and queens, and no wonderful or "magic" powers are better attested than his. Towards the close of his long and wonderful life he opened an esoteric school at Ephesus, and died at the ripe old age of one hundred years. Archangel. Highest, supreme angel. From the two Greek words, arch, "first," and angelos, "messenger."

Arhat (Sans.), also pronounced and written Arahat, Arhan, Rahat, etc., "the worthy one"; a perfected Arya, one exempt from reincarnation; "deserving Divine honours." This was the name first given to the Jain, and subsequently to the Buddhist holy men initiated into the esoteric mysteries. The Arhat is one who has entered the last and highest path, and is thus emancipated from rebirth. Arians. The followers of Arius, a presbyter of the Church in Alexandria in the fourth century. One who holds that Christ is a created and human being, inferior to God the Father, though a grand and noble man, a true adept, versed in all the divine mysteries.

Aristobulus. An Alexandrian writer, and an obscure philosopher. A Jew who tried to prove that Aristotle explained the esoteric thoughts of Moses. Aryan (Sans.) Lit., "the holy"; those who had mastered the Aryasatyani and entered the Aryamarga path to Nirvana or Moksha, the great "fourfold" path. They were originally known as Rishis. But now the name has become the epithet of a race, and our Orientalists, depriving the Hindu Brahmans of their birthright, have made Aryans of all Europeans. Since, in esotericism the four paths or stages can only be entered through great spiritual development and "growth in holiness," they are called the Aryamarga. The degrees of Arhatship, called respectively Srotapatti, Sakridagamin, Anagamin, and Arhat, or the four classes of Aryas, correspond to the four paths and truths. Aspect. The form (rupa) under which any principle in septenary man or nature manifests is called an aspect of that principle in Theosophy. Astral Body. The ethereal counterpart or double of any physical body - Doppelganger.

Astrology. The science which defines the action of celestial bodies upon mundane affairs, and claims to foretell future events from the positions of the stars. Its antiquity is such as to place it among the very earliest records of human learning. It remained for long ages a secret science in the East, and its final expression remains so to this day, its esoteric application only having been brought to any degree of perfection in the West during the lapse of time since Varaha Mihira wrote his book on Astrology, some 1400 years ago. Claudius Ptolemy, the famous geographer and mathematician who founded the system of Astronomy known under his name, wrote his Tetrabiblos, which is still the basis of modern Astrology, 135 A. D. The science of Horoscopy is studied now chiefly under four heads, viz.: (1). Mundane, in its application to meteorology, seismology, husbandry. (2). State or Civic, in regard to the future of nations, Kings, and rulers. (3). Horary, in reference to the solving of doubts arising in the mind upon any subject. (4). Genethliacal, in connection with the future of individuals from birth unto death. The Egyptians and the Chaldees were among the most ancient votaries of Astrology, though their modes of reading the stars and the modern methods differ considerably. The former claimed that Belus, the Bel or Elu of the Chaldees, a scion of the Divine Dynasty, or the dynasty of the King-gods, had belonged to the land of Chemi, and had left it to found a colony from Egypt on the banks of the Euphrates, where a temple, ministered by priests in the service of the "lords of the stars," was built. As to the origin of the science, it is known on the one hand that Thebes claimed the honour of the invention of Astrology; whereas, on the other hand, all are agreed that it was the Chaldees who taught that science to the other nations. Now Thebes antedated considerably, not only "Ur of the Chaldees," but also Nipur, where Bel was first worshipped - Sin, his son (the moon), being the presiding deity of Ur, the land of the nativity of Terah, the Sabean and Astrolater, and of Abram, his son, the great Astrologer of Biblical tradition. All tends, therefore, to corroborate the Egyptian claim. If later on the name of Astrologer fell into disrepute in Rome and elsewhere, it was owing to the frauds of those who wanted to make money of that which was part and parcel of the Sacred Science of the Mysteries, and who, ignorant of the latter, evolved a system based entirely on mathematics, instead of transcendental metaphysics with the physical celestial bodies as its upadhi or material basis. Yet, all persecutions notwithstanding, the number of adherents to Astrology among the most intellectual and scientific minds was always very great. If Cardan and Kepler were among its ardent supporters, then later votaries have nothing to blush for, even in its now imperfect and distorted form. As said in *Isis Unveiled* (I., 259), "Astrology is to exact astronomy, what psychology is to exact physiology. In astrology and psychology one has to step beyond the visible world of matter and enter into the domain of transcendent spirit."

Athenagoras. A Platonic Philosopher of Athens, who wrote an apology for the Christians in 177 A. D., addressed to Marcus Aurelius, to prove that the accusations brought against them, viz., that they were incestuous and ate murdered children, were untrue.

Atman, or **Atma** (Sans.) The Universal Spirit, the divine monad, "the seventh Principle," so called, in the exoteric "septenary" classification of man. The Supreme Soul.

Aura (Gr. and Lat.) A subtile invisible essence or fluid that emanates from human, animal, and other bodies. It is a psychic effluvium partaking of both the mind and the body, as there is both an electro-vital and at the same time an electro-mental aura; called in Theosophy the Akasic or magnetic aura. In R. C. Martyrology, a Saint.

Avatara (Sans.) Divine incarnation. The descent of a god or some exalted Being who has progressed beyond the necessity for rebirth, into the body of a simple mortal. Krishna was an Avatar of Vishnu. The Dalai-Lama is regarded as an Avatar of Avalokiteswara and the Teschu-Lama as one of Tson-Kha-pa, or Amitabha. These are two kinds of Avatars: one born from woman and the other "parentless" - Anupadaka.

B

Beness. A term coined by Theosophists to render more accurately the essential meaning of the untranslatable word Sat. The latter word does not mean "Being," for the term "Being" presupposes a sentient consciousness of existence. But as the term Sat is applied solely to the absolute principle, that universal, unknown, and ever unknowable principle which philosophical Pantheism postulates, calling it the basic root of Kosmos and Kosmos itself, it could not be translated by the simple term "Being." Sat, indeed, is not even, as translated by some Orientalists, "the incomprehensible Entity"; for it is no more an "Entity" than a non-entity, but both. It is as said absolute BENESS, not "Being"; the one, secondless, undivided and indivisible ALL - the root of nature both visible and invisible, objective and subjective, comprehensible and - never to be fully comprehended.

Bhagavat-Gita (Sans.) Lit., "the Lord's Song," a portion of the Mahabharata, the great epic poem of India. It contains a dialogue wherein Krishna - the "Charioteer" and Arjuna his chela have a discussion upon the highest spiritual philosophy. The work is pre-eminently occult or esoteric. Black Magic. Sorcery; necromancy, or the raising of the dead and other selfish abuses of abnormal powers. This abuse may be unintentional; still it has to remain "black" magic whenever anything is produced phenomenally simply for one's own gratification.

Boehme (Jacob). A mystic and great philosopher, one of the most prominent Theosophists of the mediaeval ages. He was born about 1575 at Old Diedenberg, some two miles from Gorlitz (Silesia), and died in 1624, being nearly fifty years old. When a boy he was a common shepherd, and, after learning to read and write in a village school, became an apprentice to a poor shoemaker at Gorlitz. He was a natural clairvoyant of the most wonderful power. With no education or acquaintance with science he wrote works which are now proved to be full of scientific truths; but these, as he himself says of what he wrote, he "saw as in a Great Deep in the Eternal." He had "a thorough view of the universe, as in chaos," which yet opened itself in him, from time to time, "as in a young planet," he says. He was a thorough born mystic, and evidently of a constitution which is most rare; one of those fine natures whose material envelope impedes in no way the direct, even if only occasional, intercommunication between the intellectual and spiritual Ego. It is this Ego which Jacob Boehme, as so many other untrained mystics, mistook for God. "Man must acknowledge," he writes, "that his knowledge is not his own, but from God, who manifests the Ideas of Wisdom to the Soul of Man in what measure he pleases." Had this great Theosophist been born 300 years later he might have expressed it otherwise. He would have known that the "God" who spoke through his poor uncultured and untrained brain was his own Divine Ego, the omniscient Deity within himself, and that what that Deity gave out was not "what measure he pleased," but in the measure of the capacities of the mortal and temporary dwelling IT informed. Book of the Keys. An ancient Kabalistic work. The original is no longer extant, though there may be spurious and disfigured copies and forgeries of it. Brahm (Sans.) The student must distinguish between the neuter Brahma, and the male Creator of the Indian Pantheon, Brahma. The former Brahma or Brahman is the impersonal, Supreme, and uncognizable Soul of the Universe, from the essence of which all emanates, and into which all returns; which is incorporeal, immaterial, unborn, eternal, beginningless and endless. It is all-pervading, animating the highest god as well as the smallest mineral atom. Brahma, on the other hand, the male and the alleged Creator, exists in his manifestation periodically only, and passes into pralaya, i. e., disappears and is annihilated as periodically. (Vide infra.)

Brahma's Day. A period of 2,160,000,000 years, during which Brahma, having emerged out of his Golden Egg (Hiranya Garbha), creates and fashions the material world (for he is simply the fertilizing and creative force in Nature). After this period the worlds being destroyed in turn by fire and water, he vanishes with objective nature; and then comes Brahma's Night. A period of equal duration, in which Brahma is said to be asleep. Upon awakening he recommences the process, and this goes on for an AGE of Brahma composed of alternate "Days" and "Nights," and lasting for 100 years of 2,160,000,000 each. It requires fifteen figures to express the duration of such an age, after the expiration of which the Mahapralaya or Great Dissolution sets in, and lasts in its turn for the same space of fifteen figures.

Brahm-Vidya (Sans.) The knowledge or Esoteric Science about the true nature of the two Brahmas.

Buddha (Sans.) "The enlightened." Generally known as the title of Gautama Buddha, the Prince of Kapilavastu, the founder of modern Buddhism. The highest degree of knowledge and holiness. To become a Buddha one has to break through the bondage of sense and personality; to acquire a complete perception of the real Self, and learn not to separate it from all the other Selves; to learn by experience the utter unreality of all phenomena, foremost of all the visible Kosmos; to attain a complete detachment from all that is evanescent and finite, and to live while yet on earth only in the immortal and everlasting. **Buddhi** (Sans.) Universal Soul or Mind. Mahabuddhi is a name of Mahat (q. v.); also the Spiritual Soul in man (the sixth principle exoterically), the vehicle of Atma, the seventh, according to the exoteric enumeration. **Buddhism** is the religious philosophy taught by Gautama Buddha. It is now split into two distinct churches: the Southern and Northern. The former is said to be the purer, as having preserved more religiously the original teachings of the Lord Buddha. The Northern Buddhism is confined to Thibet, China, and Nepaul. But this distinction is incorrect. If the Southern Church is nearer, and has not, in fact, departed, except perhaps in trifling dogmas, due to the many councils held after the death of the MASTER from the public or exoteric teachings of Sakyamuni, the Northern Church is the outcome of Siddharta Buddha's esoteric teachings which he confined to his elect Bikshus and Arhats. Buddhism, in fact, cannot be justly judged in our age either by one or the other of its exoteric popular forms. Real Buddhism can be appreciated only by blending the philosophy of the Southern Church and the metaphysics of the Northern Schools. If one seems too iconoclastic and stern, and the other too metaphysical and transcendental, events being overcharged with the weeds of Indian exotericism - many of the gods of its Pantheon having been transplanted under new names into Thibetan soil - it is due to the popular expression of Buddhism in both churches. Correspondentially, they stand in their relation to each other as Protestantism to Roman Catholicism. Both err by an excess of zeal and erroneous interpretations, though neither the Southern nor the Northern Buddhist clergy have ever departed from Truth consciously, still less have they acted under the dictates of priestocracy, ambition, or an eye to personal gain and power, as the later churches have.

Buddhi-Taijasi (Sans.) A very mystic term, capable of several interpretations. In Occultism, however, and in relation to the human "Principles" (exoterically), it is a term to express the state of our dual Manas, when, reunited during a man's life, it bathes in the radiance of Buddhi, the Spiritual Soul. For "Taijasi" means the radiant, and Manas, becoming radiant in consequence of its union with Buddhi, and being, so to speak, merged into it, is identified with the latter; the trinity has become one; and, as the element of Buddhi is the highest, it becomes Buddhi-Taijasi. In short, it is the human soul illuminated by the radiance of the divine soul, the human reason lit by the light of the Spirit or Divine SELF-CONSCIOUSNESS.

C

Caste. Originally the system of the four hereditary classes into which Indian population was divided: Brahman, Kshatriya, Vaisya and Shoodra - (a) descendants of Brahma; (b) warrior; (c) mercantile, and (d) the lowest or agricultural Shoodra class. From these four, hundreds of divisions and minor castes have sprung.

Causal Body. This "body," which is in reality no body at all, either objective or subjective, but Buddhi the Spiritual Soul, is so-called because it is the direct cause of the Sushupti state leading to the Turya state, the highest state of Samadhi. It is called Karanopadhi, "the basis of the cause," by the "Taraka Raj" Yogis, and in the Vedanta System corresponds to both the Vignanamaya and Anandamaya Kosha (the latter coming next to Atma, and therefore being the vehicle of the Universal Spirit). Buddhi alone could not be called a "Causal body," but becomes one in conjunction with Manas, the incarnating Entity or EGO.

180

Chela (Sans.) A disciple. The pupil of a Guru or Sage, the follower of some Adept, or a school of philosophy.

Chrestos (Gr.) The early gnostic term for Christ. This technical term was used in the fifth century B. C. by AEschylus, Herodotus and others. The Manteumata pythocresta, or the "Oracles delivered by a Pythian God" through a pythoness, are mentioned by the former (Cho. 901), and Pythocrestos is derived from chrao. Chresterion is not only "the test of an oracle," but an offering to, or for, the oracle. Chrestes is one who explains oracles, a "prophet and soothsayer," and Chresterios, one who serves an oracle or a God. The earliest Christian writer, Justin Martyr, in his first Apology, calls his co-religionists Chrestians. "It is only through ignorance that men call themselves Christians, instead of Chrestians," says Lactantius (lib. IV., cap. VII.). The terms Christ and Christians, spelt originally Chrest and Chrestians, were borrowed from the Temple vocabulary of the Pagans. Chrestos meant, in that vocabulary, "a disciple on probation," a candidate for hierophantship; who, when he had attained it, through Initiation, long trials and suffering, and had been anointed (i. e., "rubbed with oil," as Initiates and even Idols of the Gods were, as the last touch of ritualistic observance), was changed into Christos - the "purified" in esoteric or mystery language. In mystic symbology, indeed, Christes or Christos meant that the "way," the Path, was already trodden and the goal reached; when the fruits of the arduous labour, uniting the personality of evanescent clay with the indestructible INDIVIDUALITY, transformed it thereby into the immortal EGO. "At the end of the way stands the Christes," the Purifier; and the union once accomplished, the Chrestos, the "man of sorrow" became Christos himself. Paul, the Initiate, knew this, and meant this precisely, when he is made to say in bad translation, "I travail in birth again until Christ be formed in you" (Gal. iv., 19), the true rendering of which is, " . . . . until you form the Christos within yourselves." But the profane, who knew only that Chrestos was in some way connected with priest and prophet, and knew nothing about the hidden meaning of Christos, insisted, as did Lactantius and Justyn Martyr, on being called Chrestians instead of Christians. Every good individual, therefore, may find Christ in his "inner man," as Paul expresses it, (Ephes. iii., 16, 17) whether he be Jew, Mussulman, Hindu or Christian.

Christ (see CHRESTOS).

Christian Scientist. A newly-coined term for denoting the practitioners of a healing art by will. The name is a misnomer, since Buddhist or Jew, Hindu or Materialist can practise this new form of Western Yoga with like success if he can only guide and control his will with sufficient firmness. "Mental Scientists" is another rival school. These work by a universal denial of every disease and evil imaginable, and claim, syllogistically, that since Universal Spirit cannot be subject to the ailings of flesh, and since every atom is Spirit and in Spirit, and since, finally, they - the healers and the healed - are all absorbed in this Spirit or Deity, there is not, nor can there be, such a thing as disease. This prevents in nowise both Christian and Mental Scientists from succumbing to disease and nursing chronic diseases for years in their own bodies just like other ordinary mortals.

Clairaudience. The faculty - whether innate or acquired by occult training - to hear things at whatever distance.

Clairvoyance. A faculty of seeing with the inner eye or spiritual sight. As now used, it is a loose and flippant term, embracing under its meaning both a happy guess due to natural shrewdness or intuition, and also that faculty which was so remarkably exercised by Jacob Boehme and Swedenborg. Yet even these two great seers, since they could never rise superior to the general spirit of the Jewish Bible and Sectarian teachings, have sadly confused what they saw, and fallen far short of true clairvoyance.

Clemens Alexandrinus. A Church Father and voluminous writer, who had been a Neo-Platonist and a disciple of Ammonius Saccas. He was one of the few Christian philosophers between the second and third centuries of our era, at Alexandria. College of Rabbis. A college at Babylon; most famous during the early centuries of Christianity, but its glory was greatly darkened by the appearance in Alexandria of Hellenic teachers, such as Philo-Judaeus, Josephus, Aristobulus and others. The former avenged themselves on their successful rivals by speaking of the Alexandrians as Theurgists and unclean prophets. But the Alexandrian believers in thaumaturgy were not regarded as sinners and impostors when orthodox Jews were at the head of such schools of "hazim." There were colleges for teaching prophecy and occult sciences. Samuel was the chief of such a college at Ramah; Elisha, at Jericho. Hillel had a regular academy for prophets and seers; and it is Hillel, a pupil of the Babylonian College, who was the founder of the sect of the Pharisees and the great orthodox Rabbis. Cycle (Gr.) KUKLOS. The ancients divided time into endless cycles, wheels within wheels, all such periods being of various durations, and each marking the beginning or end of some event either cosmic, mundane, physical or metaphysical. There were cycles of only a few years, and cycles of immense duration, the great Orphic cycle referring to the ethnological change of races lasting 120,000 years, and that of Cassandrus of 136,000, which brought about a complete change in planetary influences and their correlations between men and gods - a fact entirely lost sight of by modern astrologers.

D

Deist. One who admits the possibility of the existence of a God or gods, but claims to know nothing of either, and denies revelation. An agnostic of olden times.

Deva (Sans.) A god, a "resplendent" Deity, Deva-Deus, from the root div, "to shine." A Deva is a celestial being - whether good, bad or indifferent - which inhabits "the three worlds," or the three planes above us. There are 33 groups or millions of them.

Devachan (Sans.) The "Dwelling of the Gods." A state intermediate between two earth-lives, and into which the Ego (Atma-Buddhi-Manas, or the Trinity made one) enters after its separation from Kama Rupa, and the disintegration of the lower principles, after the death of the body, on Earth. Dhammapada (Sans.) A work containing various aphorisms from the Buddhist Scriptures.

Dhyana (Sans.) One of the six Paramitas of perfection. A state of abstraction which carries the ascetic practising it far above the region of sensuous perception, and out of the world of matter. Lit., "contemplation." The six stages of Dhyan differ only in the degrees of abstraction of the personal Ego from sensuous life.

Dhyan Chohans (Sans.) Lit., "The Lords of Light." The highest gods, answering to the Roman Catholic Archangels. The divine Intelligences charged with the supervision of Kosmos.

Double. The same as the Astral body or "Doppelganger."

E

Ecstasis (Gr.) A psycho-spiritual state; a physical trance which induces clairvoyance, and a beatific state which brings on visions.

Ego (Lat.) "I"; the consciousness in man of the "I am I," or the feeling of I-am-ship. Esoteric philosophy teaches the existence of two Egos in man, the mortal or personal, and the higher, the divine or impersonal, calling the former "personality," and the latter "individuality." Egoity (from the word "Ego"). Egoity means "individuality" - indifferent - never "personality," as it is the opposite of Egoism or "selfishness," the characteristic par excellence of the latter.

Eidolon (Gr.) The same as that which we term the human phantom, the Astral form.

Elementals, or Spirits of the Elements. The creatures evolved in the Four Kingdoms, or Elements - Earth, Air, Fire, and Water. They are called by the Kabalists, Gnomes (of the Earth), Sylphs (of the Air), Salamanders (of the Fire), and Undines (of the Water), except a few of the higher kinds and their rulers. They are rather the forces of nature than ethereal men and women. These forces, as the servile agents of the occultist, may produce various effects; but if employed by elementaries (Kamarupas)- in which case they enslave the mediums - they will deceive. All the lower invisible beings generated on the fifth, sixth, and seventh Planes of our terrestrial atmosphere are called Elementals - Peris, Devs, Djins, Sylvans, Satyrs, Fauns, Elves, Dwarfs, Trolls, Norns, Kobolds, Brownies, Nixies, Goblins, Pinkies, Banshees, Moss People, White Ladies, Spooks, Fairies, etc., etc.

Eleusinia (Gr.) The Eleusinian Mysteries were the most famous and the most ancient of all the Greek mysteries (save the Samothracian), and were performed near the hamlet of Eleusis, not far from Athens. Epiphanius traces them to the days of Iacchos (1800 B. C.) They were held in honour of Demeter, the great Ceres, and the Egyptian Isis; and the last act of the performance referred to a sacrificial victim of atonement and a resurrection, when the Initiate was admitted to the highest degree of Epopt. The festival of the Mysteries began in the month of Boedromion (September), the time of grape-gathering, and lasted from the 15th to the 22nd - seven days. The Hebrew Feast of Tabernacles - the feast of ingatherings - in the month of Ethanim (the seventh) also began on the 15th and ended on the 22nd of that month. The name of the month (Ethanim) is derived, according to some, from Adonim, Adonia, Attenim, Ethanim, and was in bonour of Adonai, or Adonis (Tham), whose death was lamented by the Hebrews in the groves of Bethlehem. The sacrifice of "Bread and Wine" was performed both in the Eleusinia and during the Feast of Tabernacles. Emanation (The doctrine of) is in its metaphysical meaning opposed to evolution, yet one with it. Science teaches that, physiologically, evolution is a mode of generation in which the germ that develops the foetus pre-exists already in the parent, the development and final form and characteristics of that germ being accomplished by nature; and that (as in its cosmology) the process takes place blindly, through the correlation of the elements and their various compounds. Occultism teaches that this is only the apparent mode, the real process being Emanation, guided by intelligent forces under an immutable LAW. Therefore, while the Occultists and Theosophists believe thoroughly in the doctrine of Evolution as given out by Kapila and Manu, they are Emanationists rather than Evolutionists. The doctrine of Emanation was at one time universal. It was taught by the Alexandrian, as well as by the Indian philosophers, by the Egyptian, the Chaldean, and Hellenic Hierophants, and also by the Hebrews (in their Kabala, and even in Genesis). For it is only owing to deliberate mistranslation that the Hebrew word asdt was translated "angels" from the Septuagint, while it means Emanations, AEons, just as with the Gnostics. Indeed, in Deuteronomy (xxxiii. 2) the word asdt or ashdt is translated as "fiery law," whilst the correct rendering of the passage should be, "from his right went (not a fiery law, but) a fire according to law," viz., that the fire of one flame is imparted to and caught up by another - like as in a trail of inflammable substance. This is precisely Emanation, as shown in *Isis Unveiled*. "In Evolution, as it is now beginning to be understood, there is supposed to be in all matter an impulse to take on a higher form - a supposition clearly expressed by Manu and other Hindoo philosophers of the highest antiquity. The philosopher's tree illustrates it in the case of the zinc solution. The controversy between the followers of this school and the Emanationists may be briefly stated thus: The Evolutionist stops all inquiry at the borders of 'the unknowable'; the Emanationist believes that nothing can be evolved - or, as the word means, unwombed or born - except it has first been involved, thus indicating that life is from a spiritual potency above the whole." Esoteric. Hidden, secret. From the Greek Esotericos - "inner," concealed. Esoteric Bodhism. Secret wisdom or intelligence, from the Greek Esotericos, "inner," and the Sanskrit Bodhi, "knowledge," in contradistinction to Buddhi, "the faculty of knowledge or intelligence," and Buddhism, the philosophy or Law of Buddha (the Enlightened). Also written "Budhism," from Budha (Intelligence, Wisdom) the Son of Soma.

Exoteric (Gr.) Outward, public; the opposite of esoteric or hidden. Extra-Cosmic, i. e., outside of Kosmos or Nature. A nonsensical word invented to assert the existence of a personal god independent of or outside Nature per se; for as Nature, or the Universe, is infinite and limitless there can be nothing outside it. The term is coined in opposition to the Pantheistic idea that the whole Kosmos is animated or informed with the Spirit of Deity, Nature being but the garment, and matter the illusive shadows, of the real unseen Presence. Eurasians. An abbreviation of "European-Asians." The mixed coloured races; the children of the white fathers, and the dark mothers of India, and vice versa.

F

Ferho (Gnostic). The highest and greatest creative power with the Nazarene Gnostics (Codex Nazaraeus).

Fire-Philosophers. The name given to the Hermetists and Alchemists of the Middle Ages, and also to the Rosicrucians. The latter, the successors of Theurgists, regarded fire as the symbol of Deity. It was the source, not only of material atoms, but the container of the Spiritual and Psychic Forces energising them. Broadly analysed, Fire is a triple principle; esoterically, a septenary, as are all the rest of the elements. As man is composed of Spirit, Soul, and Body, plus a four-fold aspect; so is Fire. As in the works of Robert Flood (de Fluctibus), one of the famous Rosicrucians, fire contains - Firstly, a visible flame (body); secondly, an invisible, astral fire (soul); and thirdly, spirit. The four aspects are (a) heat (life), (b) light (mind), (c) electricity (Kamic or molecular powers, and (d) the synthetic essences, beyond spirit, or the radical cause of its existence and manifestation. For the Hermetist or Rosicrucian, when a flame is extinct on the objective plane, it has only passed from the seen world into the unseen; from the knowable into the unknowable.

G

Gautama (Sans.) A name in India. It is that of the Prince of Kapilavastu, son of Sudhodana, the Sakhya King of a small territory on the borders of Nepaul, born in the seventh century B. C., now called the "Saviour of the world." Gautama or Gotama was the sacerdotal name of the Sakya family. Born a simple mortal, he rose to Buddha-ship through his own personal and unaided merit; a man - verily greater than any God!

Gebirol. Salomon Ben Jehudah, called in literature Avicebron. An Israelite by birth, a philosopher, poet and kabalist; a voluminous writer and a mystic. He was born in the eleventh century at Malaga (1021), educated at Saragossa, and died at Valencia in 1070, murdered by a Mahomedan. His fellow-religionists called him Salomon, the Sephardi, or the Spaniard, and the Arabs, Abu Ayyub Suleiman-ben ya'hya Ibn Dgebirol, whilst the

Scholastics named him Avicebron (see Myers' Quabbalah). Ibn Gebirol was certainly one of the greatest philosophers and scholars of his age. He wrote much in Arabic, and most of his MSS have been preserved. His greatest work appears to be The Megoy Hayyim, i. e., The Fountain of Life, "one of the earliest exposures of the secrets of the Speculative Kabbalah," as his biographer informs us. Gnosis (Gr.) Lit. "knowledge." The technical term used by the schools of religious philosophy, both before and during the first centuries of so-called Christianity, to denote the object of their enquiry. This spiritual and sacred knowledge, the Gupta Vidya of the Hindus, could only be obtained by Initiation into Spiritual Mysteries of which the ceremonial "Mysteries" were a type. Gnostics (Gr.) The philosophers who formulated and taught the "Gnosis" or knowledge. They flourished in the first three centuries of the Christian Era. The following were eminent: Valentinus, Basilides, Marcion, Simon Magus, etc. Golden Age. The ancients divided the life cycle into the Golden, Silver, Bronze and Iron Ages. The Golden was an age of primeval purity, simplicity and general happiness.

Great Age. There were several "Great Ages" mentioned by the ancients. In India it embraced the whole Maha-Manvantara, the "Age of Brahma," each "Day" of which represents the Life Cycle of a chain, i. e., it embraces a period of Seven Rounds (vide "*Esoteric Buddhism*," by A. P. Sinnett). Thus while a "Day" and a "Night" represent, as Manvantara and Pralaya, 8,640,000,000 years, an "age" lasts through a period of 311,040,000,000,000; after which the Pralaya or dissolution of the universe becomes universal. With the Egyptian and Greeks the "Great Age" referred only to the Tropical, or Sidereal year, the duration of which is 25,868 solar years. Of the complete age - that of the Gods - they said nothing, as it was a matter to be discussed and divulged only at the Mysteries, and during the Initiation Ceremonies. The "Great Age" of the Chaldees was the same in figures as that of the Hindus. Guhya Vidya (Sans.) The secret knowledge of mystic-mantras. Gupta Vidya (Sans.) The same as Guhya Vidya. Esoteric or secret science, knowledge.

Gyges. "The ring of Gyges" has become a familiar metaphor in European literature. Gyges was a Lydian, who, after murdering the King Candaules, married his widow. Plato tells us that Gyges descending once into a chasm of the earth, discovered a brazen horse, within whose opened side was the skeleton of a man of gigantic stature, who had a brazen ring on his finger. This ring when placed on his own finger made him invisible.

H

Hades (Gr.), or Aides, the "invisible," the land of shadows; one of whose regions was Tartarus, a place of complete darkness, as was also the region of profound dreamless sleep in Amenti. Judging by the allegorical description of the punishments inflicted therein, the place was purely Karmic. Neither Hades nor Amenti were the Hell still preached by some retrograde priests and clergymen; and whether represented by the Elysian Fields or by Tartarus, they could only be reached by crossing the river to the "other shore." As well expressed in the "Egyptian Belief," the story of Charon, the ferryman (of the Styx) is to be found not only in Homer, but in the poetry of many lands. The River must be crossed before gaining the Isles of the Blest. The Ritual of Egypt described a Charon and his boat long ages before Homer. He is Khu-en-na, "the hawk-headed steersman." (See Hell.)

Hallucinations. A state produced sometimes by physiological disorders, sometimes by mediumship, and at others by drunkenness. But the cause that produces the visions has to be sought deeper than physiology. All such, particularly when produced through mediumship, are preceded by a relaxation of the nervous system, generating invariably an abnormal magnetic condition which attracts to the sufferer waves of astral light. It is these latter that furnish the various hallucinations, which, however, are not always, as physicians would explain them, mere empty and unreal dreams. No one can see that which does not exist - i.e., which is not impressed - in or on the astral waves. But a seer may perceive objects and scenes (whether past, present or future) which have no relation whatever to himself; and perceive, moreover, several things entirely disconnected with each other at one and the same time, so as to produce the most grotesque and absurd combinations. But drunkard and seer, medium and adept see their respective visions in the astral light; only while the drunkard, the madman, and the untrained medium, or one in a brain fever, see, because they cannot help it, and evoke jumbled visions unconsciously to themselves without being able to control them, the adept and the trained Seer have the choice and the control of such visions. They know where to fix their gaze, how to steady the scenes they wish to observe, and how to see beyond the upper outward layers of the astral light. With the former such glimpses into the waves are hallucinations; with the latter they become the faithful reproduction of what actually has been, is, or will be taking place. The glimpses at random, caught by the medium, and his flickering visions in the deceptive light, are transformed under the guiding will of the adept and seer into steady pictures, the truthful representation of that which he wills to come within the focus of his perception.

Hell. A term which the Anglo-Saxon race has evidently derived from the name of the Scandinavian goddess, Hela, just as the word ad, in Russian and other Slavonian tongues expressing the same conception, is derived from the Greek Hades, the only difference between the Scandinavian cold Hell, and the hot Hell of the Christians, being found in their respective temperatures. But even the idea of these overheated regions is not original with the Europeans, many people having entertained the conception of an under-world climate; as well we may, if we localise our Hell in the centre of the earth. All exoteric religions - the creeds of the Brahmans, Buddhists, Zoroastrians, Mahomedans, Jews, and the rest, made their Hells hot and dark, though many were more attractive than frightful. The idea of a hot Hell is an afterthought, the distortion of an astronomical allegory. With the Egyptians Hell became a place of punishment by fire not earlier than the 17th or 18th Dynasty, when Typhon was transformed from a God into a Devil. But at whatever time they implanted this dread superstition in the minds of the poor ignorant masses, the scheme of a burning Hell and souls tormented therein is purely Egyptian. Ra (the Sun) became the Lord of the Furnace, in Karr, the Hell of the Pharaohs, and the sinner was threatened with misery "in the heat of infernal fires." "A lion was there," says Dr. Birch, "and was called the roaring monster." Another describes the place as "the bottomless pit and lake of fire, into which the victims are thrown" (compare Revelation). The Hebrew word gai-hinnom (gehena) had never really the significance given to it in Christian orthodoxy.

Hermas, an ancient Greek writer, of whose works only a few fragments now remain extant.

Hierogrammatists (Gr.) The title given to those Egyptian priests who were entrusted with the writing and reading of the sacred and secret records. The "scribes of the secret records" literally. They were the instructors of the neophytes preparing for initiation.

Hierophant. From the Greek Hierophantes, literally "he who explains sacred things"; a title belonging to the highest adepts in the temples of antiquity, who were the teachers and expounders of the Mysteries, and the Initiators into the final great Mysteries. The Hierophant stood for the Demiurge, and explained to the postulants for Initiation the various phenomena of creation that were produced for their tuition. "He was the sole expounder of the exoteric secrets and doctrines. It was forbidden even to pronounce his name before an uninitiated person. He sat in the East, and wore as symbol of authority, a golden globe, suspended from the neck. He was also called Mystagogus." (Kenneth R. H. Mackenzie, IX., F. T. S., in The Royal Masonic Cyclopoedia.) Hillel. A great Babylonian Rabbi of the century preceding the Christian Era. He was the founder of the sect of the Pharisees, a learned and a saintly man. Hinayana (Sans.) The "Smaller Vehicle"; a Scripture and a School of the Buddhists, contrasted with the Mahayana, "The Greater Vehicle." Both schools are mystical. (See Mahayana.) Also in exoteric superstition, the lowest form of transmigration.

Homogeneity. From the Greek words homos, "the same"; and genos, "kind." That which is of the same nature throughout, undifferentiated, non-compound, as gold is supposed to be.

Hypnotism (Gr.) A name given by Dr. Braid to the process by which one man of strong will-power plunges another of weaker mind into a kind of trance; once in such a state the latter will do anything suggested to him by the hypnotiser. Unless produced for beneficial purposes, the Occultists would call it black magic or sorcery. It is the most dangerous of practices, morally and physically, as it interferes with the nerve fluids.

I

Iamblichus. A great Theosophist and an Initiate of the third century. He wrote a great deal about the various kinds of demons who appear through evocation, but spoke severely against such phenomena. His austerities, purity of life and earnestness were great. He is credited with having been levitated ten cubits high from the ground, as are some modern Yogis, and mediums. Illusion. In Occultism everything finite (such as the Universe and all in it) is called Illusion or Maya.

Individuality. One of the names given in Theosophy and Occultism to the human Higher Ego. We make a distinction between the immortal and divine and the mortal human Ego which perishes. The latter or "Personality" (personal Ego) survives the dead body but for a time in Kama Loka: the Individuality prevails for ever. Initiate. From the Latin Initiatus. The designation of anyone who was received into and had revealed to him the mysteries and secrets of either Masonry or Occultism. In times of antiquity they were those who had been initiated into the arcane knowledge taught by the Hierophants of the Mysteries; and in our modern days those who have been initiated by the adepts of mystic lore into the mysterious knowledge, which, notwithstanding the lapse of ages, has yet a few real votaries on earth.

Iswara (Sans.) The "Lord" or the personal god, divine spirit in man. Literally Sovereign (independent) existence. A title given to Siva and other gods in India. Siva is also called Iswaradeva, or sovereign deva. Iu-Kabar Zivo, Gnostic term. The "Lord of the AEons" in the Nazarene system. He is the procreator (Emanator) of the seven holy lives (the seven primal Dhyan Chohans or Archangels, each representing one of the cardinal virtues), and is himself called the third life (third Logos). In the Codex he is addressed as the Helm and Vine of the food of life. Thus he is identical with Christ (Christos) who says: "I am the true vine and my Father is the husbandman." (John xv. 1.) It is well known that Christ is regarded in the Roman Catholic Church as the "Chief of the AEons," as also is Michael, "who is as God." Such also was the belief of the Gnostics.

J

Javidan Khirad (Pers.) A work on moral precepts.

Jhana (Sans.) or **Jnana**, Knowledge: Occult Wisdom. Josephus Flavius. A historian of the first century; a Hellenized Jew who lived in Alexandria and died at Rome. He was credited by Eusebius with having written the 16 famous lines relating to Christ, which were most probably interpolated by Eusebius himself, the greatest forger among the Church Fathers. This passage, in which Josephus, who was an ardent Jew and died in Judaism, is nevertheless made to acknowledge the Messiaship and divine origin of Jesus, is now declared spurious both by most of the Christian Bishops (Lardner among others) and even by Paley (see his Evidence of Christianity). It was for centuries one of the weightiest proofs of the real existence of Jesus, the Christ.

K

Kabbalah (Heb.), or **Kabbala**. "The hidden wisdom of the Hebrew Rabbis of the middle ages derived from the older secret doctrines concerning divine things and cosmogony, which were combined into a theology after the time of the captivity of the Jews in Babylon." All the works that fall under the esoteric category are termed Kabalistic.

Kamaloka (Sans.) The semi-material plane, to us subjective and invisible, where the disembodied "personalities," the astral forms called Kama Rupa, remain until they fade out from it by the complete exhaustion of the effects of the mental impulses that created these eidolons of the lower animal passions and desires. (See Kama Rupa.) It is the Hades of the ancient Greeks and the Amenti of the Egyptians - the land of Silent Shadows.

Kama Rupa (Sans.) Metaphysically and in our esoteric philosophy it is the subjective form created through the mental and physical desires and thoughts in connection with things of matter, by all sentient beings: a form which survives the death of its body. After that death, three of the seven "principles" - or, let us say, planes of the senses and consciousness on which the human instincts and ideation act in turn - viz., the body, its astral prototype and physical vitality, being of no further use, remain on earth; the three higher principles, grouped into one, merge into a state of Devachan (q. v.), in which state the Higher Ego will remain until the hour for a new reincarnation arrives, and the eidolon of the ex-personality is left alone in its new abode. Here the pale copy of the man that was, vegetates for a period of time, the duration of which is variable according to the element of materiality which is left in it, and which is determined by the past life of the defunct. Bereft as it is of its higher mind, spirit and physical senses, if left alone to its own senseless devices, it will gradually fade out and disintegrate. But if forcibly drawn back into the terrestrial sphere, whether by the passionate desires and appeals of the surviving friends or by regular necromantic practices - one of the most pernicious of which is mediumship - the "spook" may prevail for a period greatly exceeding the span of the natural life of its body. Once the Kama Rupa has learnt the way back to living human bodies, it becomes a vampire feeding on the vitality of those who are so anxious for its company. In India these Eidolons are called Pisachas, - and are much dreaded. Kapilavastu (Sans.) The birthplace of the Lord Buddha, called the "yellow dwelling," the capital of the monarch who was the father of Gautama Buddha. Kardec, Allan. The adopted name of the Founder of the French Spiritists, whose real name was Rivaille. It was he who gathered and published the trance utterances of certain mediums and afterwards made a "philosophy" of them between the years 1855 and 1870.

Karma (Sans.) Physically, action; Metaphysically, the LAW of RETRIBUTION; the Law of Cause and Effect or Ethical Causation. It is Nemesis only in the sense of bad

Karma. It is the eleventh Nidana in the concatenation of causes and effects in orthodox Buddhism; yet it is the power that controls all things, the resultant of moral action, the metaphysical Samskara, or the moral effect of an act committed for the attainment of something which gratifies a personal desire.

There is the Karma of merit and the Karma of demerit. Karma neither punishes nor rewards; it is simply the one Universal LAW which guides unerringly and, so to say, blindly, all other laws productive of certain effects along the grooves of their respective causations. When Buddhism teaches that "Karma is that moral Kernel (of any being) which alone survives death and continues in transmigration" or reincarnation, it simply means that there remains nought after each personality, but the causes produced by it, causes which are undying, i.e., which cannot be eliminated from the Universe until replaced by their legitimate effects, and so to speak, wiped out by them. And such causes, unless compensated during the life of the person who produced them with adequate effects, will follow the reincarnated Ego and reach it in its subsequent incarnations until a full harmony between effects and causes is fully re-established. No "personality" - a mere bundle of material atoms and instinctual and mental characteristics - can, of course, continue as such in the world of pure spirit. Only that which is immortal in its very nature and divine in its essence, namely, the Ego, can exist for ever. And as it is that Ego which chooses the personality it will inform after each Devachan, and which receives through these personalities the effects of the Karmic causes produced, it is, therefore, the Ego, that Self, which is the "moral Kernel" referred to, and embodied Karma itself, that "which alone survives death." Kether (Heb.) "The Crown, the highest of the ten Sephiroth; the first of the supernal Triad. It corresponds to the Macroprosopus, Vast Countenance, or Arikh Anpin, which differentiates into Chokmah and Binah." Krishna (Sans.) The most celebrated Avatar of Vishnu, the "Saviour" of the Hindus and the most popular god. He is the eighth Avatar, the son of Devaki, and the nephew of Kansa, the Indian Herod, who while seeking for him among the shepherds and cowherds who concealed him slew thousands of their newly-born babes. The story of Krishna's conception, birth and childhood are the exact prototype of the New Testament story. The missionaries, of course, try to show that the Hindus stole the story of the Nativity from the early Christians who came to India.

Kshetragna, or Kshetragneswara (Sans.)Embodied Spirit in Occultism, the conscious Ego in its highest manifestations; the reincarnating Principle, or the "Lord" in us.

Kumara (Sans.) A virgin boy or young celibate. The first Kumaras are the seven sons of Brahma, born out of the limbs of the god in the so-called Ninth Creation. It is stated that the name was given to them owing to their formal refusal to "procreate" their species, and thus they "remained Yogis" according to the legend.

L

Labro, St. A Roman Saint solemnly beatified a few years ago. His great holiness consisted in sitting at one of the gates of Rome night and day for forty years, and remaining unwashed through the whole of that time, the result of which was that he was eaten by vermin to his bones.

Lao-Tze (Chin.) A great Sage, Saint, and Philosopher, who preceded Confucius.

Law of Retribution (vide Karma).

Linga Sharira (Sans.) "Astral body," i. e., the aerial symbol of the body. This term designates the doppelganger, or the "astral body" of man or animal. It is the eidolon of the Greeks, the vital and prototypal body, the reflection of the man of flesh. It is born before man and dies or fades out with the disappearance of the last atom of the body.

Logos (Gr.) The manifested deity with every nation and people; the outward expression or the effect of the Cause which is ever concealed. Thus, speech is the logos of thought; hence, in its metaphysical sense, it is aptly translated by the terms "Verbum," and the "Word."

Long Face. A Kabalistic term, Areekh Anpeen in Hebrew; or "Long Face"; in Greek, Macroprosopos, as contrasted with "Short Face," or Zeir Anpeen, the Microprosopos. One relates to Deity, the other to man, the "little image of the great form."

Longinus, Dionysius Cassius. A famous critic and philosopher, born in the very beginning of the third century (about 213). He was a great traveller, and attended at Alexandria the lectures of Ammonius Saccas, the founder of Neoplatonism, but was rather a critic than a follower. Porphyry (the Jew Malek or Malchus) was his pupil before he became the disciple of Plotinus. It is said of him that he was a living library and a walking museum. Towards the end of his life he became the instructor in Greek literature of Zenobia, Queen of Palmyra. She repaid his services by accusing him before the Emperor Aurelius of having advised her to rebel against the latter, a crime for which Longinus, with several others, was put to death by the Emperor in 273.

M

Macrocosm (Gr.) The "Great Universe" or Kosmos, literally. Magic. The "great" Science. According to Deveria and other Orientalists, "Magic was considered as a sacred science inseparable from religion" by the oldest and most civilised and learned nations. The Egyptians, for instance, were a most sincerely religious nation, as were, and are still, the Hindus. "Magic consists of, and is acquired by, the worship of the gods," says Plato. Could, then, a nation which, owing to the irrefragable evidence of inscriptions and papyri, is proved to have firmly believed in magic for thousands of years, have been deceived for so long a time? And is it likely that generations upon generations of a learned and pious hierarchy, many among whom led lives of self-martyrdom, holiness and asceticism, would have gone on deceiving themselves and the people (or even only the latter) for the pleasure of perpetuating belief in "miracles"? Fanatics, we are told, will do anything to enforce belief in their god or idols. To this we reply: - In such cases Brahmans and Egyptian Rekhget-amens or Hierophants, would not have popularised the belief in the power of man by magic practices, to command the services of the gods: which gods are in truth but the occult powers or potencies of Nature, personified by the learned priests themselves, who reverenced only in them the attributes of the one unknown and nameless Principle. As Proclus, the Platonist, ably puts it: "Ancient priests, when they considered that there is a certain alliance and sympathy in natural things to each other, and of things manifest to occult powers, and discovered that all things subsist in all, fabricated a sacred science from this mutual sympathy and similarity. . . . and applied for occult purposes both celestial and terrene natures, by means of which, through a certain similitude, they deduced divine natures into this inferior abode." Magic is the science of communicating with, and directing supernal supramundane potencies, as well as commanding those of lower spheres; a practical knowledge of the hidden mysteries of nature which are known only to the few, because they are so difficult to acquire without falling into sin against the law. Ancient and mediaeval mystics divided magic into three classes - Theurgia, Goetia and Natural Magic. "Theurgia has long since been appropriated as the peculiar sphere of the Theosophists and metaphysicians," says Kenneth Mackenzie. "Goetia is black magic, and 'natural' or white magic has risen with healing in its wings to the proud position of an exact and progressive study." The remarks added by our late learned brother are remarkable: "The realistic desires of modern times have contributed to bring magic into disrepute and ridicule. . . . Faith (in one's own self) is an essential element in magic, and existed long before other ideas which presume its pre-existence. It is said that it takes a wise man to make a fool; and a man's idea must be exalted almost to madness, i. e., his brain susceptibilities must be increased far beyond the low miserable status of modern civilisation, before he can become a true magician, for a pursuit of this science implies a certain amount of isolation and an abnegation of self." A very great isolation certainly, the achievement of which constitutes a wonderful phenomenon, a miracle in itself. Withal, magic is not something supernatural. As explained by Iamblichus, "they, through the sacerdotal theurgy, announce that they are able to ascend to more elevated and universal essences, and to those that are established above fate, viz., to god and the demiurgos: neither employing matter, nor assuming any other things besides, except the observation of a sensible time." Already some are beginning to recognise the existence of subtle powers and influences in nature, in which they have hitherto known nought. But, as Dr. Carter Blake truly remarks, "the nineteenth century is not that which has observed the genesis of new, nor the completion of old, methods of thought"; to which Mr. Bonwick adds, that "if the Ancients knew but little of our mode of investigation into the secrets of Nature, we know still less of their mode of research."

Magic, Black (vide supra). Sorcery, abuse of powers. Magic, Ceremonial. Magic, according to Kabalistic rites worked out, as alleged by the Rosicrucians and other mystics, by invoking Powers higher spiritually than Man, and commanding Elementals who are far lower than himself on the scale of being.

Magic, White, or "Beneficent Magic," so called, is divine magic, devoid of selfishness, love of power, of ambition or lucre, and bent only on doing good to the world in general and one's neighbour in particular. The smallest attempt to use one's abnormal powers for the gratification of self makes of these powers sorcery or Black Magic.

Mahamanvantara (Sans.) Lit., the great interludes between the Manus - the period of universal activity. Manvantara here implies simply a period of activity as opposed to Pralaya or rest - without reference to the length of the cycle.

Mahat (Sans.) Lit. "The Great One." The first principle of Universal Intelligence and consciousness. In the Puranic philosophy, the first product of root-nature or Pradhana (the same as Mulaprakriti); the producer of Manas the thinking principle, and of Ahankara, Egotism or the feeling of "I am I" in the lower Manas.

Mahatma (Sans.) Lit., "Great Soul." An adept of the highest order. An exalted being, who having attained to the mastery over his lower principles, is therefore living unimpeded by the "man of flesh." Mahatmas are in possession of knowledge and power commensurate with the stage they have reached in their spiritual evolution. Called in Pali Rahats and Arthas. Mahayana (Sans.) A school of Buddhistic philosophy; lit., the "Great Vehicle." A mystical system founded by Nagarjuna. Its books were written in the second century B. C.

Manas (Sans.) Lit., the "Mind." The mental faculty which makes of a man an intelligent and moral being, and distinguishes him from the mere animal; a synonym of Mahat. Esoterically, however, it means, when unqualified, the Higher Ego or the sentient reincarnating Principle in man. When qualified it is called by Theosophists Buddhi-Manas, or the spiritual soul, in contradistinction to its human reflection - Kama-Manas.

Manasaputra (Sans.) Lit., the "Sons of Mind" or mind-born Sons; a name given to our Higher Egos before they incarnated in mankind. In the exoteric though allegorical and symbolical Puranas (the sacred and ancient writings of Hindus), it is the title given to the mind-born Sons of Brahma, the Kumara. Manas Sutratma (Sans.) Two words meaning "mind" (Manas) and "Thread Soul" (Sutratma). It is, as said, the synonym of our Ego, or that which reincarnates. It is a technical term of Vedantic philosophy. Manas Taijasi(Sans.) Lit., the "radiant" Manas; a state of the Higher Ego which only high metaphysicians are able to realize and comprehend. The same as "Buddhi Taijasi," which see.

Mantras (Sans.) Verses from the Vedic works, used as incantations and charms. By Mantras are meant all those portions of the Vedas which are distinct from the Brahmanas, or their interpretation.

Manu (Sans.) The great Indian legislator. The name comes from the Sanskrit root man to think, MAN really standing only for Swayambhuva, the first of the Manus, who started from Swayambhu, the Self-Existent, who is hence the Logos and the progenitor of mankind. Manu is the first legislator - almost a divine being. Manvantara (Sans.) A period of manifestation, as opposed to Pralaya (dissolution or rest); the term is applied to various cycles, especially to a Day of Brahma - 4,320,000,000 Solar years - and to the reign of one Manu - 308,448,000. Lit., Manuantara - "between Manus." (See Secret Doctrine, Vol. 11, p. 68, et seq.)

Master. A translation from the Sanskrit Guru, "Spiritual teacher," and adopted by the Theosophists to designate the Adepts, from whom they hold their teachings.

Materialisations. In Spiritualism the word signifies the objective appearance of the so-called "spirits of the dead," who re-clothe themselves occasionally in matter; i. e., they form for themselves out of the materials at hand found in the atmosphere and the emanations of those present, a temporary body bearing the human likeness of the defunct, as he appeared when alive. Theosophists accept the phenomenon of "materialisation," but they reject the theory that it is produced by "Spirits," i. e., the immortal principles of disembodied persons. Theosophists hold that when the phenomena are genuine - which is a fact of rarer occurrence than is generally believed - they are produced by the larvae, the eidolons, or Kamalokic "ghosts" of the dead personalities. (See "Kamaloka" and "Kamarupa.") As Kamaloka is on the earth-plane and differs from its degree of materiality only in the degree of its plane of consciousness, for which reason it is concealed from our normal sight, the occasional apparition of such shells is as natural as that of electric balls and other atmospheric phenomena. Electricity as a fluid, or atomic matter (for Occultists hold with Maxwell that it is atomic), is ever, though invisibly, present in the air and manifests under various shapes, but only when certain conditions are present to "materialise" the fluid, when it passes from its own on to our plane and makes itself objective. Similarly with the eidolons of the dead. They are present around us, but being on another plane do not see us any more than we see them. But whenever the strong desires of living men and the conditions furnished by the abnormal constitutions of mediums are combined together, these eidolons are drawn - nay pulled down from their plane on to ours and made objective. This is necromancy; it does no good to the dead, and great harm to the living, in addition to the fact that it interferes with a law of nature. The occasional materialisation of the "astral bodies" or doubles of living persons is quite another matter. These "astrals" are often mistaken for the apparitions of the dead, since, chameleon-like, our own "elementaries" along with those of the disembodied and cosmic Elementals, will often assume the appearance of those images which are strongest in our thoughts. In short, at the so-called "materialisation seances," it is those present and the medium who create the peculiar apparition. Independent "apparitions" belong to another kind of psychic phenomena. Materialist. Not necessarily only one who believes in neither God nor soul, nor the survival of the latter, but also any person who materializes the purely spiritual; such as believe in an anthropomorphic deity, in a soul capable of burning in hell fire, and a hell and paradise as localities instead of states of consciousness. American "Substantialists," a Christian sect, are materialists, as also the so-called Spiritualists.

Maya (Sans.) Illusion; the cosmic power which renders phenomenal existence and the perceptions thereof possible. In Hindu philosophy that alone which is changeless and eternal is called reality: all that which is subject to change through decay and differentiation, and which has, therefore, a beginning and an end, is regarded as MAYA - illusion.

Mediumship. A word now accepted to indicate that abnormal psycho-physiological state which leads a person to take the fancies of his imagination, his hallucinations, real or artificial, for realities. No entirely healthy person on the physiological and psychic planes can ever be a medium. That which mediums see, hear, and sense, is "real" but untrue; it is either gathered from the astral plane, so deceptive in its vibrations and suggestions, or from pure hallucinations, which have no actual existence, but for him who perceives them. "Mediumship" is a kind of vulgarised mediatorship in which one afflicted with this faculty is supposed to become an agent of communication between a living man and a departed "Spirit." There exist regular methods of training for the development of this undesirable acquirement.

Mercavah, or Mercabah (Heb.) "A chariot. The Kabbalists say that the Supreme, after he had established the ten Sephiroth - which, in their totality, are Adam Kadmon, the Archetypal Man, used them as a chariot or throne of glory in which to descend upon the souls of men."

Mesmerism. The term comes from Mesmer, who rediscovered this magnetic force and its practical application toward the year 1775, at Vienna. It is a vital current that one person may transfer to another; and through which he induces an abnormal state of the nervous system that permits him to have a direct influence upon the mind and will of the subject or mesmerized person. Metaphysics. From the Greek meta, beyond, and physica, the things of the external material world. It is to forget the spirit and hold to the dead letter, to translate it beyond nature or supernatural, as it is rather beyond the natural, visible, or concrete. Metaphysics, in ontology and philosophy is the term to designate that science which treats of the real and permanent being as contrasted with the unreal, illusionary or phenomenal being. Microcosm. The "little" Universe meaning man, made in the image of his creator, the Macrocosm, or "great" Universe, and containing all that the latter contains. These terms are used in Occultism and Theosophy. Mishnah (Heb.) Lit., "a repetition" from the word Shanah, "to repeat" something said orally. A summary of written explanations from the oral traditions of the Jews and a digest of the Scriptures on which the later Talmud was based. Moksha (Sans.) The same as Nirvana; a post-mortem state of rest and bliss of the "Soul-pilgrim."

Monad. It is the Unity, the ONE; but in occultism it often means the unified duad, Atma-Buddhi, - or that immortal part of man which incarnating in the lower kingdoms and gradually progressing through them to Man, finds thence way to the final goal - Nirvana.

Monas (Gr.) The same as the Latin Monad; "the only," a Unit. In the Pythagorean system the Duad emanates from the higher and solitary Monas, which is thus the First Cause.

193

Monogenes (Gr.) Literally, the "only-begotten"; a name of Proserpine and other gods and goddesses, as also of Jesus.

Mundakya Upanishad (Sans.) Lit., the "Mundaka esoteric doctrine." A work of high antiquity; it has been translated by Raja Ram Mohun Roy. Mysteries (Sacred). They were enacted in the ancient temples by the initiated Hierophants for the benefit and instruction of candidates. The most solemn and occult were certainly those which were performed in Egypt by "the band of secret-keepers," as Mr. Bonwick calls the Hierophants. Maurice describes their nature very graphically in a few lines. Speaking of the Mysteries performed in Philae (the Nile-island), he says: - "It was in these gloomy caverns that the grand mystic arcana of the goddess (Isis) were unfolded to the adoring aspirant, while the solemn hymn of initiation resounded through the long extent of these stony recesses." The word "mystery" is derived from the Greek muo, "to close the mouth," and every symbol connected with them had a hidden meaning. As Plato and many of the other sages of antiquity affirm, these mysteries were highly religious, moral, and beneficent as a school of ethics. The Grecian Mysteries, those of Ceres and Bacchus, were only imitations of the Egyptian, and the author of "Egyptian Belief and Modern Thought" informs us that our own word "chapel or capella is said to be the caph-el or college of El, the solar divinity." The well-known Kabeiri are associated with the mysteries. In short, the Mysteries were in every country a series of dramatic performances, in which the mysteries of Cosmogony and nature in general were personified by the priests and neophytes, who enacted the parts of various gods and goddesses, repeating supposed scenes (allegories) from their respective lives. These were explained in their hidden meaning to the candidates for initiation and incorporated into philosophical doctrines.

Mystery Language. The sacerdotal secret "jargon" used by the initiated priests, and employed only when discussing sacred things. Every nation had its own "mystery" tongue, unknown to all save those admitted to the Mysteries. Mystic, from the Greek word mysticos. In antiquity, one belonging to those admitted to the ancient mysteries; in our own times, one who practises mysticism, holds mystic, transcendental views, etc. Mysticism. Any doctrine involved in mystery and metaphysics, and dealing more with the ideal worlds than with our matter-of-fact, actual universe.

N

Nazarene Codex. The Scriptures of the Nazarenes and of the Nabotheans also. According to sundry Church Fathers, Jerome and Epiphanius especially, they were heretical teachings, but are in fact one of the numerous Gnostic readings of cosmogony and theogony, which produced a distinct sect.

Necromancy. The raising of the images of the dead, considered in antiquity and by modern occultists as a practice of Black Magic. Iamblichus, Porphyry and other theurgists deprecated the practice no less than Moses, who condemned the "witches" of his day to death, the said witches being often only mediums, e.g., the case of the Witch of Endor and Samuel.

Neoplatonists. A school of philosophy which arose between the second and third century of our era, and was founded by Ammonius Saccas, of Alexandria. The same as the Philalethians, and the Analogeticists; they were also called Theurgists and by various other names. They were the Theosophists of the early centuries. Neo-Platonism is Platonic philosophy plus ecstasy, divine Raj-yoga. Nephesh (Heb.) "Breath of Life, Anima, Mens Vitae, appetites. The term is used very loosely in the Bible. It generally means Prana, 'life';

in the Kabbalah it is the animal passions and the animal soul." Therefore, as maintained in theosophical teachings, Nephesh is the Prana-Kamic Principle, or the vital animal soul in man.

Nirmanakaya (Sans.) Something entirely different in esoteric philosophy from the popular meaning attached to it, and from the fancies of the Orientalists. Some call the Nirmanakaya body "Nirvana with remains" (Schlagintweit), on the supposition, probably, that it is a kind of Nirvanic condition during which consciousness and form are retained. Others say that it is one of the Trikaya (three bodies) with "the power of assuming any form of appearance in order to propagate Buddhism" (Eitel's idea); again, that "it is the incarnate avatara of a deity" (ibid.)Occultism, on the other hand, says ("Voice of the Silence") that Nirmanakaya, although meaning literally a transformed "body," is a state. The form is that of the Adept or Yogi who enters, or chooses, that post-mortem condition in preference to the Dharmakaya or absolute Nirvanic state. He does this because the latter Kaya separates him for ever from the world of form, conferring upon him a state of selfish bliss, in which no other living being can participate, the adept being thus precluded from the possibility of helping humanity, or even devas. As a Nirmanakaya, however, the adept leaves behind him only his physical body, and retains every other "principle" save the Kamic, for he has crushed this out for ever from his nature during life, and it can never resurrect in his post-mortem state. Thus, instead of going into selfish bliss, he chooses a life of self-sacrifice, an existence which ends only with the life-cycle, in order to be enabled to help mankind in an invisible, yet most effective, manner. (See "Voice of the Silence," third Treatise, "The Seven Portals.") Thus a Nirmanakaya is not, as popularly believed, the body "in which a Buddha or a Bodhisattva appears on earth," but verily one who, whether a Chutuktu or a Khubilkhan, an adept or a Yogi during life, has since become a member of that invisible Host which ever protects and watches over humanity within Karmic limits. Mistaken often for a "Spirit," a Deva, God himself, &c., a Nirmanakaya is ever a protecting, compassionate, verily a guardian, angel to him who is worthy of his help. Whatever objection may be brought forward against this doctrine, however much it is denied, because, forsooth, it has never hitherto been made public in Europe, and therefore, since it is unknown to Orientalists, it must needs be a "myth of modern invention" - no one will be bold enough to say that this idea of helping suffering mankind at the price of one's own almost interminable self-sacrifice, is not one of the grandest and noblest that was ever evolved from the human brain.

Nirvana (Sans.) According to the Orientalists, the entire "blowing-out," like the flame of a candle, the utter extinction of existence. But in the exoteric explanations it is the state of absolute existence and absolute consciousness, into which the Ego of a man who had reached the highest degree of perfection and holiness during life, goes after the body dies, and occasionally, as is the case of Gautama Buddha and others, during life.

Nirvanee (Sans.) One who has attained Nirvana - an emancipated Soul. That Nirvana means something quite different from the puerile assertions of Orientalists, every scholar who has visited India, China, or Japan, is well aware. It is "escape from misery," but only from that of matter, freedom from Klesha, or Kama, and the complete extinction of animal desires. If we are told that Abhidharma defines Nirvana as "a state of absolute annihilation" we concur, adding to the last word the qualification "of everything connected with matter or the physical world," and this simply because the latter (as also all in it) is illusion or Maya. Sakyamuni Buddha said in the last moments of his life: - "the spiritual body is immortal." (Vide "Sans.-Chin. Dict.") As Mr. Eitel, the scholarly Sinologist, explains it: "The popular exoteric systems agree in defining Nirvana negatively as a state of absolute exemption from the circle of transmigration; as a state of entire freedom from all forms of existence, to begin with, freedom from all passion and exertion; a state of indifference to all sensibility" - and he might have added "death of all compassion for the world of suffering." And this is why the Bodhisattvas who prefer the Nirmanakaya to the Dharmakaya vesture stand higher in the popular estimation than the Nirvanees. But the same scholar adds that "Positively (and esoterically) they define Nirvana as the highest state of spiritual bliss, as absolute immortality through absorption of the Soul (Spirit rather) into itself, but preserving individuality, so that, e. g., Buddhas, after entering Nirvana, may re-appear on earth - i. e., in the future Manvantara."

Noumena (Gr.) The true essential nature of Being as distinguished from the illusive objects of sense.

Nous (Gr.) A Platonic term for the Higher Mind or Soul. It means Spirit as distinct from animal-Soul, Psyche; divine consciousness or mind in man. The name was adopted by the Gnostics for their first conscious AEon, which, with the Occultists, is the third logos, cosmically, and the third "principle" (from above) or Manas, in man. (Vide infra, "Nout.") Nout (Eg.) In the Egyptian Pantheon it meant the "One-only-One," because it does not proceed in the popular or exoteric religion higher than the third manifestation which radiates from the Unknowable and the Unknown in the esoteric philosophy of every nation. The Nous of Anaxagoras was the Mahat of the Hindus - Brahma, the first manifested deity - "the Mind or spirit Self-potent." This creative principle is the primum mobile of everything to be found in the Universe - its Soul or Ideation. (Vide "Seven Principles" in man.)

O

Occultism. See *Occult Sciences*.

Occult Sciences. The science of the secrets of nature - physical and psychic, mental and spiritual; called Hermetic and Esoteric Sciences. In the west, the Kabbala may be named; in the east, mysticism, magic, and Yoga philosophy. The latter is often referred to by the Chelas in India as the seventh "Darshana" (school of philosophy), there being only six Darshanas in India known to the world of the profane. These sciences are, and have been for ages, hidden from the vulgar, for the very good reason that they would never be appreciated by the selfish educated classes, who would misuse them for their own profit, and thus turn the Divine science into black magic, nor by the uneducated, who would not understand them. It is often brought forward as an accusation against the Esoteric Philosophy of the Kabbala, that its literature is full of "a barbarous and meaningless jargon," unintelligible to the ordinary mind. But do not exact Sciences - medicine, physiology, chemistry, and the rest - plead guilty to the same impeachment? Do not official scientists veil their facts and discoveries with a newly-coined and most barbarous Graeco-Latin terminology? As justly remarked by our late Brother, Kenneth Mackenzie, "to juggle thus with words, when the facts are so simple, is the art of the Scientists of the present time, in striking contrast to those of the seventeenth century, who called spades spades, and not 'agricultural implements.'" Moreover, whilst their "facts" would be as simple, and as comprehensible if rendered in ordinary language, the facts of Occult Science are of so abstruse a nature, that in most cases no words exist in European languages to express them. Finally our "jargon" is a double necessity - (a) for describing clearly these facts to one who is versed in the occult terminology; and (b) for concealing them from the profane. Occultist. One who practises Occultism, an adept in the Secret Sciences, but very often applied to a mere student.

Occult World. The name of the first book which treated of Theosophy, its history, and certain of its tenets. Written by A. P. Sinnett, then editor of the leading Indian paper, the Pioneer, of Allahabad, India. Olympiodorus. The last Neoplatonist of fame and celebrity in the school of Alexandria. He lived in the sixth century under the Emperor Justinian. There were several writers and philosophers of this name in pre-Christian as in post-Christian periods. One of these was the teacher of Proclus, another a historian in the eighth century, and so on.

Origen. A Christian Churchman, born at the end of the second century, probably in Africa, of whom little, if anything, is known, since his biographical fragments have passed to posterity on the authority of Eusebius, the most unmitigated falsifier that has ever existed in any age. The latter is credited with having collected upwards of one hundred letters of Origen (or Origenes Adamantius), which are now said to have been lost. To Theosophists, the most interesting of all the works of Origen is his "Doctrine of the Pre-existence of Souls." He was a pupil of Ammonius Saccas, and for a long time attended the lectures of this great teacher of philosophy.

P

Panaenus. A Platonic philosopher in the Alexandrian school of the Philalethians.

Pandora. In Greek Mythology, the first woman on earth, created by Vulcan out of clay to punish Prometheus and counteract his gift to mortals. Each God having made her a present of some virtue, she was made to carry them in a box to Prometheus, who, however, being endowed with foresight, sent her away, changing the gifts into evils. Thus, when his brother Epimetheus saw and married her, when he opened the box, all the evils now afflicting humanity issued from it, and have remained since then in the world.

Pantheist. One who identifies God with nature and vice versa. If we have to regard Deity as an infinite and omnipresent Principle, this can hardly be otherwise; nature being thus simply the physical aspect of Deity, or its body. Parabrahm (Sans.) A Vedantin term meaning "beyond Brahma." The Supreme and the absolute Principle, impersonal and nameless. In the Veda it is referred to as "THAT."

Paranirvana. In the Vedantic philosophy the highest form of nirvana - beyond the latter.

Parsees (or Parsis). The present Persian followers of Zoroaster, now settled in India, especially in Bombay and Guzerat; sun and fire worshippers. One of the most intelligent and esteemed communities in the country, generally occupied with commercial pursuits. There are between 50,000 and 60,000 now left in India where they settled some 1,000 years ago.

Personality. The teachings of Occultism divide man into three aspects - the divine, the thinking or rational, and the irrational or animal man. For metaphysical purposes also he is considered under a septenary division, or, as it is agreed to express it in theosophy, he is composed of seven "principles," three of which constitute the Higher Triad, and the remaining four the lower Quaternary. It is in the latter that dwells the Personality which embraces all the characteristics, including memory and consciousness, of each physical life in turn. The Individuality is the Higher Ego (Manas) of the Triad considered as a Unity. In other words the Individuality is our imperishable Ego which reincarnates and clothes itself in a new Personality at every new birth. Phallic Worship, or Sex Worship; reverence and adoration shown to those gods and goddesses which, like Siva and Durga in India, symbolise respectively the two sexes.

Philadelphians. Lit., "those who love their brother-man." A sect in the seventeenth century, founded by one Jane Leadly. They objected to all rites, forms, or ceremonies of the Church, and even to the Church itself, but professed to be guided in soul and spirit by an internal Deity, their own Ego or God within them.

Philalethians. (Vide "Neoplatonists.")

Philo-Judaeus. A Hellenized Jew of Alexandria, a famous historian and philosopher of the first century, born about the year 30 B. C., and died between the years 45 and 50 A. D. Philo's symbolism of the Bible is very remarkable. The animals, birds, reptiles, trees, and places mentioned in it are all, it is said, "allegories of conditions of the soul, of faculties, dispositions, or passions; the useful plants were allegories of virtues, the noxious of the affections of the unwise and so on through the mineral kingdom; through heaven, earth and stars; through fountains and rivers, fields and dwellings; through metals, substances, arms, clothes, ornaments, furniture, the body and its parts, the sexes, and our outward condition." (Dict. Christ. Biog.) All of which would strongly corroborate the idea that Philo was acquainted with the ancient Kabbala.

Philosopher's Stone. A term in Alchemy; called also the Powder of Projection, a mysterious "principle" having the power of transmuting the base metals into pure gold. In Theosophy it symbolises the transmutation of the lower animal nature of man into the highest divine.

Phren. A Pythagorean term denoting what we call the Kama-manas, still overshadowed by Buddhi-Manas.

Plane. From the Latin Planus (level, flat), an extension of space, whether in the physical or metaphysical sense. In Occultism, the range or extent of some state of consciousness, or the state of matter corresponding to the perceptive powers of a particular set of senses or the action of a particular force. Planetary Spirits. Rulers and governors of the Planets. Planetary Gods. Plastic. Used in Occultism in reference to the nature and essence of the astral body, or the "Protean Soul." (Vide "Plastic Soul" in the Theosophical Glossary.)

Pleroma. "Fulness"; a gnostic term used also by St. Paul. Divine world or the abode of gods. Universal space divided into metaphysical Aeons.

Plotinus. A distinguished Platonic philosopher of the third century, a great practical mystic, renowned for his virtues and learning. He taught a doctrine identical with that of the Vedantins, namely, that the spirit soul emanating from the One Deific Principle was after its pilgrimage on earth reunited to it. (Vide Theosophical Glossary.)

Porphyry (Porphyrius). His real name was Malek, which led to his being regarded as a Jew. He came from Tyre, and having first studied under Longinus, the eminent philosopher-critic, became the disciple of Plotinus, at Rome. He was a Neo-Platonist and a distinguished writer, specially famous for his controversy with Iamblichus regarding the evils attending the practice of Theurgy, but was, however, finally converted to the views of his opponent. A natural-born mystic he followed, like his master Plotinus, the pure Indian Raj-Yoga system, which, by training, leads to the union of the soul with the over-soul of the universe, and of the human with its divine soul, Buddhi-Manas. He complains, however, that in spite of all his efforts, he reached the highest state of ecstasy only once, and that when he was sixty-eight years of age, while his teacher Plotinus had experienced the supreme bliss six times during his life. (Vide "Porphyry," in the Theos. Gloss.)

Pot Amun. A Coptic term meaning "one consecrated to the god Amun," the Wisdom-god. The name of an Egyptian priest and occultist under the Ptolemies. Pragna, or Prajna (Sans.) A term used to designate the "Universal Mind." A synonym of Mahat.

Pralaya (Sans.) Dissolution, the opposite of Manvantara, one being the period of rest and the other of full activity (death and life) of a planet, or of the whole universe.

Prana (Sans.) Life Principle, the breath of life, Nephesh. Protean Soul. A name for Mayavi rupa or thought-body, the higher astral form which assumes all forms and every form at the will of an adept's thought. (Vide "Plastic Soul" in the Theos. Gloss.)

Psychism. The word is used now to denote every kind of mental phenomena, e.g., mediumship as well as the higher form of sensitiveness. A newly-coined word. Puranas (Sans.) Lit., "the ancient," referring to Hindu writings or Scriptures, of which there is a considerable number.

Pythagoras. The most famous mystic philosopher, born at Samos about 586 B. C., who taught the heliocentric system and reincarnation, the highest mathematics and the highest metaphysics, and who had a school famous throughout the world. (See for fuller particulars, Theos. Gloss.)

Q

Quaternary. The four lower "principles in man," those which constitute his personality (i.e., Body, Astral Double, Prana or life, organs of desire and lower Manas, or brain-mind), as distinguished from the Higher Ternary or Triad, composed of the higher Spiritual Soul, Mind and Atman (Higher Self).

R

Recollection, Remembrance, Reminiscence. Occultists make a difference between these three functions. As, however, a glossary cannot contain the full explanation of every term in all its metaphysical and subtle differences, we can only state here that these terms vary in their applications, according to whether they relate to the past or the present birth, and whether one or the other of these phases of memory emanates from the spiritual or the material brain; or, again, from the "Individuality" or the "Personality." Reincarnation, or Re-birth; the once universal doctrine, which taught that the Ego is born on this earth an innumerable number of times. Now-a-days it is denied by Christians, who seem to misunderstand the teachings of their own gospels. Nevertheless, the putting on of flesh periodically and throughout long cycles by the higher human Soul (Buddhi-Manas) or Ego is taught in the Bible as it is in all other ancient scriptures, and "resurrection" means only the rebirth of the Ego in another form. (Vide Theos. Gloss.) Reuchlin, John. A great German philosopher and philologist, Kabbalist and scholar. He was born at Pfortzheim in Germany, in 1455, and early in youth was a diplomat. At one period of his life he held the high office of judge of the tribunal at Tubingen, where he remained for eleven years. He was also the preceptor of Melancthon, and was greatly persecuted by the clergy for his glorification of the Hebrew Kabbala, though at the same time called the "Father of the Reformation." He died in 1522, in great poverty, the common fate of all who in those days went against the dead-letter of the Church.

S

Sacred Science. The epithet given to the occult sciences in general, and by the Rosicrucians to the Kabbala, and especially to the Hermetic philosophy.

Samadhi. The name in India for spiritual ecstasy. It is a state of complete trance, induced by means of mystic concentration.

Samkhara. One of the five Buddhist Skandhas or attributes. (Vide "Skandhas.") "Tendencies of mind."

Samma Sambuddha. The sudden remembrance of all one's past incarnations, a phenomenon of memory obtained through Yoga. A Buddhist mystic term. Samothrace. An island in the Grecian Archipelago, famous in days of old for the mysteries celebrated in its temples. These mysteries were world-renowned. Samyuttaka Nikaya. One of the Buddhist Sutras.

Sanna. One of the five Skandhas, or attributes, meaning "abstract ideas."

Seance. A term now used to denote a sitting with a medium for sundry phenomena. Used chiefly among the spiritualists.

Self. There are two Selves in men - the Higher and the Lower, the Impersonal and the Personal Self. One is divine, the other semi-animal. A great distinction should be made between the two.

Sephiroth. A Hebrew Kabalistic word, for the ten divine emanations from Ain-Soph, the impersonal, universal Principle, or DEITY. (Vide Theos. Gloss.) Skandhas. The attributes of every personality, which after death form the basis, so to say, for a new Karmic reincarnation. They are five in the popular or exoteric system of the Buddhists: i.e., Rupa, form or body, which leaves behind it its magnetic atoms and occult affinities; Vedana, sensations, which do likewise; Sanna, or abstract ideas, which are the creative powers at work from one incarnation to another; Samkhara, tendencies of mind; and Vinnana, mental powers.

Somnambulism. "Sleep walking." A psycho-physiological state, too well known to need explanation.

Spiritism. The same as the above, with the difference that the Spiritualists reject almost unanimously the doctrine of Reincarnation, while the Spiritists make of it the fundamental principle in their belief. There is, however, a vast difference between the views of the latter and the philosophical teachings of Eastern Occultists. Spiritists belong to the French School founded by Allan Kardec, and the Spiritualists of America and England to that of the "Fox girls," who inaugurated their theories at Rochester, U. S. A. Theosophists, while believing in the mediumistic phenomena of both Spiritualists and Spiritists, reject the idea of "spirits."

Spiritualism. The modern belief that the spirits of the dead return on earth to commune with the living. (See "Spiritism.")

St. Germain (Count). A mysterious personage, who appeared in the last century and early in the present one in France, England and elsewhere.

Sthula Sharira. The Sanskrit name for the human physical body, in Occultism and Vedanta philosophy.

*Sthulopadhi. The physical body in its waking, conscious state (Jagrat).

*Sukshmopadhi. The physical body in the dreaming state (Svapna), and Karanopadhi, "the causal body." *These terms belong to the teachings of the Taraka Raj Yoga School.

Summerland. The fancy name given by the Spiritualists to the abode of their disembodied "Spirits," which they locate somewhere in the Milky Way. It is described on the authority of returning "Spirits" as a lovely land, having beautiful cities and buildings, a Congress Hall, Museums, etc., etc. (See the works of Andrew Jackson Davis.)

Swedenborg (Emanuel). A famous scholar and clairvoyant of the past century, a man of great learning, who has vastly contributed to Science, but whose mysticism and transcendental philosophy placed him in the ranks of hallucinated visionaries. He is now universally known as the Founder of the Swedenborgian sect, or the New Jerusalem Church. He was born at Stockholm (Sweden) in 1688, from Lutheran parents, his father being the Bishop of West Gothland. His original name was Swedberg, but on his being ennobled and knighted in 1719 it was changed to Swedenborg. He became a Mystic in 1743, and four years later (in 1747) resigned his office (of Assessor Extraordinary to the College of Mines) and gave himself up entirely to Mysticism. He died in 1772.

T

Taijas (Sans.) From tejas "fire"; meaning the "radiant," the "luminous," and referring to the manasa rupa, "the body of Manas," also to the stars, and the star-like shining envelopes. A term in Vedanta philosophy, having other meanings besides the Occult signification just given.

Taraka Raj Yoga (Sans.) One of the Brahmanical Yoga systems, the most philosophical, and in fact the most secret of all, as its real tenets are never given out publicly. It is a purely intellectual and spiritual school of training.

Tetragrammaton (Gr.) The deity-name in four letters, which are in their English form IHVH. It is a kabalistical term and corresponds on a more material plane to the sacred Pythagorean Tetraktys. (See Theos. Gloss.) Theodidaktos (Gr.) The "God taught," a title applied to Ammonius Saccas.

Theogony. From the Greek theogonia, lit., the "Genesis of the Gods." Theosophia (Gr.) Lit., "divine wisdom or the wisdom of the gods." [For a fuller explanation of such words as "Theosophy," "Theosophists," "Theosophical Society," etc., vide the Theos. Gloss.]

Therapeutae, or Therapeuts (Gr.)A school of Jewish mystic healers, or esotericists, wrongly referred to, by some, as a sect. They resided in and near Alexandria, and their doings and beliefs are to this day a mystery to the critics, as their philosophy seems a combination of Orphic, Pythagorean, Essenian and purely Kabalistic practices. (See Theos. Gloss.)

Theurgy (from the Greek theiourgia). Rites for bringing down to earth planetary and other Spirits or Gods. To arrive at the realization of such an object, the Theurgist had to be absolutely pure and unselfish in his motives. The practice of theurgy is very undesirable and even dangerous in the present day. The world has become too corrupt and wicked for the practice of that which such holy and learned men as Ammonius, Plotinus, Porphyry and Iamblichus (the most learned Theurgist of all) could alone attempt with impunity. In our day theurgy or divine, beneficent magic is but too apt to become goetic, or in other words Sorcery. Theurgy is the first of the three subdivisions of magic, which are theurgic, goetic and natural magic.

Thread Soul. The same as Sutratma, which see.

Thumos (Gr.) A Pythagorean and Platonic term; applied to an aspect of the human soul, to denote its passionate Kamarupic condition: - almost equivalent to the Sanskrit word tamas: "the quality of darkness," and probably derived from the latter.

Timaeus (of Locris). A Pythagorean philosopher, born at Locris. He differed somewhat from his teacher in the doctrine of metempsychosis. He wrote a treatise on the Soul of the World and its nature and essence, which is in the Doric dialect and still extant.

Triad or Trinity. In every religion and philosophy - the three in One.

U

Universal Brotherhood. The sub-title of the Theosophical Society, and the first of the three objects professed by it.

Upadhi (Sans.) Basis of something, substructure; as in Occultism - substance is the upadhi of Spirit.

Upanishad (Sans.) Lit., "Esoteric Doctrine." The third Division of the Vedas, and classed with revelations (Sruti or "revealed word"). Some 150 of the Upanishads still remain extant, though no more than about twenty can be fully relied upon as free from falsification. These are all earlier than the sixth century B. C. Like the Kabala, which interprets the esoteric sense of the Bible, so the Upanishads explain the mystic sense of the Vedas. Professor Cowell has two statements regarding the Upanishads as interesting as they are correct. Thus he says: (1) These works have "one remarkable peculiarity, the total absence of any Brahmanical exclusiveness in their doctrine. . . . They breathe an entirely different spirit, a freedom of thought unknown in any earlier work except the Rig Veda hymns themselves; and (2) the great teachers of the higher knowledge (Gupta Vidya), and Brahmans, are continually represented as going to Kshatriya Kings to become their pupils" (chelas). This shows conclusively that (a) the Upanishads were written before the enforcement of caste and Brahmanical power, and are thus only second in antiquity to the Vedas; and (b) that the occult sciences or the "higher knowledge," as Cowell puts it, is far older than the Brahmans in India, or even of them as a caste. The Upanishads are, however, far later than Gupta Vidya, or the "Secret Science" which is as old as human philosophical thought itself.

V

Vahan (Sans.) "Vehicle," a synonym of Upadhi.

Vallabacharyas Sect (Sans.), or the "Sect of the Maharajas;" a licentious phallic-worshipping community, whose main branch is at Bombay. The object of the worship is the infant Krishna. The Anglo-Indian Government was compelled several times to interfere in order to put a stop to its rites and vile practices, and its governing Maharajah, a kind of High Priest, was more than once imprisoned, and very justly so. It is one of the blackest spots of India.

Vedanta (Sans.) Meaning literally, the "end of all knowledge." Among the six Darsanas or the schools of philosophy, it is also called Uttaramimansa, or the "later" Mimansa. There are those who, unable to understand its esotericism, consider it atheistical; but this is not so, as Sankaracharya, the great apostle of this school, and its populariser, was one of the greatest mystics and adepts of India.

Vidya (Sans.) Knowledge, or rather "Wisdom Knowledge."

Vinnana (Sans.) One of five Skandhas; meaning literally, "mental powers." (See "Skandhas.")

W

Wisdom-Religion. The same as Theosophy. The name given to the secret doctrine which underlies every exoteric scripture and religion.

Y

Yoga (Sans.) A school of philosophy founded by Patanjali, but which existed as a distinct teaching and system of life long before that sage. It is Yajnawalkya, a famous and very ancient sage, to whom the White Yajur Veda, the Satapatha Brahmana and the Brihak

Aranyaka are attributed and who lived in pre-Maha-bharatean times, who is credited with inculcating the necessity and positive duty of religious meditation and retirement into the forests, and who, therefore, is believed to have originated the Yoga doctrine. Professor Max Muller states that it is Yajnawalkya who prepared the world for the preaching of Buddha. Patanjali's Yoga, however, is more definite and precise as a philosophy, and embodies more of the occult sciences than any of the works attributed to Yajnawalkya.

Yogi or Yogin (Sans.) A devotee, one who practises the Yoga system. There are various grades and kinds of Yogis, and the term has now become in India a generic name to designate every kind of ascetic. Yuga (Sans.) An age of the world of which there are four, which follow each other in a series, namely, Krita (or Satya) Yuga, the golden age; Treta Yuga, Dwapara Yuga, and finally Kali Yuga, the black age - in which we now are. (See Secret Doctrine for a full description.)

Z

Zenobia. The Queen of Palmyra, defeated by the Emperor Aurelianus. She had for her instructor Longinus, the famous critic and logician in the third century A.D. (See "Longinus.")

Zivo, Kabar (or Yukabar). The name of one of the creative deities in the Nazarene Codex. (See *Isis Unveiled*.)

Zohar (Heb.) The "Book of Splendour," a Kabalistic work attributed to Simeon Ben Iochai, in the first century of our era. (See for fuller explanation Theos. Gloss.)

Zoroastrian. One who follows the religion of the Parsis, sun, or fire-worshippers.

Parchment Books is committed to publishing high quality
Esoteric/Occult classic texts at a reasonable price.

With the premium on space in modern dwellings, we also strive - within the limits of good book design - to make our products as slender as possible, allowing more books to be fitted into a given bookshelf area.

Parchment Books is an imprint of Aziloth Books, which has established itself as a publisher boasting a diverse list of powerful, quality titles, including novels of flair and originality, and factual publications on controversial issues that have not found a home in the rather staid and politically-correct atmosphere of many publishing houses.

Titles Include:

The Voice of the Silence	H P Blavatsky
The Ancient Wisdom	Annie Besant
The Masters and the Path	C W Leadbeater
Man, His True Nature & Ministry	Louis-Claude de St.-Martin
Secret Doctrines of the Rosicrucians	Magus Incognito
Corpus Hermeticum	(trans. GRS Mead)
The Virgin of the World	Hermes Trismegistus
Raja Yoga	Yogi Ramacharaka
Theosophy	Rudolf Steiner
The Interior Castle	St Teresa of Avila
The Gospel of Thomas	Anonymous
Pistis Sophia	(trans. GRS Mead)
The Signature of All Things	Jacob Boehme
The Secret Destiny of America	Manly P Hall
Practical Mysticism	Evelyn Underhill
The Rosicrucian Mysteries	Max Heindel
The Conference of Birds	Farid ud-Din Attar
Meetings With Remarkable Men	G I Gurdjieff
Life is Real Only Then, When 'I Am'	G I Gurdjieff
Psychic Self-Defence	Dion Fortune
War Is A Racket	Maj.-General Smedley D. Butler

Obtainable at all good online and local bookstores.

View Parchment Books' full list at: www.azilothbooks.com

We are a small, approachable company and would love to hear any of your comments and suggestions on our plans, products, or indeed on absolutely anything.   Aziloth is also interested in hearing from aspiring authors whom we might publish. We look forward to meeting you. Contact us at:

info@azilothbooks.com.

CATHEDRAL CLASSICS

Parchment Book's sister imprint, Cathedral Classics, hosts an array of classic literature, from ancient tomes to twentieth-century masterpieces, all of which deserve a place in your home. A small selection is detailed below:

Mary Shelley	*Frankenstein*
H G Wells	*The Time Machine; The Invisible Man*
Niccolo Machiavelli	*The Prince*
Omar Khayyam	*The Rubaiyat of Omar Khayyam*
Joseph Conrad	*Heart of Darkness; The Secret Agent*
Jane Austen	*Persuasion; Northanger Abbey*
Oscar Wilde	*The Picture of Dorian Gray*
Voltaire	*Candide*
Bulwer Lytton	*The Coming Race*
Arthur Conan Doyle	*The Adventures of Sherlock Holmes*
John Buchan	*The Thirty-Nine Steps*
Friedrich Nietzsche	*Beyond Good and Evil*
George Eliot	*Silas Marner*
Henry James	*Washington Square*
Stephen Crane	*The Red Badge of Courage*
Ralph Waldo Emmerson	*Self-Reliance, and Other Essays, (series 1&2)*
Sun Tzu	*The Art of War*
Charles Dickens	*A Christmas Carol*
Fyodor Dostoyevsky	*The Gambler; The Double*
Virginia Wolf	*To the Lighthouse; Mrs Dalloway.*
Johann W Goethe	*The Sorrows of Young Werther*
Walt Whitman	*Leaves of Grass - 1855 edition*
Confucius	*Analects*
Anonymous	*Beowulf*
Anne Bronte	*Agnes Grey*
More	*Utopia*
Farid ud-Din Attar	*The Conference of Birds*
Jack London	*Call of the Wild*
Edwin A. Abbott	*Flatland*

full list at: www.azilothbooks.com

Obtainable at all good online and local bookstores.